Class as a Dimension of Stratification

CLASS AS A DIMENSION OF STRATIFICATION

K.D. Srivastava

CENTRUM PRESS
NEW DELHI-110002 (INDIA)

CENTRUM PRESS
H.O.: 4360/4, Ansari Road, Daryaganj,
New Delhi-110002 (India)
Tel: 23278000, 23261597, 23255577, 23286875

B.O.: No. 1015, Ist Main Road, BSK IIIrd Stage,
IIIrd Phase, IIIrd Block, Bengaluru-560085 (INDIA)
Tel: 080-41723429

Email: centrumpress@gmail.com
Visit us at: www.centrumpress.com

Class as a Dimension of Stratification

First Edition, 2012

ISBN 978-93-81293-74-4

PRINTED IN INDIA

Printed at Tarun Offset, Delhi

Contents

Preface

The concept of social stratification is interpreted differently by the various theoretical perspectives of sociology. Proponents of structural-functionalism have suggested that since social stratification is commonly found in developed societies, hierarchy may be necessary in order to stabilize social structure. Talcott Parsons, an American sociologist, asserted that stability and social order are achieved by means of a universal value consensus, satisfying the functional prerequisites of a society. By contrast, conflict theories, such as Marxism, point to the inaccessibility of resources and lack of social mobility found in stratified societies. Many sociological theorists have criticized the extent to which the working classes are unlikely to advance socioeconomically; the wealthy tend to hold political power which they use to exploit the proletariat intergenerationally. Theorists such as Ralf Dahrendorf, however, have noted the tendency toward an enlarged middle-class in modern Western societies due to the necessity of an educated workforce in technological and service economies. Various social and political perspectives concerning globalization, such as dependency theory, suggest that these effects are due to the shift of workers to the third world.

'Social Structure' and 'Stratification' are core concepts in social theories. But social theories and their approaches widely differ and so do these concepts. There are major differences regarding the scope and determination of these concepts. Besides there are two major streams employing structural analysis and explanations: the Structuralists or the Structural-functionalists, or simply, Functionalists. Their use of terms, 'structure' and stratification' markedly vary. There is a second major stream of Marxists. Max Weber and Karl Marx, belonging to these two different streams use their concepts in their own ways. Further, there are the terminological problems: Temls such as 'social structure', 'social system' and 'social classes' overlap in several respects and so do 'social stratification' and 'social formation'. Besides the origins of terms such as 'structure' and 'stratification' lie with the biological and geological foundations of 19th century.

The Debate about the relevance of the concept of class is unresolved at the end of the 20th century. The past 100 years have witnessed the establishment of a capitalist society that has, on balance, revealed a strong bond between creativity and destructiveness. This bond is a source of innovation and prosperity. Average living standards within the population continuously improved during the 20th century. Economic growth triumphed while average weekly working hours were reduced. One question about class concerned the social distribution of economic wealth among different population segments. The visibly increasing rise in disposable time that people won during this historical process and the rise in income that allowed them to develop new patterns of personal consumption and leisure activities, patterns of behaviour that had already been revealed with a strange ambivalence by Riesman and colleagues (1950) during the middle of this century, are worth noting.

This work, Class as a Dimension of Stratification is a serious attempt towards realising the goal of distinguishing the fact from fiction. It highlights various aspects, factors, efforts and remedies of social stratification. This book elaborately discusses all relevant issues in comprehensive way.

—Editor

1

Introduction

Social stratification, similarly, refers to the division of a population into strata, one on top of another. There are, ofcourse, important differences between social stratification and geological stratification. By the term 'social stratification' we mean a horizontal division of a society into higher and lower social units. The human society, as such, heterogeneous in nature. It is divided into various economic, social, political and religious classes. Unstratified classless society with 'real equality' is no more than a myth. Social stratification, as pointed out by Sorokin, means the differentiation of a given population into hierarchically superimposed classes. These classes are lined with each other by the relationship of *superordination* and *subordination.* Precisely, we may say, the process by which individuals and groups are ranked in a more or less enduring hierarchy of status is known as stratification. Williams defines social stratification as "the ranking of individuals on a scale of superiority-inferiority equality, according to some commonly accepted basis of valuation.

Inequality of status is the main feature of social stratification. So, we may say, social stratification and social inequality go hand in hand. Moreover, the society attaches different rights and perquisites to different positions. Some groups are given higher status or prestige and as such they enjoy the privileges more than those who are ranked low. Stratification encourages the different social groups to restrict interaction within the strata rather than between the strata. Some draw our attention towards the interaction between the conqueror and the conquered to be the probable cause for the origin of social stratification. The conquering group set itself in an upper berth dominating the lower class of the conquered group. Racial differences accompanied by cultural dissimilarities may lead towards stratification as found to be chief factors in the American stratification.

Spengler suggests that social stratification emerged out of scarcity. In the state of scarcity, society differentiates, in terms of functions, power and assigns rights and privileges to them. Kingley Davis emphasises on the functional necessity of stratification in a society. A society must provide some incentives in the from of rewards to certain sections and have some way of distributingh these rewards differently, according to position. The rewards and their distribution, as attached to social positions, create social stratification. Moore, Davis, Parsons advocated for the division of labour responsible for the inequality of rewards, so that even if the present structure of social class were abolished, there would still remain inequalities of occupational status to replace the old class structure. To ensure the continuity of complex division of labour, this inequality of reward is essential. We generally use a very wide term 'stratification' so far, to mean class stratification which is, no doubt, the dominant type of stratification found in the modern world-in Capitalist societies deriving from differential access to private property and in Communist societies primarily from differential access to political power. Yet, there are many other kinds of stratification, such as, 'Age-set societies,' feudal 'estate' societies, and caste societies in which quite different kinds of stratification are found.

RANK

Differentiation by age, even where there are no organized groups of this kind, is one way of establishing rules of precedence and of formal respect due to certain members of a society from other members—in other words, of arranging people in *rank* order. The notions of *rank, hierarchy,* and *satisfaction* have a good deal in common, and the distinctions between them will become clearer as the argument proceeds. Rank may be ascribed on the basis of descent. There is no difficulty to an English reader in the idea of hereditary rank; we cling to our House of Lords, and a speaker at a meeting where any members of this body are present will, if he is formally correct, acknowledge their presence by addressing himself to 'Mr. Chairman, my lords, ladies, and gentlemen'. In the same way in many of the simpler societies persons belonging to certain lines of descent are regarded as superior to others, are entitled to receive formal marks of respect, and may sometimes have other privileges. The clearest case of such differentiation by rank is that of 'royal families'—the descendants of kings and chiefs. A society may be simply divided into 'royals' or 'nobles' and commoners, but there may be much more elaborate ranking systems. In Samoa, for example, every household claims the right to a hereditary title, and all these are ranked in order of precedence on the basis of genealogies that are recited on formal occasions.

Again, among the Kgatla, a Tswana tribe of Botswana, an elaborate system of ranking allocates every man to his appropriate place. The Tswna are politically dominant over numbers of people of different tribal origins. The many Tswana tribes of today have each been formed by the splitting off, at different times, of members of an existing royal lineage to establish independent chiefdoms. Each of these seceding members took with him a band of retainers of mixed origin, people who had, or whose ancestors had, at some time or other attached themselves to his service. Later, more outsiders became subjects of Tswana chiefs; sometimes they were conquered, sometimes they offered their allegiance in return for protection. These differences in origin are recognized by the Tswana, who divide the population into categories with names which can be translated 'sons of chiefs', 'servants of chiefs' and 'refugees'. The sons of chiefs are men descended from chiefs, as all true Tswana are supposed to be. They are ranked in order of their place on the genealogical tree. Every chief has a number of sons, only one of whom will succeed him. The descendants of this man's brothers are ranked in order of the original brothers' status, which derives from the ranking of their mothers (since all chiefs were polygynous in the old days). In each generation a new series of such ranks is created. The brothers of any chief (any their descendants) rank above those of this chief's father and their descendants. In important public discussions people speak in order of seniority, and wherever a number of Tswana are together they know who is the senior, and the rest accept his leadership.

Social inequality is a universal phenomenon in all societies. It can exist either in form of a hierarchy of groups or individuals or it may exist without the creation of a hierarchy. In the former case it is called social hierarchy. While in the latter case it is known as social differentiation for in almost all societies men and women are treated unequally. If social inequality manifests itself in the form of a hierarchy involving ranking of groups then it is known as social stratification, thus social stratification is a particular case of the social inequality. Social stratification is essentially a group phenomena. According to Ogburn and Nimkoff the process by which individuals and groups are ranked in a more or less enduring hierarchy of status is known as stratification. Melvin Tumin defines social stratification as an arrangement of any social group or society into a hierarchy of positions that are unequal with regard to power, property, social evaluation and psychic gratification. According to Lundberg a stratified society is one marked by inequality by differences among people that are evaluated by them as being lower and higher.

There are two approaches to the study of stratification:

Conflict Theories

According to Karl Marx in all stratified societies there are two major social groups: a ruling class and a subject class. The ruling class derives its power from its ownership and control of the forces of production. The ruling class exploits and oppresses the subject class. As a result there is a basic conflict of interest between the two classes. The various institutions of society such as the legal and political system are instruments of ruling class domination and serve to further its interests. Marx believed that western society developed through four main epochs-primitive communism, ancient society, feudal society and capitalist society. Primitive communism is represented by the societies of pre-history and provides the only example of the classless society. From then all societies are divided into two major classes-master and slaves in ancient society, lords and serfs in feudal society and capitalist and wage labourers in capitalist society.

Weber sees class in economic terms. He argues that classes develop in market economies in which individuals compete for economic gain. He defines a class as a group of individuals who share a similar position in market economy and by virtue of that fact receive similar economic rewards. Thus a person's class situation is basically his market situation. Those who share a similar class situation also share similar life chances. Their economic position will directly affect their chances of obtaining those things defined as desirable in their society. Weber argues that the major class division is between those who own the forces of production and those who do not. He distinguished the following class grouping in capitalist society:

- The propertied upper class
- The property less white collar workers
- The petty bourgeoisie
- The manual working class.

FUNCTIONALIST THEORIES

Talcott Parsons believe that order, stability and cooperation in society are based on value consensus that is a general agreement by members of society concerning what is good and worthwhile. Stratification system derives from common values it follows from the existence of values that individuals will be evaluated and therefore placed in some form of rank order. Stratification is the ranking of units in a social system in accordance with the common value system.

Those who perform successfully in terms of society's values will be ranked highly and they will be likely to receive a variety of rewards and will be accorded high prestige since they exemplify and personify common values. According to Kingsley Davis and Moore stratification exists in every known human society. All social system shares certain functional prerequisites which must be met if the system is to survive and operate efficiently. One such prerequisite is role allocation and performance.

This means that all roles must be filled. They will be filled by those best able to perform them. The necessary training for them is undertaken and that the roles are performed conscientiously. Davis and Moore argue that all societies need some mechanism for insuring effective role allocation and performance. This mechanism is social stratification which they see as a system which attaches unequal rewards and privileges to the positions in society. They concluded that social stratification is a device by which societies insure that the most important positions are conscientiously filled by the most qualified persons.

FORMS AND FUNCTIONS

Social stratification can be classified into four forms-slavery, estates, caste and class.

The Slavery System

It is an extreme form of inequality in which some individuals are owned by others as their property. The slave owner has full control including using violence over the slave. L. T Hobhouse defined slave as a man whom law and custom regard as the property of another. In extreme cases he is wholly without rights. He is in lower condition as compared with freemen. The slaves have no political rights he does not choose his government, he does not attend the public councils. Socially he is despised. He is compelled to work. The slavery system has existed sporadically at many times and places but there are two major examples of slavery-societies of the ancient world based upon slavery (Greek and Roman) and southern states of USA in the 18th and 19th centuries. According to H. J Nieboer the basis of slavery is always economic because with it emerged a kind of aristocracy which lived upon slave labour.

The Estate System

The estate system is synonymous with Feudalism. The feudal estates had three important characteristics. In the first place they were legally defined; each estate had a status with legal rights and duties, privileges and obligations. Secondly the estates represented a broad division of labor and were regarded as having definite functions. The nobility were ordained to defend all, the clergy to pray for all and the commons to provide food for all. Thirdly the feudal estates were political groups. An assembly of estates possessed political power. From this point of view the serfs did not constitute an estate until 12th century. This period saw the emergence of third estate-burghers who were a distinctive group within the system. Thus the three estates-clergy, nobility and commoners functioned like three political groups.

The Caste System

Caste is closely connected with the Hindu philosophy and religion, custom and tradition. It is believed to have had a divine origin and sanction. It is deeply rooted social institution in India. There are more than 2800 castes and sub-castes with all their peculiarities. The term caste is derived from the Spanish word caste meaning breed or lineage. The word caste also signifies race or kind. The Sanskrit word for caste is varna which means colour. The caste stratification of the Indian society had its origin in the chaturvarna system. According to this doctrine the Hindu society was divided into four main varnas-Brahmins, Kashtriyas, Vaishyas and Shudras. The Varna system prevalent during the Vedic period was mainly based on division of labour and occupation. The caste system owns its origin to the Varna system. Ghurye says any attempt to define caste is bound to fail because of the complexity of the phenomenon.

According to Risely caste is a collection of families bearing a common name claiming a common descent from a mythical ancestor professing to follow the same hereditary calling and regarded by those who are competent to give an opinion as forming a single homogeneous community. According to Maclver and Page when status is wholly predetermined so that men are born to their lot without any hope of changing it, then the class takes the extreme form of caste. Cooley says that when a class is somewhat strictly hereditary we may call it caste. M. N Srinivas sees caste as a segmentary system. Every caste for him divided into sub castes which are the units of endogamy whose members follow a common occupation, social and ritual life and common culture and whose members are governed by the same authoritative body viz the panchayat. According to Bailey caste groups are united into a system through two principles of segregation and hierarchy. For Dumont caste is not a form of stratification but as a special form of inequality. The major attributes of caste are the hierarchy, the separation and the division of labour. Weber sees caste as the enhancement and transformation of social distance into religious or strictly a magical principle. For Adrian Mayer caste hierarchy is not just determined by economic and political factors although these are important.

Main Features of Caste System

Caste system hierarchically divides the society. A sense of highness and lowness or superiority and inferiority is associated with this gradation or ranking. The Brahmins are placed at the top of the hierarchy and are regarded as pure or supreme. The degraded caste or the untouchables have occupied the other end of the hierarchy. The status of an individual is determined by his birth and not by selection nor by accomplishments. Each caste has its own customs, traditions practices and rituals. It has its own informal rules, regulations and procedures. The caste panchayats or the caste councils regulate the conduct of members. The caste system has imposed certain restrictions on the food habitats of the members these differ from caste to caste. In North India Brahmin would accept pakka food only from some castes lower than his own.

But he would not accept kachcha food prepared with the use of water at the hands of no other caste except his own. As a matter of rule and practice no individual would accept kachcha food prepared by an inferior casteman.

The caste system put restriction on the range of social relations also. The idea of pollution means a touch of lower caste man would pollute or defile a man of higher caste. Even his shadow is considered enough to pollute a higher caste man. The lower caste people suffered from certain socio-religious disabilities. The impure castes are made to live on the outskirts of the city and they are not allowed to draw water from the public wells. In earlier times entrance to temples and other places of religious importance were forbidden to them.

Educational facilities, legal rights and political representation were denied to them for a very long time. If the lower castes suffer from certain disabilities some higher caste like the Brahmins enjoy certain privileges like conducting prayers in the temples etc. There is gradation of occupations also. Some occupations are considered superior and sacred while certain others degrading and inferior. For a long time occupations were very much associated with the caste system. Each caste had its own specific occupations which were almost hereditary. There was no scope for individual talent, aptitude, enterprise or abilities. The caste system imposes restrictions on marriage also. Caste is an endogamous group. Each caste is subdivided into certain sub castes which are again endogamous. Intercaste marriages are still looked down upon in the traditional Indian society.

Functions of the Caste System

The caste system is credited to ensure the continuity of the traditional social organization of India. It has accommodated multiple communities including invading tribes in the Indian society. The knowledge and skills of the occupations have passed down from one generation to the next. Through subsystems like Jajmani system the caste system promoted interdependent interaction between various castes and communities with in a village. The rituals and traditions promoted cooperation and unity between members of the different castes.

The Dysfunctions

Caste system promoted untouchability and discrimination against certain members of the society. It hindered both horizontal and vertical social mobility forcing an individual to carry on the traditional occupation against his or her will and capacity. The status of women was affected and they were relegated to the background. The caste system divided the society into mutually hostile and conflicting groups and subgroups.

DOMINANT CASTE

This concept given by M. N Srinivas holds that a caste is dominant when it is numerically higher than the other castes.

In the Mysore village he described the peasant Okkalinga composed of nearly half of the population made up of nineteenth jati group. The Okkalinga were the biggest land owner. The chief criteria of domination of a caste are

1. Economic strength
2. Political power
3. Ritual purity
4. Numerical strength.

The dominant caste also wields economic and political power over the other caste groups. It also enjoys a high ritual status in the local caste hierarchy. The dominant caste may not be ritually high but enjoy high status because of wealth, political power and numerical strength. The presence of educated persons and high occupation rate also play an important role in deciding its dominance over other caste groupings. Sometimes a single clan of dominant caste controls a number of villages in areas. The dominant caste settle dispute between persons belonging to their own and other jati. The power of the dominant caste is supported by a norm discouraging village from seeking justice from area, govt official, court or police located outside the village. The members of the dominant caste particularly those from the wealthy and powerful families are representative of this village in dealing with the officials.

PURITY AND POLLUTION

The notions of purity and pollution are critical for defining and understanding caste hierarchy. According to these concepts, Brahmins hold the highest rank and Shudras the lowest in the caste hierarchy. The Varna System represents a social stratification which includes four varnas namely-Brahmans, Kshatriyas, Vaisyas and Shudras. The Shudras were allocated the lowest rank of social ladder and their responsibilities included service of the three Varnas. The superior castes tried to maintain their ceremonial purity. Dumont holds the notion of purity and pollution interlinked with the caste system and untouchability. The hierarchy of caste is decided according to the degree of purity and pollution. It plays a very crucial role in maintaining the required distance between different castes.

But the pollution distance varies from caste to caste and from place to place.

Dipankar Gupta observes that the notion of purity and pollution as Dumont observed is integrally linked with the institution of untouchability. But unlike untouchability the notion of purity and pollution is also a historical accretion. Over time this notion freed itself from its specific and original task of separating untouchables from the others and began to be operative at different planes of the caste system. The concept of purity and pollution plays a very crucial role in maintaining the required distance between different castes. But the pollution distance varies from caste to caste and from place to place.

SANSKRITIZATION

Prof. M. N Srinivas introduced the term sanskritization to Indian Sociology. The term refers to a process whereby people of lower castes collectively try to adopt upper caste practices and beliefs to acquire higher status. It indicates a process of cultural mobility that is taking place in the traditional social system of India. M. N Srinivas in his study of the Coorg in Karnataka found that lower castes in order to raise their position in the caste hierarchy adopted some customs and practices of the Brahmins and gave up some of their own which were considered to be impure by the higher castes. For example they gave up meat eating, drinking liquor and animal sacrifice to their deities. They imitiated Brahmins in matters of dress, food and rituals. By this they could claim higher positions in the hierarchy of castes within a generation. The reference group in this process is not always Brahmins but may be the dominant cas › of the locality. Sanskritization has occurred usually in groups who have enjoyed political and economic power but were not ranked high in ritual ranking. According to Yogendra Singh the process of sanskritization is an endogenous source of social change. Mackim Marriot observes that Sanskritic rites are often added on to non-Sanskritic rites without replacing them. Harold Gould writes, often the motive force behind Sanskritisation is not of cultural imitation per se but an expression of challenge and revolt against the socioeconomic deprivations.

CLASS SYSTEM

The class system is universal phenomenon denoting a category or group of persons having a definite status in society which permanently determines their relation to other groups. The social classes are de facto groups (not legally or religiously defined and sanctioned) they are relatively open not closed. Their basis is indisputably economic but they are more than economic groups. They are characteristic groups of the industrial societies which have developed since 17th century. The relative importance and definition of membership in a particular class differs greatly over time and between societies, particularly in societies that have a legal differentiation of groups of people by birth or occupation. In the well-known example of socioeconomic class, many scholars view societies as stratifying into a hierarchical system based on occupation, economic status, wealth, or income.

According to Ogburn and Nimkoff a social class is the aggregate of persons having essentially the same social status in a given society. Marx defined class in terms of the extent to which an individual or social group has control over the means of production. In Marxist terms a class is a group of people defined by their relationship to the means of production. Classes are seen to have their origin in the division of the social product into a necessary product and a surplus product.

Marxists explain history in terms of a war of classes between those who control production and those who actually produce the goods or services in society (and also developments in technology and the like). In the Marxist view of capitalism this is a conflict between capitalists (bourgeoisie) and wage workers (proletariat). Class antagonism is rooted in the situation that control over social production necessarily entails control over the class which produces goods — in capitalism this is the exploitation of workers by the bourgeoisie. Marx saw class categories as defined by continuing historical processes. Classes, in Marxism, are not static entities, but are regenerated daily through the productive process. Marxism views classes as human social relationships which change over time, with historical commonality created through shared productive processes.

A 17th-century farm labourer who worked for day wages shares a similar relationship to production as an average office worker of the 21st century. In this example it is the shared structure of wage labour that makes both of these individuals "working class.

"MacIver and Page defines social class as any portion of the community marked off from the rest by social status. Max Weber suggest that social classes are aggregates of individuals who have the same opportunities of acquiring goods, the same exhibited standard of living. He formulated a three component theory of stratification with social, status and party classes (or politics) as conceptually distinct elements.

- Social class is based on economic relationship to the market (owner, re-enter, employee, etc.)
- Status class has to do with non-economic qualities such as education, honour and prestige
- Party class refers to factors having to do with affiliations in the political domain

According to Weber a more complex division of labour made the class more heterogeneous. In contrast to simple income—property hierarchies, and to structural class schemes like Weber's or Marx's, there are theories of class based on other distinctions, such as culture or educational attainment. At times, social class can be related to elitism and those in the higher class are usually known as the "social elite".

For example, Bourdieu seems to have a notion of high and low classes comparable to that of Marxism, insofar as their conditions are defined by different habitus, which is in turn defined by different objectively classifiable conditions of existence.

In fact, one of the principal distinctions Bourdieu makes is a distinction between bourgeoisie taste and the working class taste. Social class is a segment of society with all the members of all ages and both the sexes who share the same general status. MacIver says whenever social intercourse is limited by the consideration of social status by distinctions between higher and lower there exists a social class.

CHARACTERISTICS OF SOCIAL CLASS

A social class is essentially a status group. Class is related to status. Different statuses arise in a society as people do different things, engage in different activities and pursue different vocations. Status in the case of class system is achieved and not ascribed. Birth is not the criterion of status. Achievements of an individual mostly decide his status. Class is almost universal phenomenon. It occurs in all the modern complex societies of the world. Each social class has its own status in the society. Status is associated with prestige. The relative position of the class in the social set up arises from the degree of prestige attached to the status. A social class is relatively a stable group. A social class is distinguished from other classes by its customary modes of behaviour.

This is often referred to as the life-styles of a particular class. It includes mode of dress, kind of living the means of recreation and cultural products one is able to enjoy, the relationship between parent and children. Life-styles reflect the specialty in preferences, tastes and values of a class. Social classes are open-groups. They represent an open social system. An open class system is one in which vertical social mobility is possible. The basis of social classes is mostly economic but they are not mere economic groups or divisions. Subjective criteria such as class-consciousness, class solidarity and class identification on the on hand and the objective criteria such as wealth, property, income, education and occupation on the other hand are equally important in the class system. Class system is associated with class consciousness. It is a sentiment that characterizes the relations of men towards the members of their own and other classes. It consists in the realization of a similarity of attitude and behaviour with members of other classes.

Sociologists have given three-fold classification of classes which consists of-upper class, middle class and lower class. Sorokin has spoken of three major types of class stratification-they are economic, political and occupational classes. Lloyd Warner shows how class distinctions contribute to social stability. Veblen analysed the consumption pattern of the rich class by the concept of conspicuous consumption. Warner has classified classes into six types-upper-upper class, upper-middle class, upper-lower class, lower-upper class, the lower middle class and lower class. Anthony Giddens's three class model is the upper, middle and lower (working) class.

JAJMANI SYSTEM

William H Wiser introduced the term Jajmani system in the vocabulary of Indian sociology through his book The Hindu Jajmani system where he described in detail how different caste group interact with each other in the production and exchange of goods and services. In different parts of India different terms are used to describe this economic interaction among the castes for example in Maharashtra the term Balutadar is used. However in sociological literature jajmani system has come to be accepted as a general term to describe the economic interaction between the castes at the village level. This system is also a ritual system concerned with the aspects of purity and pollution as with economic aspects. It functions so that the highest caste remains pure while the lowest castes absorb pollution from them. Villages are composed of number of jatis each having its occupational speciality. Jajmani system is essentially an agriculture based system of production and distribution of goods and services. Through jajmani relations these occupational jatis get linked with the land owning dominant caste. The jajmani system operates around the families belonging to the land owning dominant caste the numbers of which are called jajmans. The land owning caste occupy a privileged position in the jajmani relations. The interaction between occupational castes and the land owning castes take place within the framework of non-reciprocal and asymmetrical type of relations. The land owning castes maintain a paternalistic attitude of superiority towards their occupational castes that are called Kamins in North India. The term Kamin means one who works for somebody or serves him.

In terms of Karl Polanyi's classification of exchange system-Jajmani exchange can be termed as redistributive system of exchange. The Functionalist view of jajmani system regards it as the basis of self-sufficiency, unity, harmony and stability in the village community. However the Marxist scholars hold a very different opinion. They regard the jajmani system as essentially exploitative, characterized by a latent conflict of interest which could not crystallize due to the prevalent social setup. Thus if in future the conditions of the lower caste improve an open conflict between the lower and upper caste is inevitable. Oscar Lewis who studied Rampur village near Delhi and Biedelmn has been critical of the Jajmani system which they regard as exploitative.

According to them the members of occupational jatis are largely landless labourers and have no resources to wage a struggle against the dominant caste out of the compulsion of the need for survival. They succumb to all injustice perpetuated by the landowning dominant caste who enjoy both economic and political power. Scholars like Berreman, Harold Gould and Pauline Kolenda etc accept that there is an element of truth in both the functionalist and Marxist views of the jajmani system. They believe that consensus and harmony as well as conflict and exploitation are prevalent in the village society. According to Dumont jajmani system makes use of hereditary personal relationships to express the division of labour. This system is a ritual expression rather than just an economic arrangement. S. C Dube refers to the system as corresponding to the presentation and counter presentation by which castes as a whole are bound together in a village which is more or less universal in nature. Leach believes that the system maintains and regulates the division of labour and economic interdependence of castes.

TYPES OF SOCIETY

Socilogy recognises many types of Society and defines these types of society in a very clear manner. Following are some of those types of Society and their characteristics.

Tribal Society

According to Ralph Linton tribe is group of bands occupying a contiguous territory or territories having a feeling of unity deriving from numerous similarities in culture, frequent contacts and a certain community of interests. Ghurye calls the tribal of India as imperfectly segment of the Hindus. D. N Majumdar defines tribe as a social group with territorial affiliation endogamous with no specialization of functions ruled by tribal officers hereditary or otherwise united in language or dialect recognizing social distance with other tribes. A large section of tribal population depends on agriculture for survival. The examples of agricultural tribes are: Oraons, Mundas, Bhils, Santhals, Baigas, and Hos etc. The Toda furnish classic example of pastoral economy. Their social and economic organization is built around the buffaloes. They obtain their living through exchange. In some parts of India the tribal people are engaged in shifting cultivation.

It is known by different names-Nagas call it Jhum, Bhuiya call it Dahi and Koman, Maria of Bastar call it Penda, Khond refer to it as Podu and Saiga call it Bewar. Many subsidiary occupations like handicrafts are undertaken in the various tribal zones. These include basket-making, spinning and weaving. For e.g. Tharu depend upon furniture making, musical instruments, weapons, ropes and mats. The Korw and Agaria are well known iron-smelters producing tools for local use.

Characteristics of Tribal Society

The tribe inhabits and remains within definite and common topography. The members of a tribe possess a consciousness of mutual unity. The members of a tribe speak a common language. The members generally marry into their own group but now due to increased contact with outsiders there are instances of tribal marring outside as well. The tribes believe in ties of blood relationship between its members. They have faith in their having descended from a common, real or mythical, ancestor and hence believe in blood relationships with other members. Tribes follow their own political organization which maintains harmony. Religion is of great importance in the tribe. The tribal political and social organization is based on religion because they are granted religious sanctity and recognition.

Tribal Practices

- Joking relationships prevails in Matrilineal Hopi, Matrilineal Trobriand Islanders, Oraons and Baigas

- Group marriage prevail among Marquesans and Todas
- Couvade is practiced mainly in Khasi, Toda, Ho and Oraon
- Teknonymy in Khasis
- Ultimogeniture in Khasis
- Uxorilocal in Garos
- Matrilineal societies are present among Moplahs, Hopi, Nayars
- Polyandry practices tribes are-Todas, Ladaki Botas and Nayars
- Polygamy is found among Eskimo tribes, Crows of North America
- Levirate marriages are found in Ahirs in Haryana, Kodagus of Mysore and Jats and Gujars of UP.

PROFILES OF SOME OF THE SELECTED INDIAN TRIBES

Bhils

- Constitute the largest tribal group in India.
- Found mainly in Madhya Pradesh (Jhabua, Dhar, Kahnwa) and east Gujarat.
- Martial race; primarily agriculturalist.
- Badwas are witch finder, Pujaro are priests and Kotwal are drummers, Tadni is village headman.
- Generally endogamous
- Practice polygamy also.

Gonds

- Second largest tribal group in India.
- Dravidian background
- Found mainly in Madhya Pradesh
- Some of the tribal groups are Bastai, Marias, Murias, Prajas, Bhatras
- Dependent mainly on agriculture, cattle rearing second main occupation.

- Divided into exogamous sects or clans.
- Speak Gondi dialect.
- Lineage is traced through male lines.

Santhals

- Third largest tribal group in India believed to be of Pre-Aryan origin.
- Mainly in Santhal Paraganas of Bihar, West Bengal etc.
- Speak Santhali language.
- Naik is the village priest, Gorait is the messenger, Jogmanjhi is the headmentribal council is Parganait.
- Singlonga or Sun God is the main deity.

Todas

- Found mainly in Nilgiri Hills of South India.
- Classic example of polyandry.
- Call themselves Tora
- Badaga, Kota, Kurumbaand Irula tribes
- The word Toda is derived from Tundra, name of sacred tree of Topdas.
- Divided into two moieties called Taratharal and Teivaloil. These are endogamous units. All the sacred herd and cattle are owned by Tartharal thus they occupy a higher status.
- The clans are divided into families locally known as Kudupeli.
- Fraternal polyandry found.
- Divorce freely allowed.
- Todas have classificatory type of kinship calling many relatives or friends by some designation.
- Females have low status.
- People are governed by council of five elders called as Naim. Three members of this council come from Tarthar clans, two from Teivali clans and one from Badagas.
- Two of the main deities are Teikirizi and On.

Chenchu

- Mainly found in Andhra Pradesh on the river Krishna.
- They are mostly settled cultivators and very much influenced by neighboring plains people.
- They speak dialect of Dravidian origin.
- Now they have started living in semi-permanent huts.
- They are divided into exogamous clans and have animal totems.
- Divorce is common.
- Chenchus have traditional leader Peddamanshi.
- Bhaivov and Garelamaisama are popular local deities.

Khasis

- One of the matriarchial tribes of world.
- Have a rich economy influenced by industrialization and urbanization.
- They are mainly in Jaintia hills of Assam.
- Divided into four main sub-groups-Khynrian, Pnar, War and Bhoi.
- They speak a dialect that belongs to the Mon-Khmer branch of Austric family.
- Each of the sub-tribes is divided into a number of clans known as Kurs.
- Marriage within the clan is prohibited.
- Khasis are characterized by matrilineal descent.
- The clan is further sub-divided into sub class known as kpoh (composed of descendents of one grandmother.

AGRARIAN SOCIETY

The invention of plough marked the beginning of agrarian societies 6000 years back. According to Collins dictionary of Sociology Agrarian society refer to any form of society especially so traditional societies primarily based on agricultural and craft production rather than industrial production. Wallace and Wallace describe agrarian societies as employing animal drawn ploughs to cultivate the land. The mode of production of the agrarian society that is cultivation distinguishes it from the hunter-gatherer society which produces none of its food. The theories of Redfield and Tonnies are considered important. Robert Redfield talks about folk-urban continuum and little tradition and great tradition as his paramount focus in rural studies. Tonnies on the other hand discuss concepts of Gemeinschaft and Gesselschaft.

Characteristics of Agricultural Societies

Cultivation of land through the plough as this invention enabled the people to make a great leap forward in food production. It increased the productivity of land through the use of animals and bringing to the surface the nutrients of the soil. Combining irrigation techniques with the use of the plough increased the productivity and the crop yield. It also brought fallow land under cultivation. The size of the agricultural societies increased as it lessened the burden of large number of people who engaged themselves in other activities. Agricultural societies lead to the establishment of more elaborate political institutions like formalized government bureaucracy assisted by the legal system. It also leads to the evolution of distinct social classes-those who own the land and those who work on the other's land. Land is the major source of wealth and is individually owned. This creates major difference between the social strata. Agricultural societies provide the basis for the establishment of economic institutions.

Trade becomes more elaborate and money is medium of exchange. It also demands the maintenance of records of transaction, crop harvest, taxation, governmental rules and regulations. Religion becomes separate institution with elaborate rituals and traditions. The agricultural societies support the emergence of arts and cultural artifacts due to surplus food production people tend to divert their attention to other recreational activities. There is far more complex social structure. According to Ian Robertson the number of statuses multiplies, population size increases, cities appear, new institutions emerge, social classes arise, political and economic inequality becomes inbuilt into the social structure and culture becomes much more diversified and heterogeneous.

Industrial Society

The Industrial mode of production began some 250 years ago in Britain and from there it spread to the entire world. In the simplest sense an industrial society is a social system whose mode of production focuses primarily on finished goods manufactured with the aid of machinery. According to Wallace and Wallace in industrial societies the largest portion of the labour force is involved in mechanized production of goods and services. The term 'industrial societies' originated from Saint Simon who chose it to reflect the emerging central role of manufacturing industry in the 18th century Europe in contrast with previous pre-industrial and agrarian society.

Characteristics of Industrial Society

Industrial society is associated with the emergence of industrialization which transformed much of Europe and United States by replacing essentially agriculture based societies with industrial societies based on the use of machines and non-animal sources of energy to produce finished goods. Industrial societies are in a continual state of rapid change due to technological innovations. The high level of productivity in industrial societies further stimulates population growth where people start living in cities and urban areas. New medical technologies and improved living standards serve to extend life expectancy. The division of labour becomes complex with the availability of specialized jobs. The statuses are achieved rather than ascribed. The family and kinship as social institutions are relegated to the background. It is becomes a unit of consumption. There is breakup of joint family system and nuclear family units become prominent. The influence of religion diminishes as people hold many different and competing values and beliefs. State assumes central power in the industrial societies. Industrialism is associated with the widening gap between two social classes of 'haves' and 'have nots'. The rich or the capitalist class is seen as exploiting class and the poor class known as working class is seen as exploited. However in most of the industrial societies there is steady reduction in social inequalities. Industrial societies have given rise to number of secondary groups such as corporations, political parties, business houses and government bureaucracies, cultural and literary associations. The primary groups tend to lose their importance and secondary groups come to the prominence.

Post-Industrial Society

The concept of Post-Industrial society was first formulated in 1962 by D. Bell, and subsequently elaborated in his seminal work 'Coming of Post Industrial Society' (1974) It describes the economic and social changes in the late twentieth century. According to Bell in modern societies theoretical knowledge forms the 'axial principle of society and is the source of innovation and policy formulation. In economy this is reflected in the decline of goods production and manufacturing as the main form of economic activity, to be replaced by services. With regard to the class structure, the new axial principle fosters the supremacy of professional and technical occupations which constitute a new class, in all spheres economic, political and social decision making is influenced by new intellectual technologies and the new intellectual class. Other writers have also commented on the growing power of technocrats in economic and political life. G. K. Galbraith (1967) believes that power in the United states economy and therefore in American society as a whole lies in the hands of a technical bureaucracy of the techno-structure of large corporations, A Jouraine (1969) suggests similar technocratic control of French economic and political life.

Race

The term 'race' is often used loosely to indicate groups of men differing in appearance; language or colour. To some race means a nationality or all of humanity. Some even define race as the group which is mixed in nearly all aspects but socially designated as different. Race is scientifically defined as a group of people possessing the same biological inheritance, identified on the basis of external physical characteristics. Thus shape of head, colour of the hair, eyes, skin etc are some of the physical characteristics which are taken into account in determining race. Race is a biological concept but in course of time the members of a particular race develop a kind of consciousness. This race consciousness becomes a sociological phenomenon and it has an impact on social relations. The earliest classification of race was suggested by Huxley in 1870 who gave four principle types of classifications:

- Negroid
- Australoid
- Xanthochroid
- Melanochroid.

According to Maclver and Page the term race when properly used refers to a biological category. It refers to human states that owe their differences from one another specially their physiological differences to a remote separation of ancestry. Franz Boas defined race as a scientific concept applies only to the biological groupings of human types. Horton and Hunt defined race as a group of people somewhat different from other groups in a combination of inherited physical characteristics. Ralph Linton, an American anthropologist made a three-fold classification in The Study of Man. According to him the subdivision of Homo sapiens are breeds, races and stocks. Today breeds are encountered rather infrequently in some small primitive tribes or in some isolated mountains, though variants exist in such a group. A race consists of a number of breeds which share certain physical characteristics. The individuals constituting a race will have fewer characteristics in common than those making up a breed. A stock includes a number of races and of course its members will share even fewer characteristics.

Major Races in the World

Usually mankind is divided into three major racial stocks- the Caucasoid, the Mongoloid and the Negroid.

Determinants of Race

Physical traits are examined to determine the race but sometimes it becomes difficult to tell whether the differences of traits are hereditary or environmental. Attributes such as weight, colour of skin can be greatly modified by the environment. So the determinants can be definite as well as indefinite.

Definite: stature, structure of head, structure of nose, blood group, length of hands and feet and perimeter of chest.

Indefinite: Colour of skin, texture and colour of the hair and structure and colour of the eyes.

Races in India

Sir Herbert Risley classified the Indian population into seven racial types. The three fundamental races are-Dravidian, Mongoloid and Indo-Aryan. Four secondary races-Cytho-Dravidian, Aryo-Dravidian, Mongolo-Dravidian and Pre-Dravidian.

Though one of the major racial stocks the Negroid was not present in Risley's classification, J. H Hutton is of the view that Negrito races were the original occupants of India. The latest classification of the Indian people is made by Hutton, Guha and Majumdar. Guha lists six main races with nine subtypes:

1. The negrito
2. The Proto-Australoid
3. The Mongoloid-Palaeo-Mongoloids, Tibeto-Mongoloids
4. The Mediterranean-Palaeo-Mediterranean, Mediterranean, Oriental
5. The Western Brachycephalis-Alpiniod, Dinaric, Armenoid
6. The Nordic.

Guha has summed up his conclusions as regards the racial composition of tribal India in 1952.

1. The Kadar, the Irula and the Paniyan of South Indian with frizzly hair have an undoubted Negrito strain.
2. The tribes of Middle India belong to the Proto-Australoid group
3. The Brachycephalic Mongoloids of North Eastern India with typical features of the face and eye.
4. A slightly different Mongoloid type with medium stature, high head and medium nose living in Brahmaputra valley.

Majumdar expresses fundamental disagreement with the support of an ancient negrito-strain theory. There is no evidence in support of a Negrito racial stock in India.

Culture and Race

Differences in physical characteristics among people belonging to different races are often confused with differences in culture and behaviour. When the term race is used it combines a set of unrelated features such as physical characteristics, language, religion, cultural traditions and behaviour patterns which differentiate a given people from others. Furthermore there is invariably an implicit value judgment in this sense of the term. Some races are regarded as being naturally and inherently superior to the others. This is a wrong view. There is no necessary connection between race, language, culture and nationality. Racial features are largely determined by genetic and biological factors whereas culture and languages are learnt, acquired and transmitted through training and education. Race prejudice is based on false and irrational premise.

RURAL SOCIOLOGY

Rural life is the principal pivot around which whole Indian social life revolves. India is a land of agriculture. Its history, customs and traditions, complex social organization and unity in diversity etc can be understood by the study of rural life. Rural sociology is the scientific study of rural society. It involves a systematic study of rural society, its institutions, activities, interactions and social change. It not only deals with the social relationships of man in a rural environment but also takes urban surroundings into consideration for a comparative study.

According to A. R Desai rural sociology should be to make a systematic, scientific and comprehensive study of the rural social organization of its structure, function and objective tendencies of development and on the basis of such a study to discover the laws of its development. T. L Smith says that some investigators study social phenomena that are present only in or largely confined to the rural environment to persons engaged in agricultural occupation. Such sociological aspects and principles as one derived from the study of rural social relationships may be referred to as rural sociology. Bertrand has observed that in the broadest definition rural sociology is the study of human relationships in rural environment.

Rural sociology is a holistic study of rural social setting. It provides us with valuable knowledge about the rural social phenomena and social problems which helps us in understanding rural society and making prescriptions for its all round progress and prosperity.

ORIGIN AND DEVELOPMENT OF RURAL SOCIOLOGY

Rural sociology is a new branch of sociology with studies being carried out from 19th century. The prominent scholars engaged in rural sociology during this period were-Sir Henry Maine, Etton, Stemann, Baden Powell, Slater and Pallock etc. The period of 1890-1920 in America saw the rural societies facing many socio-economic problems which attracted the attention of the intelligentsia thus establishing study of rural society as an academic discipline. The appointment of Country life Commission by Theodore Roosevelt was an important landmark in the history of rural sociology. In 1916 the first text book on sociology was published by J. N Gillettee.

The Second World War caused heavy destruction and damage to human society which needed reconstruction. As a result rural sociology got an impetus in USA. The main concern of rural sociology came to be the understanding and diagnosing of the social and economic problems of farmers. More emphasis was placed on issues such as the internal structures of community life and the changing composition of rural populations than on their relationships with land or the social aspects of agricultural production. Theoretically rural sociology remained caught up in bipolar notions of social change whereas rural often got defined as the opposite of urban. Rurality was conceptualized as an autonomous sociological reality. The identification of rural sociology with rural society has also raised questions about its relevance in the western context where no rural areas were left anymore and almost the entire population had become urbanized.

In response to these critiques of rural sociology a new sub-discipline of sociology emerged that operated largely within the functionalist paradigm and was preoccupied with the study of the community life of rural people. This sub-discipline known as sociology of agriculture focused its attention on understanding and analyzing the social framework of agricultural production and the structures of relations centred on land. It raised questions about how and on what terms the agrarian sector was being integrated into the system of commodity production and about the unequal distribution of agricultural incomes and food among the different social categories of people.

The sociology of agriculture also distinguished itself from peasant studies on the grounds that its focus was on capitalist farming where the production was primarily for the market, not on peasants producing for their own consumption by using family labour. Thus it claimed more kinship with the tradition of the political economy of agriculture or agrarian studies. At the methodological level, historical inquiries became as relevant as ethnographic/empirical studies. Thisconceptual shift during the early 1970s also helped in bringing sociologists working on agrarian issues in the western countries closer to those concerned with agrarian transformations in the third world.

THE INDIAN CONTEXT OF RURAL SOCIOLOGY

In India the importance of rural sociology gained recognition after independence. The agrarian context occupies special status both in the social scientific literature on India and in the literature on agrarian societies in general. However unlike studies on caste, kinship, village community, gender, study of agrarian relations did not occupy a central position in Indian sociology. The first systematic study of rural India was done by D. N Majumdar followed by N. K Bose, S. C Dubey, M. N Shrinivas. However it was with the publication of Andre Be'teille's Studies in Agrarian Social Structure in 1974 that agrarian sociology gained professional respectability within the two disciplines. Peasant studies in a way arrived in India with village studies. The collection of essays, Village India, edited by Marriot with its emphasis on little communities and great communities was brought out under the direct supervision of Robert Redfield. By defining little communities not in relation to land but through other social institutions such as kinship, religion and the social organization of caste there was a shift away from looking at the rural population in relation to agriculture and land. Caste hierarchy came to be defined in terms of ritual or social interaction over institutions of commensality and marriage. According to Nelson up to the comparatively recent times the story of man is largely the story of rural man. So rural society is the basic foundation of human life, the keystone of the developmental process and the basic unit of social structure. Villages have been in existence since time immemorial unlike cities which are of more recent origin. In the Indian context rural sociology is of greater significance of the following reasons.

According to S. C Dubey from time immemorial village has been a basic and important unit in the organization of Indian social life. Unique nature of transformation of Indian society where elements of traditional and modern cultures have been juxtaposed. For rural development and solution of rural problems according to A. R Desai this systematic study of rural organization of its structure; function and evolution has not only become necessary but also urgent after the advent of independence. Growing influence of industrialization and urbanization. Village as the basic unit of study. Scientific study of village community is a prerequisite for democratic decentralization. In modern India, the need of rural sociology is very urgent and it is progressive social science gaining importance.

MAIN FEATURES OF RURAL SOCIETY

Village is a Community

The village satisfies all their needs in the village. They have a sense of unity and a feeling of amiability towards each other.

Village is a Institution

The development of villages is influenced considerably by the life of the village. In this way village is a primary institution.

Religiosity

Faith in religion and universal power is found in the life

of the villages. The major occupation is agriculture which involves dependence on nature. Farmers worship forces of nature. The life of the village is the joint family system. Family has a strict control and administrative powers over the individual. All the members of the family share the burden of the family occupation. In this way of working together the villagers maintain sense of cooperation among themselves. In the life of the villagers group feeling occupies an important place. They respect the judgment and obey the orders of their elders and the panchayats. Society, caste and panchayat have control over the individual.

CASTE STRUCTURE IN RURAL SET UP

The institution of caste represents the entire system by which the whole society is organized into different groups their interrelationships are determined, division of labour and exchange of goods and services are carried on the social roles and obligations of the individuals are prescribed. Risley defined caste as a collection of families or group of families bearing a common name claiming a common descent from a mythical ancestor, human or divine, professing to follow the same hereditary calling and forming a single homogeneous community. According to M. N Srinivas the features of caste prevailing through the past centuries may be described under 9 heads: hierarchy, restriction on food, drink and smoking; distinction in custom, dress and speech; pollution, ritual and other privileges and disabilities; caste organization and caste mobility.

a) Hierarchical division of society-Caste brings an element of hierarchy in society by dividing it into different strata, Brahmin, Kshatriya, Vaisya and Sudra on the basis of relative ritual purity. These major groups are again subdivided into a number of small groups which are also graded into various positions in terms of high or low. According to Bottomore in modern India there are perhaps some 2500 jatis in each major region. Ghurye also finds that in each linguistic region there are about 200 caste groups which are further subdivided into about 3000 smaller units each of which is endogamous and constitutes the area of effective social life for the individual.

b) Hereditary-Each caste is a hereditary group. The membership of the caste is confined to those who are born into it by an endogamous marriage relation. The status of an individual is determined by virtue of his birth. Each caste has a traditional occupation and all the members strictly follow this occupation to earn their livelihood.

c) Endogamy-Every caste is an endogamous group. This endogamous character is maintained by the rules and regulation of marriage. However gotra exogamy is maintained in each caste. Every caste is subdivided into different small units on the basis of gotra. The members of one gotra are believed to be successors of a common ancestor-hence prohibition of marriage within the same gotra.

d) Unique culture-Ghurye says that castes are small and complete social worlds in themselves marked differently from one another though subsisting within the larger society. Every caste has a distinct culture, traditions and customs which distinguish it from those of the other groups. The behavioural pattern, food habits etc is prescribed by the caste rules.

e) Closed group-Endogamy, unique culture and heredity combined together to make caste a closed group. No person can enter into a particular caste except by birth. Srinivas talks about process of Sanskritisation which takes place with in Indian society.

f) Organization-Every caste has its own organizational structure known as caste panchayat which lays down rules and regulations that have to be obeyed by the members of that caste. The internal differences and conflicts are settled in the caste panchayat which serves as a judicial system. Socially every caste group is an autonomous body having judiciary, executive and financial power of its own which it exercises over the members of that caste in the interests of the caste as a whole.

g) Rights and Privileges-These vary from caste to caste. Generally the Brahmins enjoy the most privileged position and have extensive rights which they can exercise over the members of other castes. They have a dominant position in social, political and economic fields of rural life. Such rights and privileges decrease as one descends the caste hierarchy.

ROLE OF CASTE IN RURAL SOCIETY

Caste stands as a pivot of rural social structure. It acts as the most powerful determinant of individual behaviour and social order in rural unity. Caste is the determinant of individual status and role. It determines the status of the individual as soon as he takes birth. Hutton says that the system provides him from birth a fixed social milieu from which neither wealth nor property, success nor disaster can remove him unless of course he so violates standards of behaviour lay down by the caste. Caste also guides the behaviour of an individual in his conduct, his association and interaction. It has helped maintain the continuity of social order by preserving its pattern of culture and traditions. It plays a vital role in the process of socialization by teaching individuals the culture and traditions, values and norms of their society. It unifies society in a chain by assigning different places and positions to different groups. It works as the basis of division of labour in society which keeps society away from tensions and conflicts arising out of competition for occupation, power and prestige. Caste also has a deep influence in the religious lives of rural people. The notion of karma and dharma kept social and economic system intact. Performance of rituals, worshipping of different kinds of Gods and Goddesses and celebration of festivals are determined by the caste system.

There are some negative aspects according to P. N Bose the caste system has acted essentially to impose that attitude of mind, needed to raise men from savagery but to stop them half way on progress. Caste acts as a barrier to modernization. Modernization essentially needs a change in outlook and mentality along with socio-economic development. It has hindered development as it imposes strict rules regarding occupation of different people. The society characterized by the caste system is a closed one permitting very little or no social mobility. It acts as a perpetuating force of social inequality and untouchability. It is based on inequality of status and opportunities which often creates conflict and tension in the society.

JAJMANI SYSTEM IN RURAL SOCIETY

The notion of the jajmani system was popularized by colonial ethnography. It tended to conceptualize agrarian social structure in the framework of exchange relations. In its classical construct, different caste groups specialized in specific occupations and exchanged their services through an elaborate system of division of labour. Though asymmetry in position of various caste groups was recognized what it emphasized was not inequality in rights over land but the spirit of community. Wiser argued, each served the other. Each in turn was master. Each in turn was servant. This system of inter relatedness in service within Hindu community was called the Jajmani system. Central to such a construction of exchange is the idea of reciprocity (Gouldner) with the assumption that it was a non-exploitative system where mutual gratification was supposed to be the outcome of the reciprocal exchange.

The Concept of Jajmani System

Inter-caste relations at the village level constitute vertical ties. They may be classified into economic, ritual, political and civic ties. The castes living in a village are bound together by economic ties. Generally peasant castes are numerically preponderant in villages and they need the carpenter, blacksmith and leather worker castes to perform agricultural work. Servicing castes such as priest, barber, and washerman and water carrier cater to the needs of everyone except the Harijans. Artisan castes produce goods which are wanted by every one. Most Indian villages do not have more than a few of the essential castes and depend on neighboring villages for certain services, skills and goods.

In rural India with its largely subsistence and not fully monetized economy the relationship between the different caste groups in a village takes a particular form. The essential artisan and servicing castes are paid annually in grain at harvest time. In some parts of India the artisan and servicing castes are also provided with free food, clothing, fodder and residential site. On such occasions as birth, marriage and death, these castes perform extra duties for which they are paid customary money and some gifts in kind. This type of relationship is found all over India and is called by different names-jajmani in north, Bara Batute in Maharashtra, Mirasi in Tamil Nadu and Adade in Karnataka.

Oscar Lewis defined jajmani system as that under which each caste group within a village is expected to give certain standardized services to the families of other castes. Jajmani is more than a relationship between families than between castes. Jajmani is sort of mutual give and take form of relationship in which one family is hereditarily entitled to supply goods and render services to the other in exchange of the same. The person rendering the services or supplying the goods is known as Kameen or Prajan and the person to whom the services are rendered is called a jajman. Thus under jajmani system a permanent informal bond is made between jajman and Kameen to meet each other's need for good and services.

Main Features of Jajmani System

The jajmani system is characterized by the following features:

- Unbroken relationship-Under the jajmani system the Kameen remains obliged to render the services throughout his life to a particular jajman and the jajman in turn has the responsibility of hiring services of a Kameen.
- Hereditary relationship-Jajmani rights are enjoyed hereditarily. After the death of a man his son is entitled to work as Kameen for the same jajman family of families. The son of a jajman also accepts the son of the Kameen as his Kameen.
- Multidimensional relationship-Due to the permanency of relationship both the jajman and Kameen families become mutually dependent on each other. The relationship becomes very deep. They often take part

in the personal and family affairs, family rituals and ceremonies.

- Barter exchange-Under jajmani system the payments are made mainly in terms of goods and commodities. The Kameen gets his necessities from the jajman in return of his services.

The jajmani system has gradually decayed in modern society. There are many reasons responsible for it. Modern economic system that measures everything in terms of its monetary value. The decline of belief in caste system and hereditary occupation has given a strong blow to the system. Growth of better employment opportunities outside the village and introduction of new transport options.

AGRARIAN CHANGES AFTER INDEPENDENCE IN RURAL SOCIETY

In many ways independence from colonial rule in 1947 marked the beginning of a new phase in the history of Indian agriculture. Having evolved out of a long struggle against colonial rule with the participation of the people from various social categories, the Indian state also took over the task of supervising the transformation of its stagnant and backward economy to make sure that the benefits of economic growth were not monopolized entirely by a particular section of society. It is with this background that development emerged as a strategy of economic change and an ideology of the new regime. However at the micro-level the structures that evolved during colonial rule still continued to exist.

The local interests that had emerged over a long period of time continued to be powerful in the Indian countryside even after the political climate had changed. According to Daniel Thorner the earlier structure of land relations and debt dependencies where a small section consisting of few landlords and money lenders were dominant continued to prevail in the Indian countryside. The nature of property relations, the local values that related social prestige negatively to physical labour and the absence of any surplus with the actual cultivator for investment on land ultimately perpetuated stagnation. This complex of legal, economic and social relations typical of Indian countryside served to produce an effect that Thorner described as a built-in depressor.

LAND REFORMS IN RURAL SOCIETY

The agrarian question had been an important topic of discussions for Indian freedom struggle leaders as well who wrote extensively and debated on how Indian society and economy should be reorganized. Land reforms became a question of considerable academic interest and debate in the discourse about planning and development. They were viewed as necessary for initiating modernization in agriculture. While there was a general agreement that the prevailing agrarian structures marked by absentee landlordism and semi-feudal relations of production, needed to be reorganized, two extreme positions were taken on the crucial questions-what kind of agrarian reforms were required and which would work the best? Is there an economic logic behind land reforms?

The first view was that of the institutionalists who argued that the way out for Indian agriculture lay in a radical reorganization of land ownership patterns that would not only democratize the village and revive the independent peasant economy but also increase the productivity of land. Thus the slogan came upland to the tiller. They also argued that smaller-sized holdings gave higher productivity. The second viewpoint argued against the redistribution of land on the grounds that it was both unviable as not enough land was available for everyone and that it worked against the logic of economics. The modernization of agriculture required landlords' reorientation. They needed to be motivated to cultivate their own land with wage labour and using modern technology. The land reforms would only divide the land into unviable holdings rendering them unfeasible for the use of modern technology.

However the process of agrarian reforms is inherently a political question. The choices made by the Indian state and the actual implementation of land reforms were determined by the politics of the new regime rather than by the theoretical superiority of a particular position. The Indian state chose to reorganize agrarian relations through redistribution of land but not in a comprehensive and radical manner. Joshi described it as sectorial or sectional reforms. The Government of India directed its states to abolish intermediary tenures, regulate rent and tenancy rights, confer ownership rights on tenants, impose ceilings on holdings, distribute the surplus land among the rural poor and facilitate consolidation of holdings. A large number of legislations were passed by the state government over a short period of time.

However most of the legislations provided loopholes that allowed the dominant landowners to tamper with land records by redistributing land among relatives, evicting their tenants and using other means to escape the legislations. In the absence of concerted political will land reforms could succeed only in regions where the peasantry was politically mobilized and could exert pressure from below.

Despite overall failure, land reforms succeeded in weakening the hold of absentee landlords over rural society and assisted in the emergence of a class of substantial peasants and petty landlords as the dominant political and economic group. For example in Rajasthan though the abolition of Jagirs was far from satisfactory it made considerable difference to the overall land ownership patterns and to the local and regional power structures. The Rajputs possessed much less land after the land reforms than they did before, Most of the village land had moved into the hands of those who could be called small and medium landowners. In qualitative terms most of the land begins to be self-cultivated and the incidence of tenancy declined considerably. The fear of losing land induced many potential losers to sell or rearrange their lands in a manner that escaped legislations.

However in few cases the landless labourers living in the countryside most of whom belonged to the ex-touchable castes received land. The beneficiaries by and large belonged to middle level caste groups who traditionally cultivated land as a part of the calling of their castes. While land reforms were supposed to deal with the problem of landlordism, the hold of moneylenders over the peasantry was to be weakened by providing credit through institutional sources initially by credit societies and later by the nationalized commercial banks. According to the findings of an official survey carried out immediately after Independence from colonial rule up to approximately 91% of the credit needs of cultivators were being met by informal sources of credit. Much of this came from moneylenders. Indian state planned to expand the network of cooperative credit societies. With the imposition of social control and later their nationalization, commercial banks were also asked to lend to the agricultural sector on priority basis. Over the years the dependence of rural households on informal sources has come down significantly. The assessment studies on the cooperative credit societies showed that much of their credit went to the relatively better of sections of rural society and the poor continued to depend on the more expensive informal sources. This was explained as a consequence of the prevailing structure of land tenures. The state response was to bureaucratize the cooperative societies. Though in some regions this helped in releasing credit societies from the hold of big landowners, bureaucratization also led to rampant corruption and increasing apathy among those whom they were supposed to serve. Yet despite inherent bias of institutional credit against the rural poor, its availability played an important role in making the green revolution a success and definitely helped to marginalize the professional moneylender in the rural power structure.

COMMUNITY DEVELOPMENT PROGRAMME IN RURAL SOCIETY

As a strategy of development, the CDP was different from both land reforms and the idea of making cheap institutional credit available to cultivators. CDP had emanated from the productionist approach to rural development. It was based on a notion of the harmonious village community without any significant internal differences and conflict of interests. There was hardly any mention of the unequal power relations in the village. Its objective was to provide a substantial increase in agricultural production and improvement in basic services which would ultimately lead to a transformation in the social and economic life of the village. Its basic assumption was that the Indian peasant would of his own free will and because of his felt needs immediately adopt technical improvements the moment he was shown them. The programme was launched on 2 October 1952 in a few selected blocks and it was soon extended to the entire country. However the enthusiasm with which the programme was started could not be sustained. A non-political approach to agrarian transformation resulted in helping only those who were already powerful in the village. Most of the benefits were cornered by a small section of the rural elite.

SOCIAL PATHOLOGY

Generally speaking in late 19th and early 20th century sociologists grouped together under the heading of social pathology those human actions which ran contrary to ideals of residential stability, property ownership, sobriety, thrift, habituation to work, small business enterprise, sexual discretion, family solidarity, neighbourliness and discipline of the will. In effect social problems were considered to be any forms of behaviour violating the mores from which these ideals were projected.

The concept of disorganization was developed by Thomas and Zananiecki in their famous book 'The Polish Peasant in Europe and America' According to them the term social disorganization refers to the decrease in the influence of the existing social rules of behaviour upon individual members. As a result of this there develops individuation and lack of cohesion in society. It was explained by them as a process which will automatically and inevitably create social problems.

APPROACHES TO THE STUDY OF SOCIAL DISORGANIZATION

The earliest approach to the study of social disorganization is that of the social problems. The problems were discussed without any particular sociological frame of reference both the facts and suggested reform programmes being taken from the fields in which the problems were found. Each problem was considered in complete isolation from others. It was assumed that society could progress if it would attack the mal-adjustment which delayed human advancement. Thus the social problems were the diseases of society which threatened the welfare of the group. This is not a scientific approach because social problems in one period of history are not so considered in another. Besides some of the so called social problems are not generally accepted as such. Therefore this approach is called evangelistic one. For all its imperfections and inadequacies the social problem approach contributed to the understanding of social disorganization paving the way for a more scientific analysis.

The second approach to the study of social disorganization is the bio-pyschological. It is the result of the development of the sciences; biology and psychology. The beginnings of this approach can be traced in the formulation of racial theories by Gobineau. He and his followers declared the theory that the decay of all societies is the result of racial intermixing. This is because that the races are not equal in capacity. The eugenists were of the view that there are biological differences not only between races but between individuals within the same race. Therefore society would take drastic steps to prevent conception among the mentally unfit.

This is only way open to solve social problems and for the prevention of social disorganization. This approach helps us to know that the disorganization of society is the direct result of deficiencies in the biological make-up passed on from generation through heredity.

The third approach is geographical. Geographical factors such as land, water, rainfall, climate and soil decide the superiority of a given culture or the backwardness of people. The forms of social disorganization which are explained in terms of geographical factors are crime, cultural retardation, illiteracy, suicide, divorce and insanity. Geography imposes limitation to man's ingenuity but it does not determine the patterns of social adjustment.

The fourth approach to the study of social disorganization is cultural because it explains social problems in terms of cultural processes. Thus the different forms of social-organization show institutional malfunctioning.

The fifth approach is the cultural lag frame of reference. The term cultural lag explained by Ogburn is based upon the distinction between material and non-material culture. Rapid changes takes place in the material culture whereas slow changes in non-material culture.

Changes in material culture necessitate related changes in non-material culture. According to this school the disorganization of the modern family is the result of a lag in the continued functioning of and failure to develop suitable substitutes for the old folkways and mores governing family relations. Cultural anthropologists attempt to broaden the concept cultural lag to include lack of harmonious functioning between two associated cultural traits. Thomas and Znaniecki in their Polish Peasant talk of the cultural approach. This may be called the culture conflict approach. According to them the social disorganization of the immigrant community is the result of conflict between the cultures of the old and the new worlds in which the control of the primary group breaks down.

THE NATURE OF SOCIAL DISORGANIZATION

The philosophically organic approach postulates the interdependence of culture and human nature. It must be included in the formulation of the nature of the social and personal disorganization. Human nature reflects culture in the responses of the individual mechanism. Culture includes those responses which are common to the group and which are passed from generation to generation.

Social Disorganization in a Simple Society

The social change, social disorganization and personal disorganization have their genesis in the variant behaviour of the individuals. In simple societies, however deviations in behaviour are minimum. Therefore there is a little awareness of their existence by the group. New coordination is made both for the society and for the individual with a minimum of stress and strain.

Social Disorganization in a Complex Society

The functioning of three important factors is commonly held responsible for spontaneous variations in behaviour. They are-the specialized functioning inherent in complex society. The family as a culture defining agency and cultural participation outside the particular social order.

The result is the emergence of a wide variety of various response patterns out of which develops disorganization both in society and individual. Some innovations find ready acceptance because they are related to those aspect of culture which are found outside institutional pattern. Innovations in mores, ideas and beliefs often meet with social disapproval because they vary from the accepted pattern. In simple society people revamp the discordant elements to the degree that their variance is no longer apparent. Innovations which meet with organized resistance tend to result in marked social disorganization. All positive response to social disapproval does not result in attempts to explain the variant behaviour in terms of the welfare of the group.

Social disorganization is the inevitable result until such time as the new behaviour pattern loses group support or becomes incorporated into the social order. When however social disapproval of variations is met negatively by retreat into a world of fantasy there is no corresponding social disorganization except to the extent to which the individual becomes a threat to the safety of society and its members. This point of view does not deny the causative role of social organization in the production of personal disorganization. All social change involves some social disorganization. It is important to think of social disorganization related to those aspects of social change which result in the disturbance and revamping of social institutions and of the patterns of interrelationship between them. In the same way the social responses of the individual are always in flux. But only when changes take place in the individual's pattern of adjustment to social situations which arouse social disapproval that one may speak of personal disorganization.

NATURE OF PERSONAL DISORGANIZATION

Personal disorganization represents the behaviour of the individual which deviates from the social norms. It results in social disapproval which may express itself in a wide variety of degree. The individual may also react in different ways. Social reality presents an endless confusion of social disapproval from time to time. It may be mild or violent. Accordingly individuals respond either positively or negatively to social disapproval. The most visible aspect of personal disorganization in complex societies is that in which there is mild social disapproval to which the individual responds positively. This kind of personal disorganization does not deeply disturb the social order. The second aspect of social disorganization is that in which there is violent social disapproval and yet the individual responds positively. In the third aspect in which the individual's response to social disapproval is subjective the person retreats into an individually defined inner world. His innovations lose their social character. He becomes enmeshed in the development of mechanisms which further isolate him from the normal influences of group life. This type of personal disorganization results in psychosis through which the individual tries to escape from the web of social relations and in suicide.

PERSONAL DISORGANIZATION AND SOCIAL DISORGANIZATION

Social disorganization consists of the co-ordination of individual responses as a result of the operation of consensus and control. Personal organization refers to the coordination and integration of the attitude systems within the personality. A change in the cultural context which destroys the functioning of coordination that constitutes the social order represents social disorganization. Similarly any variant behaviour which disturbs the integration of the attitude systems within the personality represents personal disorganization.

Causes of Social Disorganization

According to Maclver and Page five main factors such as psychological, biological, physical, technological and culture bring about social change. When the changes brought about these factors in the social structure are so disturbing that the present institution and other means of social control are no longer able to control them by adjusting themselves to the new situations there arise social disorganization. Factors of social disorganization at a particular period are so interrelated that it is difficult to find which factor is predominant. Elliott and Merrill observe that in order to understand the full implications of a study of social disorganization we must keep in mind the complex nature of all social phenomena. Out of man's fruitless search for unique causes has come recognition of the multiple factors which account for such characteristics of modern society as the decline in the acceptance of revealed religion the changing structure of the family, the increasing importance of the central government, and the lowering standards of morality. Others would rely on a re-constructuction of the fundamental economic institutions to bring about the changes. Still another group insists that the basis of all human woe lies in the biological field. Each of these groups however ignore the selective nature of the interpretation while on the other hand any realistic social understanding must consider all the factors related to the particular manifestation of social disorganization which is under investigation.

2

Social Structures and Stratification

STRATIFICATION

The systemic forms of inequality that divide societies and broadly impact occupational and social status. Stratification may take many forms based on wealth, gender, age, ethnicity, or some other form of distinction. Stratification is consequently a central concern of economic, anthropological, and especially sociological research. It involves not only the forms of discrimination or differential treatment that stand in the way of egalitarianism but also the larger system of rewards that structures the economy and the social order. Studies of stratification trace the evolution and reproduction of these systems; they document the ways in which groups maintain or change their positions within them; and they seek to understand the consequences of these processes for the social order.

In small-scale and low-technology societies, inequality is limited by low levels of accumulated wealth and usually organized in terms of age, gender, and kinship position. This minimizes the formation of enduringly unequal groups—youths will become elders, for example.

By contrast, larger-scale, wealthier societies are more likely to be stratified into enduringly reproduced groups or classes. While Karl Marx described all history as the history of class struggle, others distinguish class as one specific form of stratification among others. Sociologists commonly identify three major forms of stratification in complex societies: *caste* systems, with rigid borders, highly differentiated statuses, and little possibility of mobility (the caste system of India is one example; slave and/or racially segregated societies are another); the system of *estates* characteristic of European feudal societies, which distinguished between the clergy, the nobility, and the broad category of peasants, merchants, and artisans; and *class systems*, more common in modern societies. Max Weber and later Talcott Parsons described the first two systems as dominated by ascribed status, or status into which one is born. Class systems, in contrast, provided a greater margin for achieved status. The contemporaneous rise of the meritocratic ideal places a premium on achievement, in spite of the many economic, cultural, and institutional pressures that assure the general reproduction of structures of inequality.

Sociologists, especially in the United States, have devoted a great deal of attention to the question of social mobility. Despite the meritocratic ideal, the preponderance of research suggests that mobility patterns are primarily determined by structural factors, such as changes in occupational opportunities or fertility rates. Furthermore, there is strong evidence that significant social mobility among the social strata is more the exception than the rule (this is more strongly the case in Europe, where stratification is more determining of life chances than in the United States). Systems of stratification tend to reproduce themselves: children from families of a particular social class tend to follow the occupational trajectories typical of their class background.

To a considerable extent, the history of sociology is the history of efforts to explain historical and actual stratification and to develop means of addressing social inequalities. Marxism, with its theory of class stratification based on ownership of capital and its program of revolution, is one of the most prominent approaches. Weber, in contrast, contended that in modern societies there were sources of stratification other than the relationship to capital, and that not all forms of stratification aligned with one another. He defined class in terms of "life-chances," but he also stressed the partial autonomy of power—particularly the bureaucratic power so influential in modern society. In this respect, Weber anticipated the restratification of communist societies along lines of access to bureaucratic power. In addition, he proposed the concept of *status group* to describe groups whose prestige derives from cultural rather than economic or political factors. Perhaps the most significant contemporary analyst of this dimension of stratification is Pierre Bourdieu, who emphasizes the role of "cultural capital" in the negotiation of class positions.

Marx's and Weber's theories of stratification are examples of conflict theory, insofar as they see society as an arena in which people compete for power, wealth, and prestige. In contrast, Herbert Spencer and Emile Durkheim argued that some degree of inequality contributes to the functional integration of society. This view was extended by Kingsley Davis and Wilbert Moore in an influential article, "*Some Principles of Stratification*" (1945). Davis and Moore argued that all societies need some means of motivating their most competent workers to fill important and difficult occupations. This motivational problem is addressed by fashioning a hierarchy of rewards that privileges functionally important positions. Social inequality is therefore functionally necessary, because a society that fails to motivate people to perform important jobs risks collapse. Critics were quick to argue that this functionalist view neglected the question of power within systems of stratification, and that it legitimized existing inequality. This long-running exchange became known as the Davis–Moore debate, although it has faded in importance with the decline of functionalism and the rise of Marxist and poststructuralist accounts of power and ideology.

SYSTEMS OF STRATIFICATION

Learning Objectives

1. Explain the difference between open and closed societies.
2. Define the several systems of stratification.
3. Understand how Max Weber and Karl Marx differed in their view of class societies.

When we look around the world and through history, we see different types of stratification systems. These systems vary on their degree of vertical mobilityvertical mobilityMovement up or down through a society's stratification system., or the chances of rising up or falling down the stratification ladder. In some so-called *closed* societies, an individual has virtually no chance of moving up or down. *Open* societies have more vertical mobility, as some people, and perhaps many people, can move up or even down. That said, a key question is how much vertical mobility really exists in these societies. Let's look at several systems of stratification, moving from the most closed to the most open.

Slavery

The most closed system is slaveryslaveryThe ownership of people., or the ownership of people, which has been quite common in human history (Ennals, 2007). Slavery is thought to have begun 10,000 years ago, after agricultural societies developed, as people in these societies made prisoners of war work on their farms. Many of the ancient lands of the Middle East, including Babylonia, Egypt, and Persia, also owned slaves, as did ancient China and India. Slavery especially flourished in ancient Greece and Rome, which used thousands of slaves for their trade economies. Most slaves in ancient times were prisoners of war or debtors. As trade died down during the Middle Ages, so did slavery.

Slavery is the most closed system of stratification. Although U.S. slavery, depicted here, ended with the Civil War, slavery still exists today in parts of Africa, Asia, and South America.

But once Europeans began exploring the Western Hemisphere in the 1500s, slavery regained its popularity. Portuguese and Spanish colonists who settled in Brazil and Caribbean islands made slaves of thousands of Indians already living there. After most of them died from disease and abuse, the Portuguese and Spaniards began bringing slaves from Africa. In the next century, the English, the French, and other Europeans also began bringing African slaves into the Western Hemisphere, and by the 1800s they had captured and shipped to the New World some 10–12 million Africans, almost 2 million of whom died along the way. The United States, of course, is all too familiar with slavery, which remains perhaps the most deplorable experience in American history and continues to have repercussions for African Americans and the rest of American society. It increasingly divided the new nation after it won its independence from Britain and helped lead to the Civil War eight decades later. The cruel treatment of slaves was captured in Harriet Beecher Stowe's classic but controversial book *Uncle Tom's Cabin*, which ignited passions on both sides of the slavery debate.

Today slavery still exists in parts of Africa, Asia, and South America, with some estimates putting the number of slaves in the tens of millions. Today's slaves include (a) men first taken as prisoners of war in ethnic conflicts; (b) girls and women captured in wartime or kidnapped from their neighborhoods and used as prostitutes or sex slaves; (c) children sold by their parents to become child laborers; and (d) workers paying off debts who are abused and even tortured and too terrified to leave.

Estate Systems

Estate systemsestate systemA system of stratification characterized by control of land that was common during feudalism. are characterized by control of land and were common in Europe and Asia during the Middle Ages and into the 1800s. In these systems, two major estates existed: the landed gentry or nobility and the peasantry or serfs. The landed gentry owned huge expanses of land on which serfs toiled. The serfs had more freedom than slaves had but typically lived in poverty and were subject to arbitrary control by the nobility (Kerbo, 2009).

Estate systems thrived in Europe until the French Revolution in 1789 violently overturned the existing order and inspired people in other nations with its cries for freedom and equality. As time went on, European estate systems slowly gave way to class systems of stratification. After the American colonies won their independence from Britain, the South had at least one characteristic of an estate system, the control of large plots of land by a relatively few wealthy individuals and their families, but it obviously used slaves rather than serfs to work the land. Much of Asia, especially China and Japan, also had estate systems. For centuries, China's large population lived as peasants in abject conditions and frequently engaged in peasant uprisings. These escalated starting in the 1850s after the Chinese government raised taxes and charged peasants higher rents for the land on which they worked. After many more decades of political and economic strife, Communists took control of China in 1949.

Caste Systems

In a caste systemcaste systemA stratification system based on rigid placement at birth into unequal groups based on one's parents' status, with no chance of moving out of these groups., people are born into unequal groups based on their parents' status and remain in these groups for the rest of their lives. For many years, the best-known caste system was in India, where, supported by Hindu beliefs emphasizing the acceptance of one's fate in life, several major castes dictated one's life chances from the moment of birth, especially in rural areas. People born in the lower castes lived in abject poverty throughout their lives. Another caste, the *harijan*, or *untouchables*, was considered so low that technically it was not thought to be a caste at all. People in this caste were called the untouchables because they were considered unclean and were prohibited from coming near to people in the higher castes. Traditionally, caste membership in India almost totally determined an individual's life, including what job you had and whom you married; for example, it was almost impossible to marry someone in another caste. After India won its independence from Britain in 1949, its new constitution granted equal rights to the untouchables. Modern communication and migration into cities further weakened the caste system, as members of different castes now had more contact with each other. Still, caste prejudice remains a problem in India and illustrates the continuing influence of its traditional system of social stratification.

A country that used to have a caste system is South Africa. In the days of apartheid, from 1950 to 1990, a small group of white Afrikaners ruled the country. Black people constituted more than three-quarters of the nation's population and thus greatly outnumbered Afrikaners, but they had the worst jobs, could not vote, and lived in poor, segregated neighborhoods. Afrikaners bolstered their rule with the aid of the South African police, which used terror tactics to intimidate blacks (Berger, 2009).

Many observers believe a caste system also existed in the South in the United States after Reconstruction and until the civil rights movement of the 1960s ended legal segregation. A segregated system called Jim Crow dominated the South, and even though African Americans had several rights, including the right to vote, granted to them by the 13th, 14th, and 15th Amendments to the Constitution, these rights were denied in practice. Lynchings were common for many decades, and the Southern police system bolstered white rule in the South just as the South African police system bolstered white rule in that country (Litwack, 2009).

Class Systems

Many societies, including all industrial ones, have class systemsclass systemA system of stratification containing unequal groups but with a relatively high degree of social mobility.. In this system of stratification, a person is born into a social ranking but can move up or down from it much more easily than in caste systems or slave societies. This movement in either direction is primarily the result of a person's own effort, knowledge, and skills or lack of them. Although these qualities do not aid upward movement in caste or slave societies, they often do enable upward movement in class societies. Of the three systems of stratification discussed so far, class systems are by far the most open, meaning they have the most vertical mobility. We will look later at social class in the United States and discuss the extent of vertical mobility in American society.

Sociologist Max Weber, whose work on organizations and bureaucracies, also had much to say about class systems of stratification. Such systems, he wrote, are based on three dimensions of stratification: class (which we will call *wealth*), power, and prestige. WealthwealthIncome, stocks, bonds, real estate, and other dimensions of one's total material possessions. is the total value of an individual or family, including income, stocks, bonds, real estate, and other assets; powerpower. The ability to influence others to do one's bidding even if they don't want to. is the ability to influence others to do your bidding, even if they do not want to; and prestigeprestige.

In discussing these three dimensions, Weber disagreed somewhat with Karl Marx, *Sociology and the Sociological Perspective*, said our ranking in society depends on whether we own the means of production. Marx thus felt that the primary dimension of stratification in class systems was economic. Weber readily acknowledged the importance of this economic dimension but thought power and prestige also matter. He further said that although wealth, power, and prestige usually go hand-in-hand, they do not always overlap. For example, although the head of a major corporation has a good deal of wealth, power, and prestige, we can think of many other people who are high on one dimension but not on the other two. A professional athlete who makes millions of dollars a year has little power in the political sense that Weber meant it. An organized crime leader might also be very wealthy but have little prestige outside of the criminal underworld. Conversely, a scientist or professor may enjoy much prestige but not be very wealthy.

Classless Societies

Although, as noted earlier, all societies except perhaps for the simplest ones are stratified, some large nations have done their best to eliminate stratification by developing classless societies classless societies. Societies with no social stratification.. Marx, of course, predicted that one day the proletariat would rise up and overthrow the bourgeoisie and create a communist society, by which he meant a classless one in which everyone had roughly the same amount of wealth, power, and prestige. In Russia, China, and Cuba, revolutions inspired by Marx's vision occurred in the 20th century. These revolutions resulted in societies not only with less economic inequality than in the United States and other class systems but also with little or no political freedom. Moreover, governing elites in these societies enjoyed much more wealth, power, and prestige than the average citizen. Overall, the communist experiments in Russia, China, and Cuba failed to achieve Marx's vision of an egalitarian society.

Some Western European nations, such as Sweden and Denmark, have developed "social democracies" based on fairly socialist economies. Although a few have nominal monarchies, these nations have much political freedom and less economic inequality than the United States and other class societies. They also typically rank much higher than the United States on various social and economic indicators. Although these nations are not truly classless, they indicate it is possible, if not easy, to have a society that begins to fulfil Marx's egalitarian vision but where political freedom still prevails.

GROUPS AND ORGANIZATIONS

Social Issues in the News

"Arrests Made in Vandalism Spree," the headline said. In March 2010, three high school students, two juveniles and one 18-year-old, allegedly spray-painted obscenities on cars, homes, and an elementary school in Muncie, Indiana. A police captain said, "I think they just started out to do a friend's house. The thing kind of carried away after that and went nuts through the rest of the neighbourhood." The estimated damage was in the thousands of dollars and was so extensive that the 18-year-old suspect was charged with a felony. The police captain said the boys felt sorry for their vandalism. "They probably wish they could take it back, but it happened and it's a lot of damage." (Werner, 2010)

This news story depicts an unusual group activity, spray painting. It is likely that none of these teens would have done the spray painting by himself. If so, this news story reminds us of the importance of the many groups to which people typically belong. The English poet John Donne (1573–1631) once wrote, "No man is an island, entire of itself; Every man is a piece of the continent, a part of the main". Obviously meant to apply to both sexes, Donne's passage reminds us that we are all members of society. At the more micro level, we are all members of social groups and categories. The sociologists look at us more as members of groups and less as individuals, and they try to explain our attitudes and behaviour in terms of the many groups and social backgrounds from which we come. For these reasons, sociology is often considered the study of group life, group behaviour, and group processes. This chapter discusses the importance of many types of groups for understanding our behaviour and attitudes and for understanding society itself. We will see that groups are necessary for many of our needs and for society's functioning but at the same time can often lead to several negative consequences, as the story of vandalism in Muncie illustrates.

STRATIFICATION OF SOCIAL STRUCTURES

In common language we often ascribe the successes or failures of political action to certain social realities such as class, nation, caste, religion, gender and so on.

For instance, we might say that the continued prevalence of untouchability in India has effectively limited the benefits of affirmative action reaching out to dalits; or women's political participation has been thwarted by gender exploitation. We, often, say that such and such a political decision or outcome has been due to the presence or absence of certain social structures. Most of us are aware that the course of public decision-making is not merely based on rule of law or franchise in a formal sense. Such a course also depends on the operation of social forces.

Social structures are not constant. They change and reconstitute themselves. They undergo transformation with the activity of their members. They are subject to changes trough scores of ways but more specifically through political &on. In India, scholars have pointed out how the electoral process has led to the reformulation and reassertion of caste identities. Social agents or actors (members of a society) may understand their position and role in social structures diffidently.

MEANING

'Social Structure' and 'Stratification' are core concepts in social theories. But social theories and their approaches widely differ and so do these concepts. There are major differences regarding the scope and determination of these concepts. Besides there are two major streams employing structural analysis and explanations: the Structuralists or the Structural-functionalists, or simply, Functionalists. Their use of terms, 'structure' and stratification' markedly vary. There is a second major stream of Marxists.

Max Weber and Karl Marx, belonging to these two different streams use their concepts in their own ways. Further, there are the terminological problems: Temls such as 'social structure', 'social system' and 'social classes' overlap in several respects and so do 'social stratification' and 'social formation'. Besides the origins of terms such as 'structure' and 'stratification' lie with the biological and geological foundations of 19th century. Our approach to social reality today may not be in tune with such formulations.

i) Tentatively, we can say that social structures are ordered relations of parts of a whole forming an arrangement in which elements of social life are linked together. There is continuity in such relations or patterns of interaction over time. Therefore, social structures have the following two fold connotations:
   a) They are patterns of interactions between social actors or groups.
   b) They imply relative persistence, endurance and durability over time.

ii) As in the case of social structures, so with respect to social stratification, there are wide differences between social theorists. From the structural-functional perspective, Talcott Parsons says that social stratification is, "The different making of human individuals who conlpose a given social system and their treatment as superior and inferior relative to one another in certain socially significant respects."

Even if one adopts this definition, the ranking of social agents might vary widely as there may not be agreement on the criteria of ranking. If one employs a class perspective the meaning of social stratification is markedly in opposition to the functional one. Here the emphasis would not be 'ranking' but on conflict. The Social Structures used Stratification conflict is on account of exploitation centered around the relations of production. Marx makes this clear in one of his formulations of class: "In so far as millions of families live under economic conditions of existence that separate their mode of life, their interests and their culture from those of other classes and put them in hostile opposition to the latter they form a class".

Stratification leads social action in certain direction within a social system. (It's the grid through which differential communication and deference are routed). It upholds a system of order in terms of which life's opportunities are conferred on actors. Marxism suggests that under revolutionary conditions, the revolutionary masses make social stratification their primary target of attack and attempt to overhaul the relations embedded in it.

But short of revolutionary conditions, systems of stratification may enable different levels and degrees of mobility to social agents. One of the important concepts coined by the late M.N. Srinivas, an eminent Indian sociologist to denote such social mobility in India is 'Sanskritisation' i.e., upward mobility of lower castes in the caste system by adopting the beliefs, practices and rituals of the upper castes.

PERSPECTIVES ON SOCIAL STRUCTURES

Structuralists emphasise sustaining structures-One of the major intellectual tendencies where structures conceived in a variety of ways was given absolute primacy and efficacy and the subject as an agency came to be disregarded was the tendency called structuralism. In this conception structures were removed from the objective worlds and were transposed to the domain of culture, beliefs and thought. It discounted the possibility of any direct encounter with the social reality as functionalism suggested. The operation of the structures resulted in social action and transformation or provided explanations for them.

One of the earliest manifestations of this tendency was in the study of language. Hitherto, it was understood that words and language are expressions of concepts and representations of objects. Linguistic structuralism made understanding internal to language. A linguistic sign is made of sound image and a concept. The sound image relates to the sounds and syllables of the sign; the concept is a mental construct. The sound image is the signifier and the concept is the signified. Linguistic structuralism pointed out that the relation between the signifier and the signified is arbitrary, a matter of convention.

There is nothing in common between a tree and the word "tree". The crucial relation is not between the sign and the real world cf objects. It is between the sign and the overall system of language. Meaning is arrived at by the relation of differences within sound images working together to produce a positive meaning. It is the product of structure and form and not of substance, made of concepts or the signified. Language creates meaning rather than conveys it.

In the work of Levi Strauss, the social anthropologist, structure denoted something entirely different from the empirical structures of Functionalism. The structure that persists is characteristic of human social organisation as such and not the structure of a particular society associated with a scientific culture. Scientific knowledge is not induced from sensory observations; those observations should be made intelligible. He saw widely varied social practices as expressions of a theoretically constituted structure. Existing practices do not sustain a structure but a variety of social practices can be explained with reference to a single structure. Through the concept of structure he attempted to provide universal explanations. For him structures were models.

Structuralism of this kind had a deep impact on Marxism and it was developed by the French Philosopher Louis Althusser. He asserted the total separation between ideology and science and read it in the works of Marx calling it as epistemological break. Structuralism also left a deep impact in psychoanalysis particularly in the work of Jacques Lacan.

The present times have been characterised by a major revolt against structuralism in all these forms. Philosophers have called into question the assumptions and strivings of structuralists to constitute a social science in the natural science model. Post-structuralists have highlighted the historical and framework-relative character of the categories employed in social sciences and their inability to be univqrsalised. Hermeneutics argues how communication is primarily bound to cultural ambiences and decoilstructioilists expose the assumptions underlying a position and ask the possible outcomes if those assumptions are reversed. There is a great return of the subject as the seat of consciousness and deliberate pursuit. Structures to the extent they are acknowledged at all art primarily seen as the bites of the constitution of the self rather than makers of the self.

Functionalism

Functionalists, sometimes called as structural-functionalists, underplay individual human initiatives and prefer social structures. The most important representatives of this trend are Emile Durkheim, A.R. Radcliffe Brown and Talcott Parsons. They see social structures as external to individual actors.

These structures vary from one society to the other and largely explain the similarity and differences between one society and another. The behaviour of individuals in social life is to be explained with them in view. They emphasize careful satiny of social facts and identifying the patterns of interaction holding them together. They see in society a normative order that assigns duties and responsibilities, prevents deviant behaviour and ensures value consensus.

This trend does not adequately distinguish the working of the social structures and natural processes. Although it proclaims value-neutrality, it has strong bias towards maintenance of the existing social order and seeing social change as reorganisation existing social structures.

Marxian

Marxian : Importance to class-structure and economic relations as basic. Marxists have emphasised class-structure as the key to understanding societies. Classes are formed on the basis of the relation of social agents to the means of production and to social produce as a whole and the resultant solidarity or bonds that they produce. In Marxist understanding of class-structure there is an overt emphasis on economic relations. It is expressed in the metaphor of 'base' and 'superstructures'. While the economy constitutes the base, the political, cultural, ideological and legal spheres form the superstructure.

The class structure of a society primarily rests on the relation between two basic classes and the role that other classes play is marked by these basic classes. In a capitalist society, for instance, the bourgeoisie and the proletariat are the basic classes. There might be other classes such as the peasantry craftsmen, professionals, landlords etc. but the role that these classes can play is demarcated by the basic classes.

Marxists understand Classes as those that are formed through class struggle. It is in and through political struggles that classes realise their allies and demarcate their enemies.

Marxism does admit the autonomy of political, cultural and ideological structures in relation to the economic process. But they are not clear about the nature and scope of this autonomy. Marxists do admit the existence of autonomous social strata and factions but they are encapsulated within classes. They find it difficult to explain cross-class and trans-class phenomena such as identity and gender issues. While Marxists do recognise the autonomy of human agency, its relation to class-structure is highly debatable. Besides, Marxists have not adequately conceptualised the relation between class-structure, the moral donlain and the persistence of social stability. In India the relation between class structure and caste structure has been a very complex one to be explained.

Weberian

Max Weber: Multi-dimensional and integrated approach Max Weber, emphasised a multi-dimentional approach to understand social structures. He attempted to integrate structure and agency, material and normative dimensions. He highlighted the $le of the knowing subject and did not see higher as passive receptacles of the operation of the social structures.

He argued that meaning is not intrinsic to the social world waiting to be discovered through rational inquiry. Human actors interpret and construct the meaning of the social world around them. Different viewpoints embodying different values and interests, may therefore mean different readings of the social structures. Weber argued that 'unintended consequences of action' beget social structures such as markets.

Max Weber distinguished between Power and Authority. Authority is legitimate power. Legitimate authority involves an element of voluntary compliance. He identified three sources of authority: traditional, legal-rational and charismatic. Traditional authority is ascriptive and inherited; legal-rational authority is based on calculability, intellectualisation and impersonal logic of goal directed action; and charismatic authority is extraordinary personal power identified in and with a particular individual.

Weber preferred the State, and particularly the bureaucracy as the fountain of power. Power represents action likely to succeed even against opposition and resistance of those to whom it is applied. Bureaucracy embodies legal-ratianal authority which he saw as undermining other forms of authority such as traditional and charismatic. He thought that the process of rationalisation, understood as calculability, intellectualisation and impersonal and goal directed action, are increasingly overtaking human activity. This affects all institutions. He uses the metaphor of iron-cage to denote a situation where concern for means and instruments drives nut the concern for human ends.

Although Weber's conception of structure attempts to relate agency and subjectivity with external reality, it suggests little inter-subjective bond between social actors. In its absence rational-legal domain of the state alone becomes the normal social bond, suggesting the metaphor of 'iron-cage'. Weber accords little consideration. The democracy and active citizenship to sustain social relations. His understanding of the social structure under the modern conditions conception constantly calls for charismatic spells of one kind or another to sustain people's engagement with the social order. But charisma cannot be anticipated, calculated and predictable. It's a double-edged sword. Therefore, rational-legal authority will always attempt to keep it at bay. Weber does not adequately engage with the inequality of wealth, power and status. There is little to suggest that he thought that it was the responsibility of the state to promote an equalitarian order. A shared moral domain cannot arise in a Weberian framework.

Weberian and Marxian-Integration-Habermas

One of the important thinkers of our times who has carried the Weberian conception further, while maintaining an interface with Marxism, is Jurgen Habermas. He recognises the role of social structures and the calculative and predictive orientation they suggest but he also takes into account the dimension of power and domination built into them. At the same time he takes seriously the potentiality of arriving at meaning built into language communication.

SOCIAL STRATIFICATION

In the earlier section: we dealt with the issue of social structures and how tinkers of different streams like Structuralists: Functionalists, Weberians and Marxists interpreted them. We also noted differences among them. In this Section we will read about stratification or layers in a society.

Stratification has a great deal to do with the prospects of any specific political system. Aristotle suggested that the viability of constitutional government rests on a particular kind of stratification. Lenin argued for the prospect of socialist transformation of Tsarist Russia based on an understanding of its changing social stratification.

The Marxist Approach

Marx employs ownership and control over the means of production and relationship of social agents to the process of production as the criteria for social stratification. Marx also uses the concepts of strata and factions to indicate the clasting interests found in a class.

The Weberian Approach

While Marx based social stratification on class, Weber introduced a model of stratification based on CLASS, STATUS AND POWER. He understood class very differently. For him a class is composed of people who have life chances in communion as determined by their power to dispose of goods and skills for the sake of income: 'The crucial aspect of class is its situation in the market.

Status reffers to the social ranking, honour and esteem that a group is held in. These are attributes attached to particular styles of life and groups are ranked as high or low accordingly. Ranking, styles and avocations in terms of status vary from one society to the other.

Therefore, while class is universalistic, status tends to be more particularistic. For example in India the caste system is a specific mode of expression of status. Ritual ranking attached to caste becomes one of the major factors of stratification.

3

Groups, Organizations and Social Change Stratification

GROUP DYNAMICS AND BEHAVIOUR

Social scientists have studied how people behave in groups and how groups affect their behaviour, attitudes, and perceptions (Gastil, 2009). Their research underscores the importance of groups for social life, but it also points to the dangerous influences groups can sometimes have on their members.

The Importance of Group Size

The distinction made earlier between small primary groups and larger secondary groups reflects the importance of group size for the functioning of a group, the nature of its members' attachments, and the group's stability. If you have ever taken a very small class, say fewer than 15 students, you probably noticed that the class atmosphere differed markedly from that of a large lecture class you may have been in. In the small class, you got to know the professor better, and the students in the room got to know each other better. Attendance in the small class was probably more regular than in the large lecture class.

Over the years, sociologists and other scholars have studied the effects of group size on group dynamics. One of the first to do so was German sociologist Georg Simmel (1858–1918), who discussed the effects of groups of different sizes. The smallest group, of course, is the two-person group, or two-person group., such as a married couple or two people engaged to be married or at least dating steadily. In this smallest of groups, Simmel noted, relationships can be very intense emotionally (as you might know from personal experience) but also very unstable and short lived: if one person ends the relationship, the dyad ends as well.

A triadtriadA three-person group., or three-person group, involves relationships that are still fairly intense, but it is also more stable than a dyad. A major reason for this, said Simmel, is that if two people in a triad have a dispute, the third member can help them reach some compromise that will satisfy all the triad members. The downside of a triad is that two of its members may become very close and increasingly disregard the third member. As one example, some overcrowded college dorms are forced to house students in triples, or three to a room. In such a situation, suppose that two of the roommates are night owls and like to stay up very late, while the third wants lights out by 11:00 p.m. If majority rules, as well it might, the third roommate will feel very dissatisfied and may decide to try to find other roommates.

Group Leadership and Decision Making

Most groups have leaders. In the family, of course, the parents are the leaders, as much as their children sometimes might not like that. Even some close friendship groups have a leader or two who emerge over time. Virtually all secondary groups have leaders. These groups often have a charter, operations manual, or similar document that stipulates how leaders are appointed or elected and what their duties are.

Sociologists commonly distinguish two types of leaders, instrumental and expressive. An instrumental leader instrumental leader A leader whose main focus is to achieve group goals and accomplish group tasks is a leader whose main focus is to achieve group goals and accomplish group tasks. Often instrumental leaders try to carry out their role even if they alienate other members of the group. The second type is the expressive leader expressive leader A leader whose main focus is to maintain and improve the quality of relationships among group members and more generally to ensure group harmony., whose main focus is to maintain and improve the quality of relationships among group members and more generally to ensure group harmony. Some groups may have both types of leaders.

Related to the leader types is leadership *style*. Three such styles are commonly distinguished. The first, authoritarian leadership authoritarian leadership with a primary focus on achieving group goals and on rigorous compliance with group rules., involves a primary focus on achieving group goals and on rigorous compliance with group rules and penalties for noncompliance. Authoritarian leaders typically make decisions on their own and tell other group members what to do and how to do it. The second style, democratic leadership that involves extensive consultation with group members on decisions., involves extensive consultation with group members on decisions and less emphasis on rule compliance. Democratic leaders still make the final decision but do so only after carefully considering what other group members have said, and usually their decision will agree with the views of a majority of the members. The final style is laissez-faire leadership, that allows a group to function on its own.. Here the leader more or less sits back and lets the group function on its own and really exerts no leadership role.

When a decision must be reached, laissez-faire leadership is less effective than the other two in helping a group get things done. Whether authoritarian or democratic leadership is better for a group depends on the group's priorities. If the group values task accomplishment more than anything else, including how well group members get along and how much they like their leader, then authoritarian leadership is preferable to democratic leadership, as it is better able to achieve group goals quickly and efficiently. But if group members place their highest priority on their satisfaction with decisions and decision making in the group, then they would want to have a lot of input in decisions. In this case, democratic leadership is preferable to authoritarian leadership. Some small groups shun leadership and instead try to operate by *consensus*. In this model of decision making popularized by Quakers (Brown, 2009), no decision is made unless all group members agree with it. If even one member disagrees, the group keeps discussing the issue until it reaches a compromise that satisfies everyone.

If the person disagreeing does not feel very strongly about the issue or does not wish to prolong the discussion, she or he may agree to "stand aside" and let the group make the decision despite the lack of total consensus. But if this person refuses to stand aside, no decision may be possible.

A major advantage of the consensus style of decision making is psychic. Because everyone has a chance to voice an opinion about a potential decision and no decisions are reached unless everyone agrees with them, group members will ordinarily feel good about the eventual decision and also about being in the group. The major disadvantage has to do with time and efficiency. When groups operate by consensus, their discussions may become long and tedious, as no voting is allowed and discussion must continue until everyone is satisfied with the outcome. This means the group may well be unable to make decisions quickly and efficiently.

One final issue in leadership has to do with gender differences in leadership styles. Although the evidence indicates that women and men are equally capable of being good leaders, their leadership styles do tend to differ. Women are more likely to be democratic leaders, while men are more likely to be authoritarian leaders. Because of this difference, women leaders sometimes have trouble securing respect from their subordinates and are criticized for being too soft. Yet if they respond with a more masculine, or authoritarian, style, they may be charged with acting too much like a man and be criticized in ways a man would not be.

Groups, Roles, and Conformity

The groups are essential for social life, in large part because they play an important part in the socialization process and provide emotional and other support for their members. As sociologists have emphasized since the origins of the discipline during the 19th century, the influence of groups on individuals is essential for social stability. This influence operates through many mechanisms, including the roles that group members are expected to play. Secondary groups such as business organizations are also fundamental to complex industrial societies such as our own.

Social stability results because groups induce their members to conform to the norms, values, and attitudes of the groups themselves and of the larger society to which they belong. The opening news story about teenage vandalism reminds us, however, conformity to the group, or peer pressure, has a downside if it means that people might adopt group norms, attitudes, or values that are bad for some reason to hold and may even result in harm to others. Conformity is thus a double-edged sword. Unfortunately, bad conformity happens all too often, as several social-psychological experiments, to which we now turn, remind us.

Stanley Milgram and Electric Shock

Although the type of influence Asch's experiment involved was benign, other experiments indicate that individuals can conform in a very harmful way. One such very famous experiment was conducted by Yale University psychologist Stanley Milgram (1974), who designed it to address an important question that arose after World War II and the revelation of the murders of millions of people during the Nazi Holocaust. This question was, "How was the Holocaust possible?" Many people blamed the authoritarian nature of German culture and the so-called authoritarian personality that it inspired among German residents, who, it was thought, would be quite ready to obey rules and demands from authority figures.

Milgram wanted to see whether Germans would indeed be more likely than Americans to obey unjust authority. He devised a series of experiments and found that his American subjects were quite likely to give potentially lethal electric shocks to other people. During the experiment, a subject, or "teacher," would come into a laboratory and be told by a man wearing a white lab coat to sit down at a table housing a machine that sent electric shocks to a "learner." Depending on the type of experiment, this was either a person whom the teacher never saw and heard only over a loudspeaker, a person sitting in an adjoining room whom the teacher could see through a window and hear over the loudspeaker, or a person sitting right next to the teacher. The teacher was then told to read the learner a list of word pairs, such as mother-father, cat-dog, and sun-moon. At the end of the list, the teacher was then asked to read the first word of the first word pair—for example, "mother" in our list—and to read several possible matches. If the learner got the right answer ("father"), the teacher would move on to the next word pair, but if the learner gave the wrong answer, the teacher was to administer an electric shock to the learner. The initial shock was 15 volts, and each time a wrong answer was given, the shock would be increased, finally going up to 450 V, which was marked on the machine as "Danger: Severe Shock." The learners often gave wrong answers and would cry out in pain as the voltage increased. In the 200-V range, they would scream, and in the 400-V range, they would say nothing at all. As far as the teachers knew, the learners had lapsed into unconsciousness from the electric shocks and even died.

Before his study began, Milgram consulted several psychologists, who assured him that no sane person would be willing to administer lethal shock in his experiments. He thus was shocked (pun intended) to find that more than half the teachers went all the way to 450 V in the experiments, where they could only hear the learner over a loudspeaker and not see him. Even in the experiments where the learner was sitting next to the teacher, some teachers still went to 450 V by forcing a hand of the screaming, resisting, but tied-down learner onto a metal plate that completed the electric circuit.

It turned out that the learners were not actually being shocked. Instead the voice and screams heard through the loudspeaker were from a tape recorder, and the learner that some of the teachers saw was placed there by Milgram to pretend to be in agony.

Milgram concluded that people are quite willing, however reluctantly, to obey authority even if it means inflicting great harm on others. If that could happen in his artificial experiment situation, he thought, then perhaps the Holocaust was not so incomprehensible after all, and it would be too simplistic to blame the Holocaust just on the authoritarianism of German culture. Instead, perhaps its roots lay in the very conformity to roles and group norms that makes society possible in the first place. The same processes that make society possible may also make tragedies like the Holocaust possible.

The Third Wave

In 1969, concern about the Holocaust prompted Ron Jones, a high school teacher from Palo Alto, California, to conduct a real-life experiment that reinforced Milgram's findings by creating a Nazi-like environment in the school in just a few short days (Jones, 1979). He began by telling his sophomore history class about the importance of discipline and self-control. He had his students sit at attention and repeatedly stand up and sit down in quiet unison and saw their pride as they accomplished this task efficiently. All of a sudden everyone in the class seemed to be paying rapt attention to what was going on.

The next day, Jones began his class by talking about the importance of community and of being a member of a team or a cause. He had his class say over and over, "Strength through discipline, strength through community." Then he showed them a new class salute, made by bringing the right hand near the right shoulder in a curled position. He called it the Third Wave salute, because a hand in this position resembled a wave about to topple over. Jones then told the students they had to salute each other outside the classroom, which they did so during the next few days. As word of what was happening in Jones's class spread, students from other classes asked if they could come into his classroom.

On the third day of the experiment, Jones gave membership cards to every student in his class, which had now gained several new members. He told them they had to turn in the name of any student who was disobeying the class's rules. He then talked to them about the importance of action and hard work, both of which enhanced discipline and community. Jones told his students to recruit new members and to prevent any student who was not a Third Wave member from entering the classroom. During the rest of the day, students came to him with reports of other students not saluting the right way or of some students criticizing the experiment. Meanwhile, more than 200 students had joined the Third Wave.

On the fourth day of the experiment, more than 80 students squeezed into Jones's classroom. Jones informed them that the

Third Wave was in fact a new political movement in the United States that would bring discipline, order, and pride to the country and that his students were among the first in the movement. The next day, Jones said, the Third Wave's national leader, whose identity was still not public, would be announcing a grand plan for action on national television at noon.

At noon the next day, more than 200 students crowded into the school auditorium to see the television speech. When Jones gave them the Third Wave salute, they saluted back. They chanted, "Strength through discipline, strength through community," over and over, and then sat in silent anticipation as Jones turned on a large television in front of the auditorium. The television remained blank. Suddenly Jones turned on a movie projector and showed scenes from a Nazi rally and the Nazi death camps. As the crowd in the auditorium reacted with shocked silence, the teacher told them there was no Third Wave movement and that almost overnight they had developed a Nazi-like society by allowing their regard for discipline, community, and action to warp their better judgment. Many students in the auditorium sobbed as they heard his words.

The Third Wave experiment once again indicates that the normal group processes that make social life possible also can lead people to conform to standards—in this case fascism—that most of us would reject. It also helps us understand further how the Holocaust could have happened. As Jones told his students in the auditorium, "You thought that you were the elect. That you were better than those outside this room. You bargained your freedom for the comfort of discipline and superiority. You chose to accept the group's will and the big lie over your own conviction....Yes, we would all have made good Germans."

Zimbardo's Prison Experiment

In 1971, Stanford University psychologist Philip Zimbardo (1972) conducted an experiment to see what accounts for the extreme behaviors often seen in prisons: does this behaviour stem from abnormal personalities of guards and prisoners or, instead, from the social structure of prisons, including the roles their members are expected to play? His experiment remains a compelling illustration of how roles and group processes can prompt extreme behaviour.

Zimbardo advertised for male students to take part in a prison experiment and screened them out for histories of mental illness, violent behaviour, and drug use. He then assigned them randomly to be either guards or prisoners in the experiment to ensure that any behavioral differences later seen between the two groups would have to stem from their different roles and not from any preexisting personality differences had they been allowed to volunteer.

The guards were told that they needed to keep order. They carried no weapons but did dress in khaki uniforms and wore reflector sunglasses to make eye contact impossible. On the first day of the experiment, the guards had the prisoners, who wore gowns and stocking caps to remove their individuality, stand in front of their cells (converted laboratory rooms) for the traditional prison "count." They made the prisoners stand for hours on end and verbally abused those who complained. A day later the prisoners refused to come out for the count, prompting the guards to respond by forcibly removing them from their cells and sometimes spraying them with an ice-cold fire extinguisher to expedite the process. Some prisoners were put into solitary confinement. The guards also intensified their verbal abuse of the prisoners.

By the third day of the experiment, the prisoners had become very passive. The guards, several of whom indicated before the experiment that they would have trouble taking their role seriously, now were quite serious. They continued their verbal abuse of the prisoners and became quite hostile if their orders were not followed exactly. What had begun as somewhat of a lark for both guards and prisoners had now become, as far as they were concerned, a real prison.

Shortly thereafter, first one prisoner and then a few more came down with symptoms of a nervous breakdown. Zimbardo and his assistants could not believe this was possible, as they had planned for the experiment to last for 2 weeks, but they allowed the prisoners to quit the experiment. When the first one was being "released," the guards had the prisoners chant over and over that this prisoner was a bad prisoner and that they would be punished for his weakness. When this prisoner heard the chants, he refused to leave the area because he felt so humiliated. The researchers had to remind him that this was only an experiment and that he was not a real prisoner. Zimbardo had to shut down the experiment after only 6 days.

Zimbardo (1972) later observed that if psychologists had viewed the behaviors just described in a real prison, they would likely have attributed them to preexisting personality problems in both guards and prisoners. As already noted, however, his random assignment procedure invalidated this possibility. Zimbardo thus concluded that the guards' and prisoners' behavioral problems must have stemmed from the social structure of the prison experience and the roles each group was expected to play. Zimbardo (2008) later wrote that these same processes help us understand "how good people turn evil," to cite the subtitle of his book, and thus help explain the torture and abuse committed by American forces at the Abu Ghraib prison in Iraq after the United States invaded and occupied that country in 2003. Once again we see how two of the building blocks of social life—groups and roles—contain within them the seeds of regrettable behaviour and attitudes.

GROUPS, ORGANIZATIONS AND SOCIAL CHANGE

As we consider ways to try to improve our society, the role of groups and organizations becomes very important. This section briefly considers this importance.

Vehicles for Social Change

One individual can certainly make a difference, but it is much more common for any difference to be made by individuals acting together—that is, by a group. In this regard, it is very clear that groups of many types have been and will continue to be vehicles for social reform and social change of many kinds. Many of the rights and freedoms Americans enjoy today were the result of committed efforts by social reform groups and social movements of years past: the abolitionist movement, the woman suffrage movement and contemporary women's movement, the labour movement, the civil rights movement, the gay rights movement, and the environmental movement, to name just a few. Their experience reflects the wisdom of anthropologist Margaret Mead's famous quote that we should "never doubt that a small group of thoughtful, committed citizens can change the world. Indeed, it is the only thing that ever has."

In today's world, there are innumerable social service and social advocacy groups that are attempting to bring about changes to benefit a particular constituency or the greater society, and you might well belong to one of these groups on your campus or in your home community. All such groups, past, present, and future, are vehicles for social reform and social change, or at least have the potential for becoming such vehicles.

Obstacles to Social Change

Groups can bring about social reform and social change, but they can also thwart efforts to achieve a just society. For every social change and social reform effort that so many groups and organizations undertake, other groups and organizations try to block such efforts. Groups may be the building blocks of social reform and social change, but they are also the building blocks for the status quo. If the study of sociology can be said to be the study of group life, as noted earlier, the study of social reform and social change can also be said to be the study of what groups and organizations do to try to bring about social reform or to maintain the status quo.

Changing Groups and Organizations From Within

Groups and organizations are typically set in their ways and do not often change their dynamics, goals, or other key aspects. This is especially true of the formal organizations we call bureaucracies, which, as we saw, are so committed and even "stuck" to certain procedures that they become inefficient and even alienating. Groupthink can also set in and stifle creativity and keep group and organizational members from raising concerns about certain practices and/or goals.

The revealing by an employee of organizational practices that the employee believes to be illegal and/or immoral is now the common term for raising such concerns, especially when the concern involves illegal and/or potentially harmful behaviour. It is not easy to be a whistle-blower, and several individuals who have "blown the whistle" have been harassed, fired, or sued for doing so. In response to such reprisals, various federal and state laws have been passed to protect whistle-blowers. Still, it takes a certain amount of courage and no small amount of perseverance to be a whistle-blower. It is almost certain that some readers of this book will one day find themselves in a position where they, too, might have to decide whether to become a whistle-blower when they perceive some violation of the law and/or harmful behaviour to be occurring. If so, they will have great potential for changing a group or an organization from within while performing a social good for the larger society.

SOCIAL ISSUES IN THE NEWS

"More Wichita Kids Go Hungry," the headline said. In July 2009, as the United States was in a deep recession, poverty-stricken parents in Wichita, Kansas, increasingly worried about how they would be able to feed their children. As a state official explained, "We see a lot of children who regularly wonder where their next meal is coming from. Churches that used to do food drives once every two to three months are now doing them once a month." The number of children eating at one of Wichita's major food pantries had climbed by one-third from a year earlier, and the number of children classified as homeless had increased by 90% from 1,000 to 1,900. A sixth-grade girl gave life to these numbers when she wrote of her own family's situation. "My mom works very hard to support our family," she said, "[but] some days we would eat only once a day. Then Mom got her paycheck and we were really happy but then the bills started coming and we couldn't buy food because a house was more important. We would rather have a house to live in and we needed a car." (Wenzl, 2009)

This story of hunger in America's heartland reminds us that poverty is far from unknown in the richest nation in the world, especially since a severe economic recession began in 2008. The United States has long been considered a land of opportunity, but research by sociologists and other social scientists shows again and again that people differ dramatically in their opportunity to realize the American dream.

To illustrate this, imagine that you and four other people are about to begin playing the popular board game *Monopoly*. Following the rules, each player begins with $1,500. You start the game, go around the board, buy properties or land on someone else's properties, and sometimes end up in Jail or Free Parking. Like life itself, whether you eventually win or lose the game is a matter of both luck and skill.

But if *Monopoly* were *more* like real life, each player would *not* begin with $1,500. Instead, they would begin with very different amounts, because in real life some people are richer than others, and some are much poorer. In fact, reflecting the unequal distribution of wealth in the United States, one player, the richest, would begin with $6,352 of the $7,500 distributed to the five players combined. The next richest player would have $848. The third player would start with $285, while the next would have $52. The fifth and poorest player would actually begin $38 in debt! "Distribution of Starting Cash If *Monopoly* Were More Like Real Life" depicts this huge disparity in money at the beginning of the game.

Now suppose you are the player starting $38 in debt. How would you feel being this player? You can hardly afford to buy Park Place or Boardwalk. Even landing on a couple of "pay" spaces like a utility the first time you go around the board would virtually force you out of the game. If you landed in Jail, you could not afford to get out. What are your chances of winning the game? Yes, you have a chance to win, but how likely is this? The second, third, and fourth players have a better chance of winning than you do, but in the long run they obviously will not win nearly as often as the richest player, who, after all, starts out with about 85% of all the money distributed at the beginning.

Unlike most games, real life is filled with differences in wealth and other resources a society values. Sociologists refer to rankings based on these differences as social stratification of people based on wealth and other resources a society values..

Except for the simplest preindustrial societies, every society is stratified to some extent, and some societies are more stratified than others. Another way of saying this is that some societies have more *economic inequality*, or a greater difference between the best-off and the worst-off, than others. In modern society, stratification is usually determined by income and other forms of wealth, such as stocks and bonds, but resources such as power and prestige matter, too. No matter what determines it, a society's stratification has significant consequences for its members' attitudes, behaviour, and, perhaps most important of all, life chances life degree to which people succeed in life in such areas as education, income, and health—how well people do in such areas as education, income, and health. We will see examples of these consequences in the pages ahead and end with a discussion of some promising policies and programs for reducing inequality and poverty.

EXPLAINING STRATIFICATION

The Conflict View

Conflict theory's explanation of stratification draws on Karl Marx's view of class societies and incorporates the critique of the functionalist view just discussed. Many different explanations grounded in conflict theory exist, but they all assume that stratification stems from a fundamental conflict between the needs and interests of the powerful, or "haves," in society and those of the weak, or "have-nots" (Kerbo, 2009). The former take advantage of their position at the top of society to stay at the top, even if it means oppressing those at the bottom. At a minimum, they can heavily influence the law, the media, and other institutions in a way that maintains society's class structure.

Ideology and Stratification

In explaining stratification, conflict theory emphasizes ideology set of beliefs that supports the status quo., or a set of ideas that justifies the status quo. This emphasis goes back to the work of Marx, who said the ruling class shapes and even controls the ruling ideas of a society. It tries to shape these ideas so that they justify the existing order and decrease the chances that the poor will challenge it. The key goal of the ruling class here is to prevent the poor from achieving class. An awareness of one's social class membership, the structural reasons for it, and the needs arising from such membership., or an awareness of their oppression and the true reasons for it. If the poor instead do not recognize their interests as a class that does not control the means of production.

As an example, Marx called religion the "opiate of the masses." By this he meant that religious beliefs influence the poor to feel that their fate in life is God's will or a test of their belief in God. If they hold such beliefs, they will neither blame their poverty on the rich nor rebel against them. Religious beliefs help create false consciousness. Ideological beliefs bolster every system of stratification and domination. In slave societies, the dominant ideology, and one that at least some slaves accepted, was that slaves are inferior to their masters and deserve no better fate in life. When U.S. slavery existed in the South, it was commonly thought that blacks were biologically inferior and suited only to be slaves. Caste societies, as we noted earlier, have similar beliefs that justify the existence and impact of the caste system. Hitler's "final solution" likewise rested on the belief that Jews and other groups he targeted were biologically inferior and deserving of extermination.

Ideological beliefs in class societies are more subtle and complex but nonetheless influential. One of the most important beliefs in the United States is the American Dream, epitomized by the story of Abraham Lincoln. According to this belief, people born into poverty can lift themselves up by the bootstraps and become successful if they work hard enough. By implication, if people remain poor, they are not trying hard enough or have other personal deficiencies keeping them in poverty. This ideology prompts many Americans to take a blaming-the-victim approach by blaming poverty on laziness and other problems in the poor rather than on discrimination and the lack of opportunity in society. To the extent that people accept such ideological beliefs, they are less likely to criticize the existing system of stratification. Marx did not foresee the extent to which these beliefs in the United States would impede the development of class consciousness.

Symbolic Interactionism

Consistent with its micro orientation, symbolic interactionism tries to understand stratification by looking at people's interaction and understandings in their daily lives. Unlike the functionalist and conflict views, it does not try to explain why we have stratification in the first place. Rather, it examines the differences that stratification makes for people's lifestyles and their interaction with other people.

One of the most insightful analyses of stratification that fits into a symbolic interactionist framework was Thorstein Veblin's (1899/1953) famous discussion of *conspicuous consumption*, or the acquisition and display by the wealthy of lavish products that show off their wealth. The very rich do not "need" mansions or other very opulent homes, and neither do they need a motor vehicle costing upward of $100,000 or more or jewellery costing thousands and thousands of dollars. Yet they purchase these products to show off their wealth and to feel better about themselves. The lifestyles of the rich are featured in classic novels by writers such as F. Scott Fitzgerald and in classic films such as *The Philadelphia Story*, starring the formidable trio of Katharine Hepburn, Cary Grant, and James Stewart. Although one message of many of these cultural works is that money does not always bring happiness, it remains true, as Fitzgerald once wrote, "Let me tell you about the very rich. They are different from you and me."

Examples of the symbolic interactionist framework are also seen in the many literary works and films that portray the difficulties that the rich and poor have in interacting on the relatively few occasions when they do interact. For example, in the film *Pretty Woman*, Richard Gere plays a rich businessman who hires a prostitute, played by Julia Roberts, to accompany him to swank parties and other affairs. Roberts has to buy a new wardrobe and learn how to dine and behave in rich social settings, and much of the film's humour and poignancy come from her awkwardness in learning the lifestyle of the rich.

If there are many dramatic and humorous accounts of the "lifestyles of the rich and famous," there are also many sociological and other accounts of lives of the poor. Poverty is discussed later in this chapter, but for now it is sufficient to say that the poor often lead lives of quiet desperation and must find many ways of coping with the fact of being poor. Studies of the poor, too, reflect the symbolic interactionist perspective.

GLOBAL STRATIFICATION

Classifying Global Stratification

For the sake of clarity and simplicity, the best way to understand global stratification is to think of the world composed of three categories of nations, based on their degree of wealth or poverty, their level of industrialization and economic development, and related factors. Over the decades, scholars and international organizations such as the United Nations and World Bank have used various classification systems containing three categories.

One of the first typologies came into use after World War II and classified nations as falling into the *First World*, *Second World*, and *Third World*. The First World was generally the western, capitalist democracies of North America and Europe and certain other nations (Australia, New Zealand, Japan). The Second World was the nations belonging to the Soviet Union, while the Third World was all the remaining nations, almost all of them from Central and South America, Africa, and Asia. Although this classification was useful for several reasons, the demise of the Soviet Union by the end of 1991 caused it to fall out of favor.

A replacement typology placed nations into *developed*, *developing*, and *undeveloped* categories, respectively. Although this typology was initially popular, critics said that calling nations "developed" made them sound superior, while calling nations "undeveloped" made them sound inferior. Although this classification scheme is still used, it, too, has begun to fall out of favor.

Today a popular typology simply ranks nations into groups called *wealthy* (or *high-income*) nations, *middle-income nations*, and *poor* (or *low-income*) nations. This classification has the advantage of being based on the most important economic difference among the nations of the world: how much income and wealth they have. At the risk of being somewhat simplistic, the other important differences among the world's nations all stem from their degree of wealth or poverty.

Wealthy Nations

The wealthy nations are the most industrialized nations, and they consist primarily of the nations of North America and Western Europe; Australia, Japan, and New Zealand; and certain other nations in the Middle East and Asia. Many of them were the first nations to become industrialized starting in the 19th century, when the Industrial Revolution began, and their early industrialization certainly contributed to the great wealth they enjoy today. Yet it is also true that many Western European nations were also wealthy before the Industrial Revolution, thanks in part to the fact that they had been colonial powers and acquired wealth from the resources of the lands that they colonized. Although wealthy nations constitute only about one-fifth of the world's population, they hold about four-fifths of the world's entire wealth. They are the leading nations in industry, high finance, and information technology. Although each of the world's wealthy nations is internally stratified to a greater or lesser degree, these nations as a group live a much more comfortable existence than middle-income nations and, especially, poor nations. People in wealthy nations are more educated and healthier, and they enjoy longer lives. At the same time, wealthy nations use up more than their fair share of the world's natural resources, and their high level of industrialization causes them to pollute and otherwise contribute to climate change to a far greater degree than is true of nations in the other two categories.

Middle-Income Nations

Middle-income nations are generally less industrialized than wealthy nations but more industrialized than poor nations. They consist primarily of nations in Central and South America, Eastern Europe, and parts of Africa and Asia and constitute about one-third of the world's population. There is much variation in income and wealth within the middle-income category, even within the same continent. In South America, for example, the gross national income per capita in Chile, adjusted to U.S. dollars, is $13,270 (2008 figures), compared to only $4,140 in Bolivia (Population Reference Bureau, 2009). Thus many international organizations and scholars find it useful to further divide middle-income nations into upper-middle-income nations and lower-middle-income nations. Not surprisingly, many more people in the latter nations live in dire economic circumstances than those in the former nations. In Bolivia, for example, 30% of the population lives on less than $2 per day, compared to only 5% in Chile.

Poor Nations

Poor nations are certainly the least industrialized and most agricultural of all the world's countries. This category consists primarily of nations in Africa and parts of Asia and constitutes roughly half of the world's population.

By any standard, people in these nations live a desperate existence in the most miserable conditions possible. They suffer from AIDS and other deadly diseases, live on the edge of starvation, and lack indoor plumbing, electricity, and other modern conveniences that most Americans take for granted. Most of us have seen unforgettable photos or video of African children with stick-thin limbs and distended stomachs symptomatic of severe malnutrition. We revisit their plight in a later section on the consequences of global stratification.

Explaining Global Stratification

Explanations of global stratification parallel those of U.S. inequality in their focus on individual versus structural problems. One type of explanation takes an individual, blaming-the-victim approach by in effect blaming the people in the poorest nations for their own poverty, while a second explanation takes a more structural approach in blaming the situation of the poorest nations on their treatment by the richest ones. Again there is evidence to support both types of explanations, but many sociologists favor the more structural explanation.

Modernization Theory

The individual explanation is called modernization theory. The view that global stratification results from a failure of poor nations to have the beliefs, values, and practices necessary for industrialization and rapid economic growth. (Rostow, 1990). According to this theory, rich nations became wealthy because early on they were able to develop the "correct" beliefs, values, and practices—in short, the correct culture—for trade, industrialization, and rapid economic growth to occur. These cultural traits include a willingness to work hard, to abandon tradition in favor of new ways of thinking and doing things, and to adopt a future orientation rather than one aimed toward the present.

Modernization theory has direct relevance for the experience of Western Europe. According to the theory, Western European nations began to emerge several centuries ago as economic powers because their populations adopted the kinds of values and practices just listed.

According to Max Weber (1904/1958), one of the founders of sociology, Western Europe was able to do this because the Protestant Reformation diminished the traditional distrust of the Catholic Church for material success and social and economic change. The new Protestant ethic that Western Europeans adopted stressed the importance of hard work and material success in one's lifetime, rather than the traditional emphasis on rewards in an afterlife.

According to modernization theory, nations in other parts of the world never became wealthy and remain poor today because they never developed the values and practices just listed. Instead, they continued to follow traditional beliefs and practices that stymied industrial development and modernization.

As should be clear, modernization theory has much in common with the culture of poverty theory discussed earlier. It attributes the poverty of poor nations to their failure to develop the "proper" beliefs, values, and practices necessary for economic success both at the beginning of industrialization during the 19th century and in the two centuries that have since transpired. Because modernization theory implies that people in poor nations do not have the talent and ability to improve their lot, it falls into the functionalist explanation of stratification.

Dependency Theory

The structural explanation for global stratification is called dependency theory. The view that global stratification results from colonialization and exploitation of the poorest nations by the richest ones.. Not surprisingly, this theory's views sharply challenge modernization theory's assumptions (Packenham, 1992). Whereas modernization theory attributes global stratification to the "wrong" cultural values and practices in the poorest nations, dependency theory blames global stratification on the exploitation of these nations by the rich ones. According to this view, the poor nations never got the chance to pursue economic growth because early on they were conquered and colonized by European ones. The European nations stole the poor nation's resources and either enslaved their populations or used them as cheap labour. Because dependency theory implies that poor nations remain poor because of lack of opportunity owing to exploitation by wealthy nations, it falls into the conflict perspective on stratification.

In today's world, huge multinational corporations continue to exploit the labour and resources of the poorest nations, say dependency theorists. Often these corporations work hand-in-hand with corrupt officials in the poor nations to strengthen their economic stake in the countries. An example of this dynamic occurred during the 1990s in the poor western African country of Nigeria, where the Royal Dutch/Shell oil company at the time was pumping half of that nation's oil. Activists in southern Nigeria began to claim that Shell's oil drilling was destroying their land and that Shell was paying them too little for their oil. In response to their protests, the government sent in police at Shell's request, with Shell paying some of the police costs. The police put down the activists' dissent by destroying several villages and killing 2,000 people.

Which makes more sense, modernization theory or dependency theory? As with many theories, both make sense to some degree, but both have their faults. Modernization theory places too much blame on poor nations for their own poverty and ignores the long history of exploitation of poor nations by rich nations and multinational corporations alike. For its part, dependency theory cannot explain why some of the poorest countries are poor even though they were never European colonies; neither can it explain why some former colonies such as Hong Kong have been able to attain enough economic growth to leave the rank of the poorest nations. Together, both theories help us understand the reasons for global stratification, but most sociologists would probably favor dependency theory because of its emphasis on structural factors in the world's historic and current economy.

Effects of Global Stratification

Global stratification greatly affects the life chances of people around the world. As noted earlier, people in the poorest nations live in some of the worst conditions possible. AIDS, malaria, starvation, and other deadly diseases are common. Many children die before reaching adolescence, and many adults die before reaching what in the richest nations would be considered their middle age. Many people in the poorest nations are illiterate, and a college education remains as foreign to them as their way of life would be to us.

One of the most important indicators of a nation's well-being is infant mortality (the number of infant deaths during the first year of life for every 1,000 births), and the global picture of infant mortality presents sad, striking evidence of the difference that a nation's poverty makes. Because of poor prenatal and postnatal nutrition, disease, and the other dire conditions facing people in the poorest nations, their rates of infant mortality are shockingly high and manifest one tragic effect of global poverty.

4

Race and Ethnicity Discrimination

RACE AND ETHNICITY

The goal of this tutorial is to help you objectively analyse the phenomena of race and ethnicity as well as some of the world wide patterns of discrimination based on them. In doing this, it is important to suspend our own biases as much as possible and to take a cultural relativity approach. That is to say, we must not let our own cultural biases get in the way of understanding the lives of other people. This is a very difficult task given the emotionally charged feelings and deep beliefs that most people have concerning race and ethnicity. However, suspending these attitudinal barriers in order to gain a better understanding of the phenomena is worth the effort.

Have you ever asked yourself what are the defining characteristics of being "white" or "black" in America today? Is it solely a matter of skin color? Are other factors as important or even more important? What makes someone "Hispanic" or "Latino." Is it language? Country of origin? Cultural traditions? Family values? Religion? Skin color? Can you be "white" or "black" and Hispanic at the same time? Can you be a non-Spanish speaking member of one of Mexico's Indian communities and be Hispanic? Are people from Spain and Portuguese speaking Brazilians Hispanic? The answers to these questions probably are not entirely clear to you nor are they to most Americans. It addition, the answers very likely will differ depending on the region of America in which you live. The ways in which we personally acquire our own group identities are often complex. Similarly, the way we assign group identity to others is not always straight forward. Race and ethnic group labels in America are not clearly based on criteria that everyone understand, agree with, and can easily use. As a result, someone else may label you in a way that you consider inaccurate and very offensive. This can instantly create a barrier to open communication even if the slight was unintended.

To comprehend the human diversity of the United States or any other country, it is important to first understand the criteria commonly used for making group distinctions. These generally are based on cultural and/or biological factors. Americans tend to see each other in terms of age, economic class, religion, gender, ethnicity, and race. We are usually a member of a particular group for each of these criteria. Which of our group identities is most important varies with the social situation. In America today, gender, ethnicity, and race often have the most far ranging impacts on us as individuals.

Ethnicity refers to selected cultural and sometimes physical characteristics used to classify people into groups or categories considered to be significantly different from others. Commonly recognized American ethnic groups include American Indians, Latinos, Chinese, African Americans, European Americans, etc. In some cases, ethnicity involves merely a loose group identity with little or no cultural traditions in common. This is the case with many Irish and German Americans. In contrast, some ethnic groups are coherent subcultures with a shared language and body of tradition. Newly arrived immigrant groups often fit this pattern.

It is important not to confuse the term minority with ethnic group. Ethnic groups may be either a minority or a majority in a population. Whether a group is a minority or a majority also is not an absolute fact but depends on the perspective. For instance, in some towns along the southern border of the U.S., people of Mexican ancestry are the overwhelming majority population and control most of the important social and political institutions but are still defined by state and national governments as a minority. In small homogenous societies, such as those of hunters and gatherers and pastoralists, there is essentially only one ethnic group and no minorities.

For many people, ethnic categorization implies a connection between biological inheritance and culture. They believe that biological inheritance determines much of cultural identity. If this were true, for instance, African American cultural traits, such as "black English", would stem from genetic inheritance. We now know that this is not true—biological race and culture are not the same thing. The pioneering English anthropologist Edward Tylor may have been the first scientist to understand this fact and to state it in print. In 1871, he wrote that cultural traits are entirely learned. Subsequently, a baby can be placed into another culture shortly after birth and can be thoroughly enculturated to that culture, regardless of their skin color, body shape, and other presumed racial features. For example, both women in the photographs on the right are genetically African, but they do not speak the same language nor do they share any other significant cultural patterns due to the fact that they were brought up in very different societies. The African American woman is far more similar culturally to her European American neighbours than to the West African woman from Senegal.

A race is a biological subspecies, or variety of a species, consisting of a more or less distinct population with anatomical traits that distinguish it clearly from other races. This biologist's definition does not fit the reality of human genetic variation today. We are an extremely homogenous species genetically. As a matter of fact, all humans today are 99.9% genetically identical, and most of the variation that does occur is in the difference between males and females and our unique personal traits. This homogeneity is very unusual in the animal kingdom. Even our closest biological relatives, the chimpanzees have 2-3 times more genetic variation than people. Orangutans have 8-10 times more variation.

It is now clear that our human "races" are primarily cultural creations, not biological realities. The commonly held belief in the existence of human biological races is based on the false assumption that anatomical traits, such as skin color and specific facial characteristics, cluster together in single distinct groups of people. They do not. There are no clearly distinct "black", "white", or other races.

The popularly held view of human races ignores the fact that anatomical traits supposedly identifying a particular race are often found extensively in other populations as well. This is due to the fact that similar natural selection factors in different parts of the world often result in the evolution of similar adaptations. For instance, intense sunlight in tropical latitudes has selected for darker skin color as a protection from intense ultraviolet radiation. As a result, the dark brown skin color characteristic of sub-Saharan Africans is also found among unrelated populations in the Indian subcontinent, Australia, New Guinea, and elsewhere in the Southwest Pacific.

The actual patterns of biological variation among humans are extremely complex and constantly changing. They can also be deceptive. All of us could be classified into a number of different "races", depending on the traits that are emphasized. For example, if people are sorted on the basis of stature or blood types, the geographic groupings will be clearly different from those defined on the basis of skin color. Using the B blood type for defining races, Australian Aborigines would be lumped together with most Native Americans. Some Africans would be in the same race as Europeans while others would be categorized with Asians.

Historically in the Western World, human "races" have been defined on the basis of a small number of superficial anatomical characteristics that can be readily identified at a distance, thereby making discrimination easier. Focusing on such deceptive distinguishing traits as skin color, body shape, and hair texture causes us to magnify differences and ignore similarities between people. It is also important to remember that these traits are no more accurate in making distinctions between human groups than any other genetically inherited characteristics. All such attempts to scientifically divide humanity into biological races have proven fruitless.

In the final analysis, it is clear that people, not nature, create our identities. Ethnicity and supposed "racial" groups are largely cultural and historical constructs. They are primarily social rather than biological phenomena. This does not mean that they do not exist. To the contrary, "races" are very real in the world today. In order to understand them, however, we must look into culture and social interaction rather than biology.

Racial discrimination differentiates between individuals on the basis of real and perceived racial differences, and has been official government policy in several countries, such as South Africa in the apartheid era, and the USA.

In the United States, racial profiling of minorities by law enforcement officials has been called racial discrimination. As early as 1865, the Civil Rights Act provided a remedy for intentional race discrimination in employment by private employers and state and local public employers. The Civil Rights Act of 1871 applies to public employment or employment involving state action prohibiting deprivation of rights secured by the federal constitution or federal laws through action under colour of law. Title VII is the principal federal statute with regard to employment discrimination prohibiting unlawful employment discrimination by public and private employers, labour organizations, training programs and employment agencies based on race or colour, religion, gender, and national origin.

Within the criminal justice system in some Western countries, minorities are convicted and imprisoned disproportionately when compared with whites. In 1998, nearly one out of three black men between the ages of 20-29 were in prison or jail, on probation or parole on any given day in the United States. First Nations make up about 2% of Canada's population, but account for 18% of the federal prison population as of 2000. According to the Australian government's June 2006 publication of prison statistics, indigenous peoples make up 24% of the overall prison population in Australia. In 2004, Maori made up just 15% of the total population of New Zealand but 49.5% of prisoners. Maori were entering prison at 8 times the rate of non-Maori. A quarter of the people in England's prisons are from an ethnic minority. The Equality and Human Rights Commission found that five times more black people than white people per head of population in England and Wales are imprisoned. Experts and politicians said over-representation of black men was a result of decades of racial prejudice in the criminal justice system.

Racism

Racism is the belief that the genetic factors which constitute race are a primary determinant of human traits and capacities and that racial differences produce an inherent superiority of a particular race. Racism's effects are called "racial discrimination." In the case of institutional racism, certain racial groups may be denied rights or benefits, or receive preferential treatment.

Racial discrimination typically points out taxonomic differences between different groups of people, although anyone may be discriminated against on an ethnic or cultural basis, independently of their somatic differences. According to the United Nations conventions, there is no distinction between the term racial discrimination and ethnicity discrimination. There is some evidence that the meaning of the term has changed over time, and that earlier definitions of racism involved the simple belief that human populations are divided into separate races. Many biologists, anthropologists, and sociologists reject this taxonomy in favor of more specific and/or empirically verifiable criteria, such as geography, ethnicity, or a history of endogamy.

Definitions

Although the term racism usually denotes race-based prejudice, violence, dislike, discrimination, or oppression, the term can also have varying and contested definitions. *Racialism* is a related term, sometimes intended to avoid these negative meanings. According to the *Oxford English Dictionary*, racism is a belief or ideology that all members of each racial group possess characteristics or abilities specific to that race, especially to distinguish it as being either superior or inferior to another racial group or racial groups.

The *Merriam-Webster's Dictionary* defines racism as a belief that race is the primary determinant of human traits and capacities and that racial differences produce an inherent superiority or inferiority of a particular racial group, and that it is also the prejudice based on such a belief. The *Macquarie Dictionary* defines racism as: "the belief that human races have distinctive characteristics which determine their respective cultures, usually involving the idea that one's own race is superior and has the right to rule or dominate others."

Legal

The UN does not define "racism", however it does define "racial discrimination": according to the United Nations Convention on the Elimination of All Forms of Racial Discrimination, *the term "racial discrimination" shall mean any distinction, exclusion, restriction or preference based on race, colour, descent, or national or ethnic origin which has the purpose or effect of nullifying or impairing the recognition, enjoyment or exercise, on an equal footing, of human rights and fundamental freedoms in the political, economic, social, cultural or any other field of public life.*

This definition does not make any difference between discrimination based on ethnicity and race, in part because the distinction between the two remains debatable among anthropologists. Similarly, in British law the phrase *racial group* means "any group of people who are defined by reference to their race, colour, nationality (including citizenship) or ethnic or national origin".

Sociological

Some sociologists have defined racism as a system of group privilege. In *Portraits of White Racism*, David Wellman has defined racism as "culturally sanctioned beliefs, which, regardless of intentions involved, defend the advantages whites have because of the subordinated position of racial minorities". Sociologists Noël A. Cazenave and Darlene Alvarez Maddern define racism as "...a highly organized system of 'race'-based group privilege that operates at every level of society and is held together by a sophisticated ideology of colour/'race' supremacy. Sellers and Shelton (2003) found that a relationship between racial discrimination and emotional distress was moderated by racial ideology and public regard beliefs. That is, racial centrality appears to promote the degree of discrimination African American young adults perceive whereas racial ideology may buffer the detrimental emotional effects of that discrimination. Racist systems include, but cannot be reduced to, racial bigotry,". Sociologist and former American Sociological Association president Joe Feagin argues that the United States can be characterized as a "total racist society"

"Police harassment and brutality directed at black men, women, and children are as old as American society, dating back to the days of slavery and Jim Crow segregation. Such police actions across the nation today reveal important aspects of... the commonplace discriminatory practices of individual whites... [and] white dominated institutions that allow or encourage such practices.."

TYPES

Racial Discrimination

Racial discrimination is treating people differently through a process of social division into categories not necessarily related to races. Racial segregation policies may officialize it, but it is also often exerted without being legalized. Researchers, including Dean Karlan and Marianne Bertrand, at the MIT and the University of Chicago found in a 2003 study that there was widespread discrimination in the workplace against job applicants whose names were merely perceived as "sounding black". These applicants were 50% less likely than candidates perceived as having "white-sounding names" to receive callbacks for interviews. In contrast, institutions and courts have upheld discrimination against whites when it is done to promote a diverse work or educational environment, even when it was shown to be to the detriment of qualified applicants. The researchers view these results as strong evidence of unconscious biases rooted in the United States' long history of discrimination (i.e. Jim Crow laws, etc.)

Institutional

Institutional racism (also known as structural racism, state racism or systemic racism) is racial discrimination by governments, corporations, religions, or educational institutions or other large organizations with the power to influence the lives of many individuals. Stokely Carmichael is credited for coining the phrase *institutional racism* in the late 1960s. He defined the term as "the collective failure of an organization to provide an appropriate and professional service to people because of their colour, culture or ethnic origin".

Maulana Karenga argued that racism constituted the destruction of culture, language, religion and human possibility, and that the effects of racism were "the morally monstrous destruction of human possibility involved redefining African humanity to the world, poisoning past, present and future relations with others who only know us through this stereotyping and thus damaging the truly human relations among peoples."

Economic

Historical economic or social disparity is alleged to be a form of discrimination which is caused by past racism and historical reasons, affecting the present generation through deficits in the formal education and kinds of preparation in the parents' generation, and, through primarily unconscious racist attitudes and actions on members of the general population. (e.g. A member of race Y, Mary, has her opportunities adversely affected (directly and/or indirectly) by the mistreatment of her ancestors of race Y.)

A hypothesis embraced by classical economists is that competition in a capitalist economy decreases the impact of discrimination. The thinking behind the hypothesis is that discrimination imposes a cost on the employer, and thus a profit-driven employer will avoid racist hiring policies.

Although a capitalist economy would avoid discrimination in order to avoid extra cost, this can be avoided in other ways. A capitalist company for example may use racist hiring policies as it deviates towards the "cultural norm".

These "norms" albeit unquestioned are evident within society. In a predominantly white society when hiring a person of colour into a position of management this may then cause disputes, and damage communications between other employers. Thus the company would be economically put in a deficit because of the discrimination of other companies, as they invoke discrimination and isolate that company. Although this may be a radical, over exaggerated point of view, it portrays how pervasive racism is and how company will some time deviate towards racist hiring policies in order to henceforth be not isolated, thus preventing the company from going into an economic deficit. (Burton 2009:1)

For decades, African American farmers said they were unjustly being denied farm loans or subjected to longer waits for loan approval because of racism, and accused the U.S. Department of Agriculture (USDA) of not responding to their complaints.

During the Spanish colonial period, Spaniards developed a complex caste system based on race, which was used for social control and which also determined a person's importance in society. While many Latin American countries have long since rendered the system officially illegal through legislation, usually at the time of independence, prejudice based on degrees of perceived racial distance from European ancestry combined with one's socioeconomic status remain, an echo of the colonial caste system.

Almost uniformly, people who are darker-skinned and of indigenous descent make up the peasantry and working classes, while lighter-skinned, Spanish-descent Latin Americans are in the ruling elite.

DECLARATIONS AGAINST RACIAL DISCRIMINATION

In 1950, UNESCO suggested in *The Race Question* —a statement signed by 21 scholars such as Ashley Montagu, Claude Lévi-Strauss, Gunnar Myrdal, Julian Huxley, etc. — to "drop the term *race* altogether and instead speak of ethnic groups". The statement condemned scientific racism theories which had played a role in the Holocaust. It aimed both at debunking scientific racist theories, by popularizing modern knowledge concerning "the race question," and morally condemned racism as contrary to the philosophy of the Enlightenment and its assumption of equal rights for all. Along with Myrdal's *An American Dilemma: The Negro Problem and Modern Democracy* (1944), *The Race Question* influenced the 1954 U.S. Supreme Court desegregation decision in "Brown v. Board of Education of Topeka". The United Nations uses the definition of racial discrimination laid out in the *International*

Convention on the Elimination of All Forms of Racial Discrimination, adopted in 1966:...*any distinction, exclusion, restriction or preference based on race, colour, descent, or national or ethnic origin which has the purpose or effect of nullifying or impairing the recognition, enjoyment or exercise, on an equal footing, of human rights and fundamental freedoms in the political, economic, social, cultural or any other field of public life.*

In 2001, the European Union explicitly banned racism along with many other forms of social discrimination in the Charter of Fundamental Rights of the European Union, the legal effect of which, if any, would necessarily be limited to Institutions of the European Union: "Article 21 of the charter prohibits discrimination on any ground such as race, colour, ethnic or social origin, genetic features, language, religion or belief, political or any other opinion, membership of a national minority, property, disability, age or sexual orientation and also discrimination on the grounds of nationality."

Ideology

As an ideology, racism existed during the 19th century as "scientific racism", which attempted to provide a racial classification of humanity. Although such racist ideologies have been widely discredited after World War II and the Holocaust, racism and of racial discrimination have remained widespread all over the world. Some examples of this in present day are statistics including, but not limited to, the ratio of black men in prison to free black men vs. other races, physical abilities and mental ability statistics, and other data gathered by scientific groups. While these statistics are accurate, and can show trends, it's inappropriate in most countries to assume that because a particular race has a high crime or low literacy rate, that the entire race of people automatically are criminals or unintelligent.

It was already noted by DuBois that, in making the difference between races, it is not race that we think about, but culture: "...a common history, common laws and religion, similar habits of thought and a conscious striving together for certain ideals of life" Late 19th century nationalists were the first to embrace contemporary discourses on “race”, ethnicity and “survival of the fittest” to shape new nationalist doctrines. Ultimately, race came to represent not only the most important traits of the human body, but was also regarded as decisively shaping the character and personality of the nation.

According to this view, culture is the physical manifestation created by ethnic groupings, as such fully determined by racial characteristics. Culture and race became considered intertwined and dependent upon each other, sometimes even to the extent of including nationality or language to the set of definition. Pureness of race tended to be related to rather superficial characteristics that were easily addressed and advertised, such as blondness. Racial qualities tended to be related to nationality and language rather than the actual geographic distribution of racial characteristics. In the case of Nordicism, the denomination “Germanic” became virtually equivalent to superiority of race.

Bolstered by some nationalist and ethnocentric values and achievements of choice, this concept of racial superiority evolved to distinguish from other cultures, that were considered inferior or impure. This emphasis on culture corresponds to the modern mainstream definition of racism: “Racism does not originate from the existence of ‘races’. It *creates* them through a process of social division into categories: anybody can be racialised, independently of their somatic, cultural, religious differences.”

This definition explicitly ignores the fiery polemic on the biological concept of race, still subject to scientific debate. In the words of David C. Rowe “A racial concept, although sometimes in the guise of another name, will remain in use in biology and in other fields because scientists, as well as lay persons, are fascinated by human diversity, some of which is captured by race.”

Until recent history this racist abuse of physical anthropology has been politically exploited. Apart from being unscientific, racial prejudice became subject to international legislation. For instance, the Declaration on the Elimination of all Forms of Racial Discrimination, adopted by the United Nations General Assembly on November 20, 1963, address racial prejudice explicitly next to discrimination for reasons of race, colour or ethnic origin. Racism has been a motivating factor in social discrimination, racial segregation, hate speech and violence (such as pogroms, genocides and ethnic cleansings). Despite the persistence of racial stereotypes, humour and epithets in much everyday language, racial discrimination is illegal in many countries.

Ironically, anti-racism has also become a political instrument of abuse. Some politicians have practised *race baiting* in an attempt to win votes. In a reversal of values, anti-racism is being propagated by despots in the service of obscurantism and the suppression of women. Philosopher Pascal Bruckner claimed that *"Anti-racism in the UN has become the ideology of totalitarian regimes who use it in their own interests."*

Ethnic Nationalism

After the Napoleonic Wars, Europe was confronted with the new "nationalities question," leading to ceaseless reconfigurations of the European map, on which the frontiers between the states had been delimited during the 1648 Peace of Westphalia. Nationalism had made its first striking appearance with the invention of the *levée en masse* by the French revolutionaries, thus inventing mass conscription in order to be able to defend the newly founded Republic against the *Ancien Régime* order represented by the European monarchies. This led to the French Revolutionary Wars (1792–1802) and then to the Napoleonic conquests, and to the subsequent European-wide debates on the concepts and realities of nations, and in particular of nation-states. The Westphalia Treaty had divided Europe into various empires and kingdoms (Ottoman Empire, Holy Roman Empire, Swedish Empire, Kingdom of France, etc.), and for centuries wars were waged between princes (*Kabinettskriege* in German).

Modern nation-states appeared in the wake of the French Revolution, with the formation of patriotic sentiments for the first time in Spain during the Peninsula War (1808–1813 – known in Spanish as the Independence War). Despite the restoration of the previous order with the 1815 Congress of Vienna, the "nationalities question" became the main problem of Europe during the Industrial Era, leading in particular to the 1848 Revolutions, the Italian unification completed during the 1871 Franco-Prussian War, which itself culminated in the proclamation of the German Empire in the Hall of Mirrors in the Palace of Versailles, thus achieving the German unification.

Meanwhile, the Ottoman Empire, the "sick man of Europe", was confronted with endless nationalist movements, which, along with the dissolving of the Austrian-Hungarian Empire, would lead to the creation after World War I of the various nation-states of the Balkans, with "national minorities" in their borders. Ethnic nationalism, which advocated the belief in a hereditary membership of the nation, made its appearance in the historical context surrounding the creation of the modern nation-states.

One of its main influences was the Romantic nationalist movement at the turn of the 19th century, represented by figures such as Johann Herder (1744–1803), Johan Fichte (1762–1814) in the *Addresses to the German Nation* (1808), Friedrich Hegel (1770–1831), or also, in France, Jules Michelet (1798–1874). It was opposed to liberal nationalism, represented by authors such as Ernest Renan (1823–1892), who conceived of the nation as a community which, instead of being based on the *Volk* ethnic group and on a specific, common language, was founded on the subjective will to live together ("the nation is a daily plebiscite", 1882) or also John Stuart Mill (1806–1873).

Ethnic nationalism quickly blended itself with scientific racist discourses, as well as with "continental imperialist" discourses, for example in the pan-Germanism discourses, which postulated the racial superiority of the German Volk. The Pan-German League (*Alldeutscher Verband*), created in 1891, promoted German imperialism, "racial hygiene" and was opposed to intermarriage with Jews. Another, popular current, the *Völkisch movement*, was also an important proponent of the German ethnic nationalist discourse, which it also combined with modern antisemitism. Members of the Völkisch movement, in particular the Thule Society, would participate in the founding of the German Workers' Party (DAP) in Munich in 1918, the predecessor of the NSDAP Nazi party. Pan-Germanism and played a decisive role in the interwar period of the 1920s–1930s.

These currents began to associate the idea of the nation with the biological concept of a "master race" (often the "Aryan race" or "Nordic race") issued from the scientific racist discourse. They conflated nationalities with ethnic groups, called "races", in a radical distinction from previous racial discourses which posited the existence of a "race struggle" inside the nation and the state itself. Furthermore, they believed that political boundaries should mirror these alleged racial and ethnic groups, thus justifying ethnic cleansing in order to achieve "racial purity" and also to achieve ethnic homogeneity in the nation-state.

Such racist discourses, combined with nationalism, were not however limited to pan-Germanism. In France, the transition from Republican, liberal nationalism, to ethnic nationalism, which made nationalism a characteristic of far-right movements in France, took place during the Dreyfus Affair at the end of the 19th century. During several years, a nation-wide crisis affected French society, concerning the alleged treason of Alfred Dreyfus, a French Jewish military officer. The country polarized itself into two opposite camps, one represented by Émile Zola, who wrote *J'accuse* in defence of Alfred Dreyfus, and the other represented by the nationalist poet Maurice Barrès (1862–1923), one of the founders of the ethnic nationalist discourse in France. At the same time, Charles Maurras (1868–1952), founder of the monarchist *Action française* movement, theorized the "anti-France," composed of the "four confederate states of Protestants, Jews, Freemasons and foreigners". Indeed, to him the first three were all "internal foreigners," who threatened the ethnic unity of the French people.

ETHNIC CONFLICTS

Debates over the origins of racism often suffer from a lack of clarity over the term. Many use the term "racism" to refer to more general phenomena, such as xenophobia and ethnocentrism, although scholars attempt to clearly distinguish those phenomena from racism as an ideology or from scientific racism, which has little to do with ordinary xenophobia. Others conflate recent forms of racism with earlier forms of ethnic and national conflict. In most cases, ethno-national conflict seems to owe itself to conflict over land and strategic resources. In some cases ethnicity and nationalism were harnessed to rally combatants in wars between great religious empires.

Notions of race and racism often have played central roles in such ethnic conflicts. Historically, when an adversary is identified as "other" based on notions of race or ethnicity (particularly when "other" is construed to mean "inferior"), the means employed by the self-presumed "superior" party to appropriate territory, human chattel, or material wealth often have been more ruthless, more brutal, and less constrained by moral or ethical considerations. According to historian Daniel Richter, Pontiac's Rebellion saw the emergence on both sides of the conflict of "the novel idea that all Native people were 'Indians,' that all Euro-Americans were 'Whites,' and that all on one side must unite to destroy the other." Basil Davidson insists in his documentary, *Africa: Different but Equal*, that racism, in fact, only just recently surfaced—as late as the 19th century, due to the need for a justification for slavery in the Americas.

The idea of slavery as an "equal-opportunity employer" was denounced with the introduction of Christian theory in the West. Maintaining that Africans were "subhuman" was the only loophole in the then accepted law that "men are created equal" that would allow for the sustenance of the Triangular Trade. New peoples in the Americas, possible slaves, were encountered, fought, and ultimately subdued, but then due to European diseases, their populations drastically decreased. Through both influences, theories about "race" developed, and these helped many to justify the differences in position and treatment of people whom they categorized as belonging to different races.

Juan Ginés de Sepúlveda argued that, during the Valladolid controversy in the middle of the 16th century, the Native Americans were natural slaves because they had no *souls*. In Asia, the Chinese and Japanese Empires were both strong colonial powers, with the Chinese making colonies and vassal states of much of East Asia throughout history, and the Japanese doing the same in the 19th–20th centuries. In both cases, the

Asian imperial powers believed they were ethnically and racially preferenced too.

Academic Variants

Owen 'Alik Shahadah comments on this racism by stating: "Historically Africans are made to sway like leaves on the wind, impervious and indifferent to any form of civilization, a people absent from scientific discovery, philosophy or the higher arts. We are left to believe that almost nothing can come out of Africa, other than raw material."

Scottish philosopher and economist David Hume said, "I am apt to suspect the Negroes to be naturally inferior to the Whites. There scarcely ever was a civilised nation of that complexion, nor even any individual, eminent either in action or in speculation. No ingenious manufacture among them, no arts, no sciences." German philosopher Immanuel Kant stated: "The yellow Indians do have a meagre talent. The Negroes are far below them, and at the lowest point are a part of the American people."

In the 19th century, the German philosopher Georg Wilhelm Friedrich Hegel declared that "Africa is no historical part of the world." Hegel further claimed that blacks had no "sense of personality; their spirit sleeps, remains sunk in itself, makes no advance, and thus parallels the compact, undifferentiated mass of the African continent".

Fewer than 30 years before Nazi Germany started World War II, the German Otto Weininger, claimed: "A genius has perhaps scarcely ever appeared amongst the negroes, and the standard of their morality is almost universally so low that it is beginning to be acknowledged in America that their emancipation was an act of imprudence".

The German conservative Oswald Spengler remarked on what he perceived as the culturally degrading influence of Africans in modern Western culture: in *The Hour of Decision* Spengler denounced "the 'happy ending' of an empty existence, the boredom of which has brought to jazz music and Negro dancing to perform the Death March for a great Culture". During the Nazi era, German scientists rearranged academia to support claims of a grand "Aryan" agent behind the splendors of all human civilizations, including India and Ancient Egypt.

Scientific Variants

The modern biological definition of race developed in the 19th century with scientific racist theories. The term *scientific racism* refers to the use of science to justify and support racist beliefs, which goes back to at least the early 18th century, though it gained most of its influence in the mid-19th century, during the New Imperialism period. Also known as academic racism, such theories first needed to overcome the Church's resistance to positivist accounts of history, and its support of monogenism, that is that all human beings were originated from the same ancestors, in accordance with creationist accounts of history.

These racist theories put forth on scientific hypothesis were combined with unilineal theories of social progress which postulated the superiority of the European civilization over the rest of the world. Furthermore, they frequently made use of the idea of "survival of the fittest", a term coined by Herbert Spencer in 1864, associated with ideas of competition which were named social Darwinism in the 1940s. Charles Darwin himself opposed the idea of rigid racial differences in *The Descent of Man* (1871) in which he argued that humans were all of one species, sharing common descent. He recognised racial differences as varieties of humanity, and emphasised the close similarities between people of all races in mental faculties, tastes, dispositions and habits, while still contrasting the culture of the "lowest savages" with European civilization.

At the end of the 19th century, proponents of scientific racism intertwined themselves with eugenics discourses of "degeneration of the race" and "blood heredity." Henceforth, scientific racist discourses could be defined as the combination of polygenism, unilinealism, social darwinism and eugenism. They found their scientific legitimacy on physical anthropology, anthropometry, craniometry, phrenology, physiognomy and others now discredited disciplines in order to formulate racist prejudices. Before being disqualified in the 20th century by the American school of cultural anthropology (Franz Boas, etc.), the British school of social anthropology (Bronishaw Malinowski, Alfred Radcliffe-Brown, etc.), the French school of ethnology (Claude Lévi-Strauss, etc.), as well as the discovery of the neo-Darwinian synthesis, such sciences, in particular anthropometry, were used to deduce behaviours and psychological characteristics from outward, physical appearances.

The neo-Darwinian synthesis, first developed in the 1930s, eventually led to a gene-centred view of evolution in the 1960s. According to the Human Genome Project, the most complete mapping of human DNA to date indicates that there is no clear genetic basis to racial groups. While some genes are more common in certain populations, there are no genes which exist in all members of one population and no members of any other.

Heredity and Eugenics

The first theory of eugenics was developed in 1869 by Francis Galton (1822–1911), who used the then popular concept of *degeneration*. He applied statistics to study human differences and the alleged "inheritance of intelligence", foreshadowing future uses of "intelligence testing" by the anthropometry school. Such theories were vividly described by the writer Émile Zola (1840–1902), who started publishing in 1871 a twenty-novel cycle, *Les Rougon-Macquart*, where he linked heredity to behaviour. Thus, Zola described the high-born Rougons as those involved in politics (*Son Excellence Eugène Rougon*) and medicine (*Le Docteur Pascal*) and the low-born Macquarts as those fatally falling into alcoholism (*L'Assommoir*), prostitution (*Nana*), and homicide (*La Bête humaine*).

During the rise of Nazism in Germany, some scientists in Western nations worked to debunk the regime's racial theories. A few argued against racist ideologies and discrimination, even if they believed in the alleged existence of biological races. However, in the fields of anthropology and biology, these were minority positions until the mid-20th century. According to the 1950 UNESCO statement, *The Race Question*, an international project to debunk racist theories had been attempted in the mid-1930s. However, this project had been abandoned. Thus, in 1950, UNESCO declared that it had resumed:

Up again, after a lapse of fifteen years, a project which the International Institute for Intellectual Cooperation has wished to carry through but which it had to abandon in deference to the appeasement policy of the pre-war period. The race question had become one of the pivots of Nazi ideology and policy. Masaryk and Beneš took the initiative of calling for a conference to re-establish in the minds and consciences of men everywhere the truth about race... Nazi propaganda was able to continue its baleful work unopposed by the authority of an international organisation.

The Third Reich's racial policies, its eugenics programs and the extermination of Jews in the Holocaust, as well as Romani people in the Porrajmos (the Romani Holocaust) and others minorities led to a change in opinions about scientific research into race after the war. Changes within scientific disciplines, such as the rise of the Boasian school of anthropology in the United States contributed to this shift. These theories were strongly denounced in the 1950 UNESCO statement, signed by internationally renowned scholars, and titled *The Race Question*.

UNDERSTANDING SEX AND GENDER

Although the terms *sex* and *gender* are sometimes used interchangeably and do in fact complement each other, they nonetheless refer to different aspects of what it means to be a woman or man in any society.

Sex: The anatomical and other biological differences between females and males that are determined at the moment of conception and develop in the womb and throughout childhood and adolescence. refers to *the anatomical and other biological differences between females and males that are determined at the moment of conception and develop in the womb and throughout childhood and adolescence*. Females, of course, have two X chromosomes, while males have one X chromosome and one Y chromosome. From this basic genetic difference spring other biological differences. The first to appear are the different genitals that boys and girls develop in the womb and that the doctor (or midwife) and parents look for when a baby is born (assuming the baby's sex is not already known from ultrasound or other techniques) so that the momentous announcement,

"It's a boy!" or "It's a girl!" can be made. The genitalia are called primary sex characteristics. Anatomical and other biological differences between females and males that begin developing in the womb., while the other differences that develop during puberty are called secondary sex characteristicss. Biological differences between females and males that emerge during puberty and stem from hormonal differences between the two sexes. In this difficult period of adolescents' lives, boys generally acquire deeper voices, more body hair, and more muscles from their flowing testosterone. Girls develop breasts and wider hips and begin menstruating as nature prepares them for possible pregnancy and childbirth. For better or worse, these basic biological differences between the sexes affect many people's perceptions of what it means to be female or male, as we shall soon discuss.

Gender as a Social Construction

If sex is a biological concept, then gender. The social and cultural differences a society assigns to people based on their biological sex is a social concept. It refers to *the social and cultural differences a society assigns to people based on their (biological) sex*. A related concept, gender roles. A society's expectations of people's behaviour and attitudes based on whether they are females or males., refers to *a society's expectations of people's behaviour and attitudes based on whether they are females or males*. Understood in this way, gender, like race as discussed, *Race and Ethnicity*, is a *social construction*. How we think and behave as females and males is not etched in stone by our biology but rather is a result of how society expects us to think and behave based on what sex we are. As we grow up, we learn these expectations as we develop our gender identity. Individuals' beliefs about themselves as either females or males., or our beliefs about ourselves as females or males.

Sexual Orientation

Preference for sexual relationships with individuals of the opposite sex, the same sex, or both sexes refers to a person's preference for sexual relationships with individuals of the other sex (*heterosexuality*), one's own sex (*homosexuality*), or both sexes (*bisexuality*). The term also increasingly refers to *trans gendered* individuals, those whose behaviour, appearance, and/or gender identity fails to conform to conventional norms. Trans gendered individuals include *transvestites* (those who dress in the clothing of the opposite sex) and *transsexuals* (those whose gender identity differs from the physiological sex and who sometimes undergo a sex change).

It is difficult to know precisely how many people are gay, lesbian, bisexual, or trans gendered. One problem is conceptual. For example, what does it mean to be gay or lesbian? Does one need to actually have sexual relations with a same-sex partner to be considered gay? What if someone is attracted to same-sex partners but does not actually engage in sex with such persons? What if someone identifies as heterosexual but engages in homosexual sex for money (as in certain forms of prostitution) or for power and influence (as in much prison sex)? These conceptual problems make it difficult to determine the extent of homosexuality.

A second problem is empirical. Even if we can settle on a definition of homosexuality, how do we then determine how many people fit this definition? For better or worse, our best evidence of the number of gays and lesbians in the United States comes from surveys of national samples of Americans in which they are asked various questions about their sexuality. Although these are anonymous surveys, obviously at least some individuals may be reluctant to disclose their sexual activity and thoughts to an interviewer. Still, scholars think the estimates from these surveys are fairly accurate but that they probably underestimate by at least a small amount the number of gays and lesbians.

A widely cited survey carried out by researchers at the University of Chicago found that 2.8% of men and 1.4% of women identified themselves as gay/lesbian or bisexual, with greater percentages reporting having had sexual relations with same-sex partners or being attracted to same-sex persons. In the 2008 General Social Survey, 2.2% of men and 3.5% of women identified themselves as gay/lesbian or bisexual. Among individuals having had any sexual partners since turning 18, 2.2% of men reported having had at least some male partners, while 4.6% of women reported having had at least some female partners. Although precise numbers must remain unknown, it seems fair to say that between about 2% and 5% of Americans are gay/lesbian or bisexual.

If it is difficult to determine the number of people who are gay/lesbian or bisexual, it is even more difficult to determine why some people have this sexual orientation while most do not have it. Scholars disagree on the "causes" of sexual orientation. Some scholars attribute it to unknown biological factor(s) over which individuals have no control, just as individuals do not decide whether they are left-handed or right-handed. Supporting this view, many gays say they realized they were gay during adolescence, just as straights would say they realized they were straight during their own adolescence. Other scholars say that sexual orientation is at least partly influenced by cultural norms, so that individuals are more likely to identify as gay or straight depending on the cultural views of sexual orientation into which they are socialized as they grow up. At best, perhaps all we can say is that sexual orientation stems from a complex mix of biological and cultural factors that remain to be determined.

The Development of Gender Differences

What accounts for differences in female and male behaviour and attitudes? Do the biological differences between the sexes account for differences between these other differences? Or do these latter differences stem, as most sociologists think, from cultural expectations and from differences in the ways in which the sexes are socialized? These are critical questions, for they ask whether the differences between boys and girls and women and men stem more from biology or from society. The biological explanations for human behaviour implicitly support the status quo. If we think behavioral and other differences between the sexes are due primarily to their respective biological makeups, we are saying that these differences are inevitable or nearly so and that any attempt to change them goes against biology and will likely fail.

As an example, consider the obvious biological fact that women bear and nurse children and men do not. Couple this with the common view that women are also more gentle and nurturing than men, and we end up with a "biological recipe" for women to be the primary caretakers of children. Many people think this means women are therefore much better suited than men to take care of children once they are born, and that the family might be harmed if mothers work outside the home or if fathers are the primary caretakers. To the extent this belief exists, women may not want to work outside the home or, if they choose to do so, they face difficulties from employers, family, and friends. Conversely, men may not even think about wanting to stay at home and may themselves face difficulties from employees, family, and friends if they want to do so. A belief in a strong biological basis for differences between women and men implies, then, that there is little we can or should do to change these differences. It implies that "anatomy is destiny," and destiny is, of course, by definition inevitable.

This implication makes it essential to understand the extent to which gender differences do, in fact, stem from biological differences between the sexes or, instead, stem from cultural and social influences. If biology is paramount, then gender differences are perhaps inevitable and the status quo will remain. If culture and social influences matter much more than biology, then gender differences can change and the status quo may give way. With this backdrop in mind, let's turn to the biological evidence for behavioral and other differences between the sexes and then examine the evidence for their social and cultural roots.

Biology and Gender

Several biological explanations for gender roles exist, and we discuss two of the most important ones here. One explanation is from the related fields of sociobiology and evolutionary psychology and argues an evolutionary basis for traditional gender roles.

Scholars advocating this view reason as follows. In prehistoric societies, few social roles existed. A major role centered on relieving hunger by hunting or gathering food. The other major role centered on bearing and nursing children. Because only women could perform this role, they were also the primary caretakers for children for several years after birth. And because women were frequently pregnant, their roles as mothers confined them to the home for most of their adulthood. Meanwhile, men were better suited than women for hunting because they were stronger and quicker than women. In prehistoric societies, then, biology was indeed destiny: for biological reasons, men in effect worked outside the home (hunted), while women stayed at home with their children.

Evolutionary reasons also explain why men are more violent than women. In prehistoric times, men who were more willing to commit violence against and even kill other men would "win out" in the competition for female mates. They thus were more likely than less violent men to produce offspring, who would then carry these males' genetic violent tendencies. By the same token, men who were prone to rape women were more likely to produce offspring, who would then carry these males' "rape genes." This early process guaranteed that rape tendencies would be biologically transmitted and thus provides a biological basis for the amount of rape that occurs today.

If the human race evolved along these lines, sociobiologists and evolutionary psychologists continue, natural selection favoured those societies where men were stronger, braver, and more aggressive and where women were more fertile and nurturing. Such traits over the millennia became fairly instinctual, meaning that men's and women's biological natures evolved differently. Men became, by nature, more assertive, daring, and violent than women, and women are, by nature, more gentle, nurturing, and maternal than men. To the extent this is true, these scholars add, traditional gender roles for women and men make sense from an evolutionary standpoint, and attempts to change them go against the sexes' biological natures. This in turn implies that existing gender inequality must continue because it is rooted in biology. As the title of a book presenting the evolutionary psychology argument summarizes this implication, "biology at work: rethinking sexual equality" (Browne, 2002).

Critics challenge the evolutionary explanation on several grounds. First, much greater gender variation in behaviour and attitudes existed in prehistoric times than the evolutionary explanation assumes. Second, even if biological differences did influence gender roles in prehistoric times, these differences are largely irrelevant in today's world, in which, for example, physical strength is not necessary for survival. Third, human environments throughout the millennia have simply been too diverse to permit the simple, straightforward biological development that the evolutionary explanation assumes. Fourth, evolutionary arguments implicitly justify existing gender inequality by implying the need to confine women and men to their traditional roles.

Recent anthropological evidence also challenges the evolutionary argument that men's tendency to commit violence, including rape, was biologically transmitted. This evidence instead finds that violent men have trouble finding female mates who would want them and that the female mates they find and the children they produce are often killed by rivals to the men. The recent evidence also finds those rapists' children are often abandoned and then die. As one anthropologist summarizes the rape evidence, "The likelihood that rape is an evolved adaptation [is] extremely low. It just wouldn't have made sense for men in the [prehistoric epoch] to use rape as a reproductive strategy, so the argument that it's preprogrammed into us doesn't hold up".

A second biological explanation for traditional gender roles centres on hormones and specifically on testosterone, the so-called male hormone. One of the most important differences between boys and girls and men and women in the United States and many other societies is their level of aggression. Simply put, males are much more physically aggressive than females and in the United States commit about 85%–90% of all violent crimes.

To see whether testosterone does indeed raise aggression, investigators typically assess whether males with higher testosterone levels are more aggressive than those with lower testosterone levels. Several studies find that this is indeed the case. For example, a widely cited study of Vietnam-era male veterans found that those with higher levels of testosterone had engaged in more violent behaviour. However, this correlation does not necessarily mean that their testosterone increased their violence: as has been found in various animal species, it is also possible that their violence increased their testosterone. Because studies of human males can't for ethical and practical reasons manipulate their testosterone levels, the exact meaning of the results from these testosterone-aggression studies must remain unclear, according to a review sponsored by the National Academy of Sciences.

Another line of research on the biological basis for sex differences in aggression involves children, including some as young as ages 1 or 2, in various situations. They might be playing with each other, interacting with adults, or writing down solutions to hypothetical scenarios given to them by a researcher.

In most of these studies, boys are more physically aggressive in thought or deed than girls, even at a very young age. Other studies are more experimental in nature. In one type of study, a toddler will be playing with a toy, only to have it removed by an adult. Boys typically tend to look angry and to try to grab the toy back, while girls tend to just sit there and whimper. Because these gender differences in aggression are found at very young ages, researchers often say they must have some biological basis. However, critics of this line of research counter that even young children have already been socialized along gender lines, a point to which we return later. To the extent this is true, gender differences in children's aggression may simply reflect socialization and not biology.

In sum, biological evidence for gender differences certainly exists, but its interpretation remains very controversial. It must be weighed against the evidence, to which we next turn, of cultural variations in the experience of gender and of socialization differences by gender. One thing is clear: to the extent we accept biological explanations for gender, we imply that existing gender differences and gender inequality must continue to exist. This implication prompts many social scientists to be quite critical of the biological viewpoint. As Linda L. Lindsey (2011) notes, "Biological arguments are consistently drawn upon to justify gender inequality and the continued oppression of women." In contrast, cultural and social explanations of gender differences and gender inequality promise some hope for change. Let's examine the evidence for these explanations.

Culture and Gender

Some of the most compelling evidence against a strong biological determination of gender roles comes from anthropologists, whose work on preindustrial societies demonstrates some striking gender variation from one culture to another. This variation underscores the impact of culture on how females and males think and behave.

Margaret Mead (1935) was one of the first anthropologists to study cultural differences in gender. In New Guinea she found three tribes—the Arapesh, the Mundugumor, and the Tchambuli—whose gender roles differed dramatically. In the Arapesh both sexes were gentle and nurturing. Both women and men spent much time with their children in a loving way and exhibited what we would normally call maternal behaviour. In the Arapesh, then, different gender roles did not exist, and in fact, both sexes conformed to what Americans would normally call the female gender role.

The situation was the reverse among the Mundugumor. Here both men and women were fierce, competitive, and violent. Both sexes seemed to almost dislike children and often physically punished them. In the Mundugumor society, then, different gender roles also did not exist, as both sexes conformed to what we Americans would normally call the male gender role.

In the Tchambuli, Mead finally found a tribe where different gender roles did exist. One sex was the dominant, efficient, assertive one and showed leadership in tribal affairs, while the other sex liked to dress up in frilly clothes, wear makeup, and even giggle a lot. Here, then, Mead found a society with gender roles similar to those found in the United States, but with a surprising twist. In the Tchambuli, women were the dominant, assertive sex that showed leadership in tribal affairs, while men were the ones wearing frilly clothes and makeup.

Mead's research caused a firestorm in scholarly circles, as it challenged the biological view on gender that was still very popular when she went to New Guinea. In recent years, Mead's findings have been challenged by other anthropologists. Among other things, they argue that she probably painted an overly simplistic picture of gender roles in her three societies. Other anthropologists defend Mead's work and note that much subsequent research has found that gender-linked attitudes and behaviour do differ widely from one culture to another (S. Morgan, 1989). If so, they say, the impact of culture on what it means to be a female or male cannot be ignored.

Extensive evidence of this impact comes from anthropologist George Murdock, who created the Standard Cross-Cultural Sample of almost 200 preindustrial societies studied by anthropologists. Murdock (1937) found that some tasks in these societies, such as hunting and trapping, are almost always done by men, while other tasks, such as cooking and fetching water, are almost always done by women. These patterns provide evidence for the evolutionary argument presented earlier, as they probably stem from the biological differences between the sexes. Even so there were at least some societies in which women hunted and in which men cooked and fetched water.

More importantly, Murdock found much greater gender variation in several of the other tasks he studied, including planting crops, milking, and generating fires. Men primarily performed these tasks in some societies, women primarily performed them in other societies, and in still other societies both sexes performed them equally. Women are the primary weavers in about 61% of the societies that do weaving, men are the primary weavers in 32%, and both sexes do the weaving in 7% of the societies. Murdock's findings illustrate how gender roles differ from one culture to another and imply they are not biologically determined.

An example of this intermediary gender category may be found in India, where the *hirja* role involves males who wear women's clothing and identify as women (Reddy, 2006). The *hirja* role is an important part of Hindu mythology, in which androgynous figures play key roles both as humans and as gods. Today people identified by themselves and others as *hirjas* continue to play an important role in Hindu practices and in Indian cultural life in general. Serena Nanda (1997) calls *hirjas* "human beings who are neither man nor woman" and says they are thought of as "special, sacred beings" even though they are sometimes ridiculed and abused.

Anthropologists have found another androgynous gender composed of women warriors in 33 Native American groups in North America. Walter L. Williams (1997) calls these women "amazons" and notes that they dress like men and sometimes even marry women. In some tribes girls exhibit such "masculine" characteristics from childhood, while in others they may be recruited into "amazonhood." In the Kaska Indians, for example, a married couple with too many daughters would select one to "be like a man." When she was about 5 years of age, her parents would begin to dress her like a boy and have her do male tasks. Eventually she would grow up to become a hunter.

The androgynous genders found by anthropologists remind us that gender is a social construction and not just a biological fact. If culture does affect gender roles, socialization is the process through which culture has this effect. What we experience as girls and boys strongly influences how we develop as women and men in terms of behaviour and attitudes. To illustrate this important dimension of gender, let's turn to the evidence on socialization.

Socialization and Gender

The Family

Socialization into gender roles begins in infancy, as almost from the moment of birth parents begin to socialize their children as boys or girls without even knowing it. Many studies document this process (Lindsey, 2011). Parents commonly describe their infant daughters as pretty, soft, and delicate and their infant sons as strong, active, and alert, even though neutral observers find no such gender differences among infants when they do not know the infants' sex. From infancy on, parents play with and otherwise interact with their daughters and sons differently. They play more roughly with their sons—for example, by throwing them up in the air or by gently wrestling with them—and more quietly with their daughters. When their infant or toddler daughters cry, they warmly comfort them, but they tend to let their sons cry longer and to comfort them less. They give their girls dolls to play with and their boys "action figures" and toy guns. While these gender differences in socialization are probably smaller now than a generation ago, they certainly continue to exist. Go into a large toy store and you will see pink aisles of dolls and cooking sets and blue aisles of action figures, toy guns, and related items.

Peers

Peer influences also encourage gender socialization. As they reach school age, children begin to play different games based on their gender. Boys tend to play sports and other competitive team games governed by inflexible rules and relatively large numbers of roles, while girls tend to play smaller, cooperative games such as hopscotch and jumping rope with fewer and more flexible rules. Although girls are much more involved in sports now than a generation ago, these gender differences in their play as youngsters persist and continue to reinforce gender roles. For example, they encourage competitiveness in boys and cooperation and trust among girls. Boys who are not competitive risk being called "sissy" or other words by their peers. The patterns we see in adult males and females thus have their roots in their play as young children.

Sociology Making a Difference

In considering the debate, discussed in the text, between biology and sociology over the origins of gender roles, some widely cited studies by sociologists over gender differences in children's play and games provide important evidence for the importance of socialization.

Janet Lever (1978) studied fifth-grade children in three different communities in Connecticut. She watched them play and otherwise interact in school and also had the children keep diaries of their play and games outside school. One of her central aims was to determine how complex the two sexes' play and games were in terms of such factors as number of rules, specialization of roles, and size of the group playing. In all of these respects, Lever found that boys' play and games were typically more complex than girls' play and games. She attributed these differences to socialization by parents, teachers, and other adults and argued that the complexity of boys' play and games helped them to be better able than girls to learn important social skills such as dealing with rules and coordinating actions to achieve goals.

Meanwhile, Barrie Thorne (1993) spent many months observing fourth and fifth graders in two different working-class communities in California and Michigan sit in class and lunchrooms and play on the school playgrounds. Most children were white, but several were African American or Latino. As you might expect, the girls and boys she observed usually played separately from each other, and the one-sex groups in which they played were very important for the development of their gender identity, with boys tending to play team sports and other competitive games and girls tending to play cooperative games such as jump rope. These differences led Thorne to conclude that gender-role socialization stems not only from practices by adults but also from the children's own activities without adult involvement. When boys and girls did interact, it was often "girls against the boys" or vice-versa in classroom spelling contests and in games such as tag. Thorne concluded that these "us against them" contests helped the children learn that boys and girls are two different and antagonistic sexes and that gender itself is antagonistic, even if there were also moments when both sexes interacted on the playground in more relaxed, noncompetitive situations. Boys also tended to disrupt girls' games more than the reverse and in this manner both exerted and learned dominance over females. In all of these ways, children were not just the passive recipients of gender-role socialization from adults (their teachers), but they also played an active role in ensuring that such socialization occurred.

The studies by Lever and Thorne were among the first to emphasize the importance of children's play and peer relationships for gender socialization. They also called attention to the importance of the traits and values learned through such socialization for outcomes later in life. The rise in team sports opportunities for girls in the years since Lever and Thorne did their research is a welcome development that addresses the concerns expressed in their studies, but young children continue to play in the ways that Lever and Thorne found. To the extent children's play has the consequences just listed, and to the extent these consequences impede full gender inequality, these sociological studies suggest the need for teachers, parents, and other adults to help organize children's play that is more egalitarian along the lines discussed by Lever, Thorne, and other scholars. In this way, their sociological work has helped to make a difference and promises to continue to do so.

Schools

School is yet another agent of gender socialization (Klein, 2007). First of all, school playgrounds provide a location for the gender-linked play activities just described to occur. Second, and perhaps more important, teachers at all levels treat their female and male students differently in subtle ways of which they are probably not aware. They tend to call on boys more often to answer questions in class and to praise them more when they give the right answer. They also give boys more feedback about their assignments and other school work. At all grade levels, many textbooks and other books still portray people in gender-stereotyped ways. It is true that the newer books do less of this than older ones, but the newer books still contain some stereotypes, and the older books are still used in many schools, especially those that cannot afford to buy newer volumes.

Mass Media

Gender socialization also occurs through the mass media. On children's television shows, the major characters are male. On Nickelodeon, for example, the very popular SpongeBob SquarePants is a male, as are his pet snail, Gary; his best friend, Patrick Star; their neighbor, Squidward Tentacles; and SpongeBob's employer, Eugene Crabs. Of the major characters in Bikini Bottom, only Sandy Cheeks is a female. For all its virtues, *Sesame Street* features Bert, Ernie, Cookie Monster, and other male characters. Most of the Muppets are males, and the main female character, Miss Piggy, depicted as vain and jealous, is hardly an admirable female role model. As for adults' prime-time television, more men than women continue to fill more major roles in weekly shows, despite notable women's roles in shows such as *The Good Wife* and *Grey's Anatomy*.

Women are also often portrayed as unintelligent or frivolous individuals who are there more for their looks than for anything else. Television commercials reinforce this image. Cosmetic ads abound, suggesting not only that a major task for women is to look good but also that their sense of self-worth stems from looking good. Other commercials show women becoming ecstatic over achieving a clean floor or sparkling laundry. Judging from the world of television commercials, then, women's chief goals in life are to look good and to have a clean house. At the same time, men's chief goals, judging from many commercials, are to drink beer and drive cars.

Women's and men's magazines reinforce these gender images (Milillo, 2008). Most of the magazines intended for teenage girls and adult women are filled with pictures of thin, beautiful models, advice on dieting, cosmetic ads, and articles on how to win and please your man. Conversely, the magazines intended for teenage boys and men are filled with ads and articles on cars and sports, advice on how to succeed in careers and other endeavors, and pictures of thin, beautiful (and sometimes nude) women. These magazine images again suggest that women's chief goals are to look good and to please men and that men's chief goals are to succeed, win over women, and live life in the fast lane.

Religion

Another agent of socialization, religion, also contributes to traditional gender stereotypes. Many traditional interpretations of the Bible yield the message that women are subservient to men (Tanenbaum, 2009). This message begins in Genesis, where the first human is Adam, and Eve was made from one of his ribs. The major figures in the rest of the Bible are men, and women are for the most part depicted as wives, mothers, temptresses, and prostitutes; they are praised for their roles as wives and mothers and condemned for their other roles. More generally, women are constantly depicted as the property of men. The Ten Commandments includes a neighbor's wife with his house, ox, and other objects as things not to be coveted (Exodus 20:17), and many biblical passages say explicitly that women belong to men, such as this one from the New Testament:

Wives be subject to your husbands, as to the Lord. For the husband is the head of the wife as Christ is the head of the Church. As the Church is subject to Christ, so let wives also be subject in everything to their husbands.

Several passages in the Old Testament justify the rape and murder of women and girls. The Koran, the sacred book of Islam, also contains passages asserting the subordinate role of women (Mayer, 2009).

A Final Word on the Sources of Gender

Scholars in many fields continue to debate the relative importance of biology and of culture and socialization for how we behave and think as girls and boys and as women and men. The biological differences between females and males lead many scholars and no doubt much of the public to assume that masculinity and femininity are to a large degree biologically determined or at least influenced. In contrast, anthropologists, sociologists, and other social scientists tend to view gender as a social construction. Even if biology does matter for gender, they say, the significance of culture and socialization should not be underestimated. To the extent that gender is indeed shaped by society and culture, it is possible to change gender and to help bring about a society where both men and women have more opportunity to achieve their full potential.

GENDER INEQUALITY

We have said that the women's movement changed American life in many ways but that gender inequality persists. Let's look at examples of such inequality, much of it taking the form of institutional discrimination, which, *Race and Ethnicity*, can occur even if it is not intended to happen. We start with gender inequality in income and the workplace and then move on to a few other spheres of life.

Income and Workplace Inequality

In the last few decades, women have entered the workplace in increasing numbers, partly, and for many women mostly, out of economic necessity and partly out of desire for the sense of self-worth and other fulfillment that comes with work. This is true not only in the United States but also in other nations, including Japan, where views of women are more traditional than those in the United States. In February 2010, 58.9% of U.S. women age 16 or older were in the labour force, compared to only 43.3% in 1970; comparable figures for men were 71.0% in 2010 and 79.7% in 1970 (U.S. Census Bureau, 2009). Thus while women's labour force participation continues to lag behind men's, they have narrowed the gap. The figures just cited include women of retirement age. When we just look at younger women, labour force participation is even higher. For example, 76.1% of women aged 35–44 were in the labour force in 2008, compared to only 46.8% in 1970.

Learning From Other Societies

The United Nations Development Programme ranks nations on a "gender empowerment measure" of women's involvement in their nation's economy and political life. Of the 93 nations included in the measure, Norway ranks first, while Japan ranks 54th, the lowest among the world's industrial nations (Watkins, 2007). This contrast provides some lessons for the status of women in the United States, which ranked only 15th.

Japan has historically been a nation with very traditional gender expectations. As the image of the woman's *geisha* role in Japan illustrates, Japanese women have long been thought to be men's helpmates and subordinates. As Linda Schneider and Arnold Silverman (2010) put it.

The subordination of women is built into Japanese institutions, shaping family life, education, and the economy. Women are seen as fundamentally different from men and inferior to men. Almost everyone assumes that the purpose of a woman's life is to serve others: her children, her husband, perhaps her in-laws, the men at work.

Many more Japanese women work outside the home now than just a few decades ago and now make up almost half the labour force. However, the percentage of all management jobs held by women was just 10.1% in 2005, up only slightly from its 6.6% level in 1985. Japan's work culture that demands 15-hour days is partly responsible for this low percentage, as it is difficult for women to meet this expectation and still bear and raise children. Another reason is outright employment discrimination. Although Japan enacted an equal opportunity law for women's employment in 1985, the law is more symbolic than real because the only penalty it provides for violations is the publication of the names of the violators (Fackler, 2007).

In sharp contrast, Norway has made a concerted effort to boost women's involvement in the business and political worlds. Like other Nordic countries (Denmark, Finland, Sweden) that also rank at the top of the United Nations gender empowerment measure, Norway is a social democratic welfare state characterized by extensive government programs and other efforts to promote full economic and gender equality. Its government provides day care for children and adult care for older or disabled individuals, and it also provides 44 weeks of paid parental leave after the birth of a child. Parents can also work fewer hours without losing income until their child is 2 years of age. All of these provisions mean that women are much more likely than their American counterparts to have the freedom and economic means to work outside the home, and they have taken advantage of this opportunity. As a recent analysis concluded, It has been extremely important for women that social rights have been extended to cover such things as the caring of young children and elderly, sick and disabled members of society. In the Nordic countries, women have been more successful than elsewhere in combining their dual role as mothers and workers, and social policy arrangements are an integral part of the gender equality policy.

While the United States ranks much higher than Japan on the UN's gender empowerment measure, it ranks substantially lower than Norway and the other Nordic nations. An important reason for these nations' higher ranking is government policy that enables women to work outside the home if they want to do so. The experience of these nations indicates that greater gender equality might be achieved in the United States if it adopted policies similar to those found in these nations that make it easier for women to join and stay in the labour force.

The Gender Gap in Income

Despite the gains women have made, problems persist. Perhaps the major problem is a gender gap in income. Women have earned less money than men ever since records started being kept. In the United States in the early 1800s, full-time women workers in agriculture and manufacturing earned less than 38% of what men earned.

By 1885 they were earning about 50% of what men earned in manufacturing jobs. As the 1980s began, full-time women workers' median weekly earnings were about 65% of men's. Women have narrowed the gender gap in earnings since then: their weekly earnings now (2009) are 80.2% of men's among full-time workers (U.S. Census Bureau, 2010). Still, this means that for every $10,000 men earn, women earn only about $8,002. To turn that around, for every $10,000 women earn, men earn $12,469. This gap amounts to hundreds of thousands of dollars over a lifetime of working.

Although such practices and requirements are now illegal, they still continue. The sex segregation they help create contributes to the continuing gender gap between female and male workers. Occupations dominated by women tend to have lower wages and salaries. Because women are concentrated in low-paying jobs, their earnings are much lower than men's.

Studies of comparable worth. The idea that women's and men's jobs may be of roughly equal value and thus deserve the same pay, even though women's jobs typically pay less than men's jobs support this argument. Researchers rate various jobs in terms of their requirements and attributes that logically should affect the salaries they offer: the importance of the job, the degree of skill it requires, the level of responsibility it requires, the degree to which the employee must exercise independent judgment, and so forth. They then use these dimensions to determine what salary a job should offer. Some jobs might be "better" on some dimensions and "worse" on others but still end up with the same predicted salary if everything evens out.

When researchers make their calculations, they find that certain women's jobs pay less than men's even though their comparable worth is equal to or even higher than the men's jobs. For example, a social worker may earn less money than a probation officer, even though calculations based on comparable worth would predict that a social worker should earn at least as much. The comparable worth research demonstrates that women's jobs pay less than men's jobs of comparable worth and that the average working family would earn several thousand dollars more annually if pay scales were re-evaluated based on comparable worth and women paid more for their work.

Even when women and men work in the same jobs, women often earn less than men (Sherrill, 2009), and men are more likely than women to hold leadership positions in these occupations.

Census data provide ready evidence of the lower incomes women receive than men even in the same occupations. For example, female marketing and sales managers earn only 68% of what their male counterparts earn; female human resource managers earn only 68% of what their male counterparts earn; female claims adjusters earn only 83%; female accountants earn only 72%; female elementary and middle school teachers earn only 90%; and even female secretaries and clerical workers earn only 86% (U.S. Department of Labour, 2008). When variables like number of years on the job, number of hours worked per week, and size of firm are taken into account, these disparities diminish but do not disappear altogether, and it is very likely that sex discrimination (conscious or unconscious) by employers accounts for much of the remaining disparity.

Litigation has suggested or revealed specific instances of sex discrimination in earnings and employment. In July 2009, the Dell computer company, without admitting any wrongdoing, agreed to pay $9.1 million to settle a class action lawsuit, brought by former executives, that alleged sex discrimination in salaries and promotions (Walsh, 2009). Earlier in the decade, a Florida jury found Outback Steakhouse liable for paying a woman site development assistant only half what it paid a man with the same title. After she trained him, Outback assigned him most of her duties, and when she complained, Outback transferred her to a clerical position. The jury awarded her $2.2 million in compensatory and punitive damages (U.S. Equal Employment Opportunity Commission, 2001).

Some of the sex discrimination in employment reflects the existence of two related phenomena, the glass ceiling. The invisible barrier facing women as they try to advance in the workplace and the glass escalator. The smooth path afforded men in promotion in the workplace, especially in occupations primarily filled by women.. Women may be promoted in a job only to find they reach an invisible "glass ceiling" beyond which they cannot get promoted, or they may not get promoted in the first place.

In the largest U.S. corporations, women constitute only about 16% of the top executives, and women executives are paid much less than their male counterparts. Although these disparities stem partly from the fact that women joined the corporate ranks much more recently than men, they also reflect a glass ceiling in the corporate world that prevents qualified women from rising up above a certain level (Hymowitz, 2009). Men, on the other hand, can often ride a "glass escalator" to the top, even in female occupations. An example is seen in elementary school teaching, where principals typically rise from the ranks of teachers. Although men constitute only about 20% of all public elementary school teachers, they account for about 44% of all elementary school principals (National Centre for Education Statistics, 2009).

Whatever the reasons for the gender gap in income, the fact that women make so much less than men means that female-headed families are especially likely to be poor. In 2008, about 31% of these families lived in poverty, compared to only 6.7% of married-couple families (U.S. Census Bureau, 2010). The term *feminization of poverty* refers to the fact that female-headed households are especially likely to be poor. The gendering of poverty in this manner is one of the most significant manifestations of gender inequality in the United States.

Sexual Harassment

Another workplace problem (including schools) is sexual harassment. Unwelcome sexual advances, requests for sexual favours, or physical conduct of a sexual nature used as a condition of employment or promotion or that interferes with an individual's job performance and creates an intimidating or hostile environment., which, as defined by federal guidelines and legal rulings and statutes, consists of unwelcome sexual advances, requests for sexual favours, or physical conduct of a sexual nature used as a condition of employment or promotion or that interferes with an individual's job performance and creates an intimidating or hostile environment.

Although men can be, and are, sexually harassed, women are more often the targets of sexual harassment, which is often considered a form of violence against women. This gender difference exists for at least two reasons, one cultural and one structural.

The cultural reason centres on the depiction of women and the socialization of men. As our discussion of the mass media and gender socialization indicated, women are still depicted in our culture as sexual objects who exist for men's pleasure. At the same time, our culture socializes men to be sexually assertive. These two cultural beliefs combine to make men believe that they have the right to make verbal and physical advances to women in the workplace. When these advances fall into the guidelines listed here, they become sexual harassment.

The second reason that most targets of sexual harassment are women is more structural. Reflecting the gendered nature of the workplace and of the educational system, typically the men doing the harassment are in a position of power over the women they harass. A male boss harasses a female employee, or a male professor harasses a female student or employee. These men realize that subordinate women may find it difficult to resist their advances for fear of reprisals: a female employee may be fired or not promoted, and a female student may receive a bad grade.

How common is sexual harassment? This is difficult to determine, as the men who do the sexual harassment are not about to shout it from the rooftops, and the women who suffer it often keep quiet because of the repercussions just listed. But anonymous surveys of women employees in corporate and other settings commonly find that 40%–65% of the respondents report being sexually harassed. In a survey of 4,501 women physicians, 36.9% reported being sexually harassed either in medical school or in their practice as physicians. Sexual harassment cases continue to make headlines.

In one recent example, the University of Southern Mississippi paid $112,500 in September 2009 to settle a case brought by a women's tennis graduate assistant against the school's women's tennis coach; the coach then resigned for personal reasons (Magee, 2009). That same month, the CEO of a hospital in Washington State was reprimanded after a claim of sexual harassment was brought against him, and he was also fired for unspecified reasons (Mehaffey, 2009).

Sexual Orientation and Inequality

A recent report by a task force of the American Psychological Association stated that "same-sex sexual and romantic attractions, feelings, and behaviours are normal and positive variations of human sexuality". A majority of Americans do not share this opinion. In the 2008 General Social Survey, 52% of respondents said that "sexual relations between two adults of the same sex" is "always wrong."

Although this figure represents a substantial decline from the survey's 1973 finding of 74%, it is clear that many Americans remain sharply opposed to homosexuality. Not surprisingly, then, sexual orientation continues to be the source of much controversy and no small amount of abuse and discrimination directed toward members of the gay, lesbian, bisexual, and trans gendered community.

These individuals experience various forms of abuse, mistreatment, and discrimination that their heterosexual counterparts do not experience. In this respect, their sexuality is the source of a good deal of inequality. For example, gay teenagers are very often the targets of taunting, bullying, physical assault, and other abuse in schools and elsewhere that sometimes drives them to suicide or at least to experience severe emotional distress.

In 38 states, individuals can be denied employment or fired from a job because of their sexual orientation, even though federal and state laws prohibit employment discrimination for reasons related to race and ethnicity, gender, age, religious belief, and national origin. And in 45 states as of April 2010, same-sex couples are legally prohibited from marrying. In most of these states, this prohibition means that same-sex couples lack hundreds of rights, responsibilities, and benefits that spouses enjoy, including certain income tax and inheritance benefits, spousal insurance coverage, and the right to make medical decisions for a partner who can no longer communicate because of disease or traumatic injury (Gerstmann, 2008).

Household Inequality

The Family, but for now the discussion will centre on housework. Someone has to do housework, and that someone is usually a woman. It takes many hours a week to clean the bathrooms, cook, shop in the grocery store, vacuum, and do everything else that needs to be done.

The best evidence indicates that women married to or living with men spend two to three times as many hours per work on housework as men spend. This disparity holds true even when women work outside the home, leading sociologist Arlie Hochschild (1989) to observe in a widely cited book that women engage in a "second shift" of unpaid work when they come home from their paying job.

The good news is that gender differences in housework time are smaller than a generation ago. The bad news is that a large gender difference remains. As one study summarized the evidence on this issue, "women invest significantly more hours in household labour than do men despite the narrowing of gender differences in recent years". In the realm of household work, then, gender inequality persists.

SOCIAL INEQUALITY

Social inequality is one of the fundamental injustices that we recognize as human beings, since every human is involved in this injustice as either perpetrators and beneficiaries or victims and sufferers. Rousseau addresses the origin of social inequality in his Discourse on the Origin of Inequality. He gives a riveting account of how he supposed man in the state of nature was like and he charts the developing stages of man until it leads him ultimately to the blossoming of civil man, where the rich perpetrate and the poor suffer inequality. The account that Rousseau gives is one that is convincing, consistent, and based on reasonable conclusions drawn from conjectured premises.

Rousseau begins his account of the origin of social inequality by first distinguishing it from natural inequality. "The other may be called moral or political inequality, because it depends on a kind of convention and is established, or at least authorized, by the consent of men".

He does this to clarify any confusion of the two terms the reader may have and to stress the difference between the natural state and the civil state of man.

The artificiality of social inequality should not be linked to the state of nature. Rousseau distances social inequality from any natural origin and restricts it to social or proto-social origins so as to solidify his position that social inequality only arose with the advent of society. With this point established, Rousseau proceeds to conjecture what humans were like in the state of nature to further illustrate the unlikelihood that natural man had social inequality. "The investigations that may be undertaken [...] only for hypothetical and conditional reasonings,".

In order to explain how social inequality came about, Rousseau hypothesizes how man must have been before the introduction of social inequality. As mentioned before, man in the state of nature is without social inequality so Rousseau focuses on natural man. Part One of the Discourse is entirely devoted to this task and in the process he introduces and elaborates on two key principles, that of pity and self-preservation.

Self-preservation is present in both natural and civil man and in any living being. There need not be any compelling argument here; it is almost self-evident. A species not concerned with self-preservation is eliminated in the game of life by the laws of nature. Pity is what is at issue with Rousseau and he argues that in natural man, pity and self-preservation are balanced while in civil man, pity has slowly ebbed. "His fellow man can be killed with impunity underneath his window."

Natural man is simple, his passions few. Passions are created, rather than being overridden or forgotten, in society. The main passion that is overridden in society is pity and the forgetting of this pity is instrumental in transforming natural man into civil man. To highlight the importance of the loss of pity, Rousseau explores what is instituted in the stead of pity.

Pity is a concept that Rousseau mentions repeatedly in his text and we can see how highly he regarded pity as a virtue. If such an important virtue exists less in civil man, what is qualified to replace it? Rousseau contends that "laws, mores, and virtue" are what take the place of pity. By praising pity and grouping laws and virtue with mores, it seems that he regards laws as disdainful and partly responsible for the depravity of civil man.

Later on, he explicitly explores whether or not laws are ill-suited to restrict crimes that the most violent passions commit and goes as far as to suggest that laws may well be the cause of such crimes! "the least one should expect of them would be that they call a halt to an evil that would not exist without them." Laws as a trademark of society are deemed to be ineffective by Rousseau and maybe even responsible for brewing the evils that exist in societal man. But Rousseau is sketchy here, he seems to be suggesting that man is good before the introduction of laws but isn't the purpose of laws meant to make man good?

We have to remember that property only exists if there are laws to enforce the exclusion of others. Somehow, pity is replaced by laws, laws may cause evils, laws form when society form, and inequality is an injustice seen as a product of these factors. The connection he draws between laws, society, and pity will later help him justify how inequality arises from property. Rousseau discusses these details meticulously in order to show a gradual transformation from natural man without social inequality to civil or societal man, who is afflicted with property and thus social inequality.

The development of the concept of property, for Rousseau, comes out of several different revolutions of the human race.

As man began to use crude tools and build simple huts he set the gears of social inequality into motion. Co-habitation and cooperation within a type of proto-family was instituted. Gender roles led to the development of sexual inequality. Sexual inequality is the beginning of the institution of social inequality as a whole. Rousseau writes, "Women became more sedentary [...] while the man went to seek their common subsistence."

The division of labour within the proto-family brought about leisure time for man, the division of labour outside the proto-family marked the beginning of the concept of property. Rousseau states, "equality disappeared, property came into existence, labour became necessary."

Man is now interdependent because he can no longer satisfy his needs with only his own labour. Rousseau notes that "From the cultivation of land, there necessarily followed the division of land;" Once there is division of land, property is propelled from being property of all to property of one, exclusive of others. Similarly, a man who puts his labour into something, of which he needs to trade to another individual in order to get what he wants, will have a conception that he owns what he put his labour into, that it is his property, and that he can and should exclude it from others.

Rousseau contends, "It is labour alone that, in giving the cultivator a right [...] it is easily transformed to property." Law is needed to enforce the right to property. Exclusion of others and infringement of this exclusion by others are what leads to injury and to injustice. The division of property plays an extremely important and central role in the account of origin of social inequality that Rousseau gives. If one man has something (that nature did not give him at birth) that another man does not have, then inequality has shifted from being natural to artificial, or social. By describing man in the pre-property and post-property states, Rousseau tries to show that if man never progressed (or declined) past the division of labour and property, full-fledged inequality in the social sense would not have developed.

Critics of Rousseau's position might contend that his argument is inconsistent and not sound. They may attack his use of the state of nature as the basis for most of his key ideas by saying his account of natural man is only conjectural and hypothetical. Rousseau admits that such an account can only be conjectural and but there seems to be no other way to return to the state of nature. "I cannot make a determination among them except on the basis of conjecture."

Rousseau even mentions that the state of nature probably never existed, "concerning this subject should not be taken for historical truths,". We as modern readers must consider the time period that Rousseau is writing in and the audience that he intended the Discourse for. It was extremely undesirable to assert the origins of man that contradicted with what was held to be fact by the Church. Given that Rousseau's account is of the imagination, it does not discount much from the body of his argument. His argument follows and adheres to the concepts introduced in the state of nature, even though his premises are hypothetical.

Another criticism of the Discourse might point to the inconsistencies in his hypothetical account of developing man. Again, he does not purport to give a narrative or documentary of how natural man transformed into civil man; he doesn't even acknowledge that natural man must have existed the way he has described him.

"I admit that, since the events I have to describe could have taken place in several ways," If we accept the basic elements of his argument, that man in the state of nature was mostly solitary and without property, we agree to his distinction between natural and moral inequality, then we can disregard minor inconsistencies in his account of man in his developing stages and still agree that it follows that property created artificial or social inequality amongst humans. What makes a man unequal in relation to another man is when he possesses more or less than his fellow man. Private property is what allows this to happen.

While many problems occur in discussing the origins of social inequality and anything else not empirically accessible, it is nevertheless an important exercise in understanding ourselves. In exploring the origin of social inequality among men, one is necessarily constrained by not having any facts of the past to base your conclusions of the present on. Rousseau recognizes and addresses this handicap in his text and skilfully argues in spite of the hindrance.

He does what he can with what is given to him. Drawing conclusions that flow naturally from his premises, Rousseau makes his argument so strong that if the premises had any hint of truth in it, his argument would hold. Rousseau, in his Discourse on the Origin of Inequality, demonstrates how one argues successfully for a topic where the premises can only be hypothetical.

5

Social Inequality and Aspects of Social Stratification

Many People have argued that the semantics of class has lost its earlier attractiveness. The rising importance of dimensions such as age, gender, nationality, race, political attitudes, and the multitude of choices in organizing one's life course has rendered the debate about the concept of class obsolete. Some argue that the semantics of class no longer seems appropriate for analysing and interpreting society. This perception is closely connected to the emergence of entirely new topics such as individualization and the plurality of life styles. My main thesis is that the currently expanding discussion on life style is not necessarily a substitute but an important supplement to the tradition of social stratification research. What people "are" and what people "do" can no longer be conceptualized by a simple one-to-one-fit. The concept of life style can provide a link between social rank and social practice. The logic of how people organize their leisure time and how they spend their income is not a simple mirror of income level but must be regarded as being embedded in social behaviour.

SOCIAL STRATIFICATION

The Debate about the relevance of the concept of class is unresolved at the end of the 20th century. The past 100 years have witnessed the establishment of a capitalist society that has, on balance, revealed a strong bond between creativity and destructiveness. This bond is a source of innovation and prosperity (Bogenhold 1995). Average living standards within the population continuously improved during the 20th century. Economic growth triumphed while average weekly working hours were reduced. One question about class concerned the social distribution of economic wealth among different population segments. The visibly increasing rise in disposable time that people won during this historical process and the rise in income that allowed them to develop new patterns of personal consumption and leisure activities, patterns of behaviour that had already been revealed with a strange ambivalence by Riesman and colleagues (1950) during the middle of this century, are worth noting.

From a historical perspective, we see production and consumption constantly changing (Becher 1980). This is reflected in a rapidly changing succession of topics in the history of economic and social thought (Stihler 1998). Whereas Max Weber ([1905/1906] 1993) attributed the success of the industrial revolution to the Protestant ethic, our contemporary understanding of that success is different. Economy and society are increasingly dependent on the levels of effective consumer demand. A constant rise in the production of goods must find a market outlet. If ascetism served as a foundation for the development of a capitalist economic system in Max Weber's world, then the connection between production and demand, that is the cycle of production, sale, and consumption, has in our understanding become the foundation for the modern economic society: no production without demand and vice versa.

The enormous rise in productivity in European countries since the middle of the 19th century has led to changes in social and occupational structures as well. If more and more can be produced with less and less labour, then transport and trade will become more important. In Germany in 1882, for example, it was estimated that for every person in trade and transport there were nine laborers in the factories. By 1996 this ratio had been reduced to about 1 to 2.5.

This development, among other things, makes the growing role of income distribution within economy even more important. In other words, the ratio between those who produce and those who transport and trade, administer and organize, has changed.

The reduction in working hours, along with a simultaneous rise in purchasing power in the long-term development has supplied the social framework for new demands. We now speak about "entertainment" and "tourist" industries. Due to the rapid growth of social wealth, it is becoming ever more interesting for sociologists to see how disposable time is used and how leisure practices relate to money income. The change in the context of economic and social structures has led to a continuous change in the ratio between blue collar workers and white collar workers. These changes have also influenced the expansion of the classical category of the working class.

Max Weber described the Janus-faced nature of a formally "free" contract form of wage labour in his socio-legal observations: a contract that obeys the law of the most powerful on the labour market (Weber 1972:Sec. VII). The process of continuing proletarianization and the accompanying development of an objectified world in an "iron cage" (Weber 1979: Sec. 188) must indeed be seen as one of the most important innovations of this century.

In the history of social thought, many well-known positions on the issue of social stratification can be interpreted as a constant dialogue with the epochal Marxist theses. The works of authors such as Max Weber (1972), Emil Lederer (1912), Werner Sombart ([1927]1987), Theodor Geiger (1932, 1949), Ralf Dahrendorf (1959), Stanislaw Ossowski (1963), Goldthorpe et al. (1968), Anthony Giddens (1973), and Daniel Bell (1974) are cases in point. It was above all the dichotomous and bipolar division of society into blocks of uniform individuals (bourgeoisie and proletariat) that Gotz Briefs described as "sweet simplicity" in his article "Proletariat" (Briefs 1931:458) at the beginning of the 1930s. This conception is too simplistic to characterize a society that is ever becoming more and more differentiated.

Regarding the analysis of social stratification in the 20th century, it seems that the occupational and economic differentiations within society have become too complex to be able to reduce these distinctions to a single common denominator. Geiger referred to this problem in one of his later works, "Die Klassengesellschaft im Schmelztiegel" ("The Class Society in the Melting Pot") published in 1949. He expressed it as follows: "Everything seems to be gliding now, a clear definable structure is hardly to be found. However, certain tendencies toward a shift in class can be seen... which lately seem to stretch right through the Marxist class ranks" (Geiger 1949:147). Geiger explicitly characterized this stratification that stretches straight through these Marxist class ranks as "horizontal stratification." This type of stratification is "first and foremost of the utmost socio-cultural importance".

Geiger's view of a "horizontal stratification" is the essence of the following considerations. My thesis is that Geiger's analysis was already conceptually drawn up by Georg Simmel ([1900] 1978), Thorstein Veblen (1899), and Max Weber ([1921] 1972). The present discussion on so-called individualization and pluralization that is popular in Germany has been built on this earlier literature and has not made reference to Geiger's work.

THE ANALYSIS OF LIFE STYLES

Contemporary Discussion of the pluralization of life styles reflects the fact that the level of vertical differentiation in terms of financial resources has little to do with the level of cultural expression as a form of individual life practice. Ulrich Beck's (1986) book Risk Society holds the view that the evidence within life practice for bonding in a specific class constellation has disappeared. His opinion is that biographies are becoming even more "open." Societies that are becoming increasingly complex multiply the possible life courses of individuals and thus, due to institutional handicaps and handicaps in life-history, result in "kits for possible biographic combinations" (Beck 1986:217).

It is of utmost importance that the question of choice of life styles is connected to the diversification and individualization of life situation: The more distinct autonomy becomes in reference to the use of time and money, the more open-ended the question becomes in which concrete practice this use materializes. Benjamin Zablocki and Rosabeth Moss Kanter (1976) clearly pointed this out more than two decades ago. This is the perfect link to the discussion of life styles, which presently seems to be held with growing enthusiasm.

The concept of "life styles" is often used in differing ways. In the Zapf et al. formulation (1987), for example, "life style" is a relatively stable pattern of organizing everyday life within the framework of a given life-situation, taking account available resources. Different forms of organizing household work and employment, alternate patterns of consumption, varying living-patterns, how time is used, and even plans for the future with their specific planning contents and planning horizons are, on an empirical level, among the most important elements in constructing a life style chart.

Consequently, life styles reveal specific patterns with various components and a large range of influences that sociologists specializing in one thematic area and different academic disciplines have treated disparately. These studies include consumer research and market research, election polls, tourist polls, sociology of leisure-time and time itself, women's studies, household economics, urban and regional studies, education studies, biographic research studies, sociology of religion and family, to mention just a few. All of these research programs have their own empirical research traditions and have made contributions to the field of research known as "life style research." Typologies for life styles already exist in each and every one of these fields of research (especially in the case of electoral poll research, market research, and research into leisure activities). However, for the most part these results tend to summarize a situation and are inadequate for sociological stratificationary research.

The central issue addressed by this paper is what sociology of social structures can be linked to the topic of life styles. The central question may be phrased as follows: Is the analysis of life styles a useful "extension" to the now largely accepted theory of individualization and does it offer an important contribution to a (better) understanding of social inequality? A principal benefit in life style analysis is that it appears to provide a cultural point of view that allows social heterogeneity to be linked to a cultural embedding in a historical life form. Thus, a varied composition of differing patterns of life organization can be drawn in connection with vertical and horizontal disparities, adequately reflecting the complex network of distribution and relationships in contemporary structures of inequality.

DISTRIBUTION AND STATUS

The Relationship between material "possession" and its appropriate use in terms of a concrete cultural use of material resources was a topic in the sociological contemplations of the classic authors whose pioneering works do not always seem to gather the necessary attention today. The insights propounded by Georg Simmel, Max Weber, or even Thorstein Veblen, whose ideas developed in completely different contexts in styles of life, have not been systematically pursued and have been revived in connection with Bourdieu's socio-cultural studies.

While Veblen pointed out the "conspicuous consumption" of the upper classes in his Theory of the Leisure Class (1899), Simmel was generally more interested in the outlines of the modern style of life in a time when society was not only experiencing cultural change but was also going through turbulent economic changes as well. For example, in Simmel's The Philosophy of Money (1978), he examined in detail this modern "style of life," which complicates human relationships. Complications are seen in the ever increasing detachment in social circles and the replacement of traditional rhythms in social life by more complex forms as well as in an increase in the tempo in which society was changing. These distinctions in every day culture can be seen in Simmel (1978) as a growing "multiplicity" of cultural styles that are forever changing. This led to Simmel's following definition of life styles:

> Indeed, the mere existence of style is in itself one of the most significant instances of distancing. Style, as the manifestation of our inner feelings, indicates that these feelings no longer immediately gush out but take on a disguise the moment they are revealed. Style, as the general form of the particular, is a veil that imposes a barrier and a distance in relation to the recipient of the expression of these feelings. (1978:473)

Weber also explored the concept of life style. However, unlike Simmel, Weber did not pay any special attention to the term and it was not among the central definitions (Grunbegriffe) to be found in "Economy and Society" (Weber 1972). Weber often used it synonymously with Lebensfuhrung (life-conduct). The concept of life style within the framework of his Protestant Ethics is mostly used as a caricature of the modern and "standardized free" way of living. References are to be found to class structures where "life style" is expressed as being an expressively cultural moment in consumption and in social inclusion and exclusion of groups.

Pierre Bourdieu's elaborations on the subject of "distinction" first appeared in France in 1979. It has had a lasting influence and inspiration on the current debate about life styles. Bourdieu's works can probably be described as being a sociology of culture based on Veblen and Simmel, influenced by Weber.

Bourdieu sees the social world in terms of a metaphor: Consider a multi-dimensional social sphere in which different groups of actors reflect, on the one hand, the sphere of social position and, on the other hand, the sphere of life styles. Material distribution in the sense of different social positions is portrayed in one sphere, whereas in the other sphere the provisions of cultural resources are staked out and manifested in the form of varying life styles. He thereby places the "sphere of social positions" in analytical contrast to the "sphere of life styles." Of course, both of these spheres are virtually interlocked with one another.

However, Bourdieu did not leave it at that, but, what is more, used the concept of disposition as a central term. Life-requirements are strengthened by a process of institutionalization, which forms the actor's habitus. It is this disposition that is repeated by practice and reinforced by existing life styles. The connections between structure habitus, and practice are to be seen as loose hinges. Differing forms of life styles are now rationalized by using the connection between disposition and practice. Finally, the effect of different life styles on a symbolic level is evaluated by means of "distinction."

Bourdieu's concept has an interesting effect when looking at social stratification and life styles, especially where Bourdieu has benefitted from Simmel's discussion. For example, directly linking his sociocultural analysis with a socio-structural dimension: if inequalities in a differentiated distribution struggle, or rather are no longer directly expressed by such struggle but are expressed or symbolized by distinctive practices, then Bourdieu's way of looking at this topic is a subject of current interest and relevance. Bourdieu (1979) has thus linked Weber's class observations with an empirical study in subtle representative areas such as holiday locations, house/flat furnishing, etc., studies that overall were based in France. Radically refined social inequalities can be portrayed as reflecting different styles of practice.

Of course it does pose great difficulties to transpose this method onto another method of application without a lot of bother while also taking theoretical and empirical components into account. An oscillation between pure empiricism components on the one hand and grand theory on the other hand can be seen in the current discussion. We can reach an understanding for life styles on a general level by using Bourdieu's admittedly somewhat problematic concept of habitus. Correspondingly, life styles attain a sort of independent self-logic, so that in the end they are indeed a product of human action but do have their own objective independent existence as well—an independent existence that opposes other types of life styles designed by people themselves.

However, it's surprising that Bourdieu does not search for explicit links to establish academic forms of social network analysis although the relationship between Bourdieu's approach and social network analysis is a close one. The cultural stratification analysis of society into forms of differing life styles is linked to communicative mechanisms of social closure. The ability of life styles to communicate is still treated symbolically. Style is stylized in order to present it to the public. Style is transformed by interpretative schemes and tastes into a construct of the social and object worlds and is, above all, defined by difference. With this in mind, communication and affiliation to certain social networks are based on the immediate level as sharing common signs.

The current sociological discussion of life styles makes no reference to this classic sociologist. For this reason, I would now like to return to the central question treating the relationship between social stratification and life styles. The issue at question is whether the concept of life styles can become an addition to or a substitution for traditional research in social stratification. The debate between Clark and Lipset (1991), Flout, Brooks, and Manza (1993), Pakulski (1993), and finally Clark, Lipset, and Rempel (1993) on the question of whether social classes are dying owe, above all, its origins to the fact that different concepts exist about what class or social class consists of. Ossowoski's old criticism (1963) of Marx, that in his work a gradual, functional, and dichotomic class scheme is found that is often practically jumbled up, is still the case today. Max Weber differentiates social classes in his class terminology by the terms Erwerbsklassen and Besitzklassen. However, one problem is that authors more often than not lean on one set definition of a particular author without being conscious of others' interpretations of the same definitions.

A basic question is: Is class just a descriptive category of distribution, or is it also part of a definite "class consciousness," no matter how defined; do we also require further information on forms of class mobility? Goldthorpe and Marshall, for example, supply a broadly interpreted concept:

Class analysis, in our sense, has as its central concern the study of relationships among class structures, class mobility, class-based inequalities and class-based action. More specifically, it explores the interconnections between positions defined by employment relations in labour markets and production units in different sectors of national economies; the processes through which individuals and families are distributed and redistributed among these positions over time; and the consequences thereof for their life-chances and for the social identities that they adopt and the social values and interest that they pursue. (1992:382).

However, such a far reaching claim is in danger of not being realized in practical research. Aage Soerensen (1991) came to the conclusion in his discussion on the equally popular approach of John Goldthorpe and Erik Olin Wright that it is important to classify positions as a result of material processes of distribution within vertical stratification. However, both approaches, Goldthorpe's as well as Wright's, have missed the mark. Both remained on the level of descriptive analysis: The two main uses of the concept of class in recent stratification research are Goldthorpe's analysis of mobility from a class formation perspective and Wright's analysis of income inequality generated in the labour market. The main problem with both efforts is that a satisfactory theory of how class generates inequality within the labour market is not available... In general, one does not need to identify positions as classes or in some other manner use class analysis to make use of the idea that positions are relevant.

On balance, positions of social inequality can be differentiated and classified in the sense of social differences without having to rely on one of the various sociological connotations of class. In one sense, class or rather class-situation is just a result of the distribution processes in ongoing labour market processes. To use Luhmann's terms: class is the "distribution of division" (Luhmann 1985:129) and classes are heuristic classifications. The degree to which contemporary societies are egalitarian is a question that must be researched empirically. Glancing at the differing empirical results within the German discussion, Mayer and Blossfeld (1990) claim that a trend towards a greater rigidity in social inequalities is evident and increasing. Blossfeld and Shavit (1993) showed in their evaluation of educational opportunities in 13 different countries that rapid educational expansion did not reduce inequalities of educational opportunities. They concluded:

> As a consequence of educational expansion societies can produce a higher average level of educational attainment from one birth cohort to the next, without changing the educational opportunities of children from different social strata.... Thus, the modernization theorists' hypothesis that educational opportunities must be turned on its head: expansion actually facilitates to a large extent the persistence of inequalities in educational opportunity. (1993:22)

If it is correct that the hierarchy of material inequality between people has remained relatively stable, then what is hiding behind the discussion of life styles? My argument is that this change in the discussion reflects the asymmetry between social situations that are conditioned by distribution on the one hand and by corresponding cognitive relevant structures among actors, on the other. This has not only resulted in a relative decoupling between locations on the vertical-material stratification scale and choice of behaviour (Nieuwbeerta 1995) but numerous patterns of consumption and leisure activities are also to be found that cannot be directly derived from positions on the stratification scale. A relative dissociation is to be found between social distribution structures. Increasing inequalities in industrial societies and growing unemployment in many contemporary societies do not necessarily lead to political action and unique class consciousness.

Clark and Lipset (1991) observed that "new forms of social stratification are emerging" (1991:397). In fact, social reality seems to be becoming so increasingly diverse and complex that it has to be studied in a different way. There are new lines and topics of social conflict, new social movements have appeared, ethnic differences have become more obvious, as well as gender issues. If life style research is the answer, what is the question? The question is to what extent should we take the cultural determination of life-forms beyond the material and/or structural survey of life-chances into account? It is a question of the relationship between life-chances and life styles.

Weber noticed this earlier noncongruence in distribution situations, cultural attitudes, and patterns of behaviour when he distinguished "class" from "status." He wanted to convey that classification into classes represents one thing, and human social organizations and socialization represents something else. This early foundation for the discussion on life styles, which Simmel had formulated in broader terms, had already been integrated and taken into consideration by Weber. To quote Weber himself, "Classes can be divided according to their relationships to production how they acquire goods, 'status' according to the principle in which goods in the form of specific types of life styles are consumed".

LIFE STYLE RESEARCH

Many features of life style research still seem rather indefinite. The semantic delimitation of life styles compared with other categories such as mentalities, mileus or sub-cultures does not seem to exist. A greater part of the discussions on life styles is due to the discomfort with vertical stratification models. Since the forms of possession in vertical class situations are not inevitably transposed into the presumed corresponding sociological practice forms, the need for innovatative sociological tools for theoretical and empirical surveys on the organization and articulation of life has now arisen. However, the latter forms will not necessarily become empty and obsolete due to the former; both can complement each other wisely.

The fact that these issues are only now gaining ground is connected with the internal logic in the development of new topics and theses in the academic discussion. The mainstream discussion is now asking questions about the congruence between material "possession" and cultural stylization, an issue that has already been mentioned by a series of authors many decades ago. The more differentiated modern societies become, the greater becomes the possible scope for expressively staging social life. The better the material provisions, the broader the margins will become, from which one or the other form can be selected.

However, even among social positions that already are at the lower end of the stratification scale, the broadening of competing social expressions is obvious. Let us look at the category of unemployed persons. No average expected type of behaviour among unemployed persons exists. Within this category no process of common socialization (Vergemeinschaftung) has taken place. Their individual biographical histories are far too different: their occupational qualifications, their training prerequisites, their aspirations, and living requirements are too different.

The intersection of (vertical) stratification sociology with socio-cultural issues can provide important answers to sociologically relevant patterns of life styles in modern societies. Joseph A. Schumpeter had already mentioned briefly in a general chapter in his book Capitalism, Socialism and Democracy (1942) that the development or capitalist life styles can easily and perhaps most impressively he described with the genesis of modern lounge suits (Schumpeter [1942]

1947:126). This example indicates that studying social change can include the process by which social and economic structures are differentiated as well as the processes of cultural change. The sociology of the stratification of unequal material distribution situations is important. How the system of classification is determined is another question that can be dealt with separately. However, these levels of distribution cannot be directly translated into either specific value patterns within society or in cultural attitudes as an expression of social life. These issues need to be dealt with by the sociology of life styles.

RANKING AND SOCIAL INEQUALITY

Ranking is a characteristic of complex societies in which different persons within a society have different quantities or qualities of power, rights and responsibilities. As societies grow in complexity, different tasks are assigned to specific people, called craft specialization. Sometimes specialization leads to status changes.

The study of ranking and social inequality in archaeology is based on the anthropological and economic studies of Elman Service (*Primitive Social Organization*, 1962) and Morton Fried (*Evolution of Political Societies*, 1967).

Service and Fried argued that there are two ways in which ranking of people in a society is arrived at: achieved and ascribed status. Achieved status results from being a warrior, artisan, shaman, or other useful profession or talent. and ascribed status (inherited from a parent or other relative). Ascribed status is based on kinship, which as a form of social organization ties the status of an individual within a group to descent, such as dynastic kings or hereditary rulers.

Ranking and Archaeology

In egalitarian societies, goods and services are spread relatively evenly among the population. High-ranking individuals in a community can be identified archaeologically by studying human burials, where differences in grave contents, the health of an individual or his or her diet can be examined. Ranking can also be established by the difference sizes of houses, the locations within a community, or the distribution of luxury or status items within a community.

THE STRUCTURE OF INEQUALITY AND THE POLITICS OF REDISTRIBUTION

The model of redistributive politics proposed by Romer (1975) and developed by Meltzer and Richard (1981) does not provide an adequate explanation of variation in the extent of government redistribution across OECD countries. As commonly noted, the limitations of the RMR model may be attributed to its assumptions about either the demand for or supply of redistribution (or to both). In this paper, we focus on the demand for redistribution and propose an alternative way to think about the preferences of the median voter or, less stringently, the preferences of middle-income voters. In so doing, we assume that the preferences of middle-income voters are critical to the politics of redistribution and set aside, for the time being, the question of how these preferences are translated into policy. Our empirical analysis will explore the role of partisanship as an intervening variable. However, our core argument, about middle-income preferences, does not depend on staking a strong position in debates about whether parties cater to core constituencies or the median voter.

Like a number of recent political-economy models, most notably Iversen and Soskice (2006), our theoretical framework posits a society consisting of three classes or social groups defined by income: the poor, the middle, and the affluent. So long as no one class constitutes a majority of the electorate, redistributive policy will be set by a coalition of two groups and such coalitions will almost certainly include the middle-income group. These propositions are, of course, stylized simplifications, but we believe they capture core features of advanced industrial societies and serve the useful purpose of focusing our attention on the question of whether middle-income voters will ally with the poor or the affluent.

In the theoretical model proposed by Iversen and Soskice (2006), the answer to this question depends on the ability of parties to make credible commitments under different electoral rules. Under majoritarian rules, middle-income voters will be inclined to support Centre-Right parties because they fear that Centre-Left parties will revert to the preferences of their core constituency once in government. The interests of middle-income voters are more closely aligned with the first-order preferences of the affluent (no redistribution) than with those of the poor (redistribution form the non-poor to the poor).

However, proportional representation provides for parties that represent the middle-income group alone, making possible the formation of Centre-Left coalition governments committed to redistributing income from the affluent to the benefit of the middle and the poor alike. A crucial feature of the Iversen-Soskice model is that the middle-income group never imposes (redistributive) taxes on itself. By contrast, the model of redistribution that underlies our approach allows for this possibility or, alternatively, for the possibility that the middle-income group will claim a less-than-equal share of the redistributive benefits that the poor and the middle jointly derive from taxing the affluent.

The RMR model's conception of short-term income maximization as the foundation for preferences over redistributive policy is surely too narrow. We can distinguish two broad alternatives to the RMR approach to preferences. One alternative shares the RMR model's emphasis on material self-interest, but posits that individuals calculate the costs and benefits of redistribution with a more extended time horizon, or in a more "enlightened" manner. Insurance against future income losses or the recognition of negative externalities associated with inequality (Alesina and Giuliano 2009) might motivate affluent individuals to support redistributive policies that do not benefit them immediately. The other alternative holds that other-regarding motivations of an altruistic nature also matter; in other words, individuals are (sometimes) willing to forego some income for the benefit of others. Our core argument builds on this latter approach, which emphasizes that individuals should be viewed not as atomized maximizers of self-interest, however enlightened, but as members of social groups or networks.

The notion of social affinity features prominently in recent studies of how racial and ethnic fractionalization affects demand for redistribution. Luttmer's (2001) influential analysis of individual-level support for welfare spending in the US provides strong evidence of what he refers to as *racial group loyalty*. According to Luttmer's analysis, individuals living in neighborhoods with many welfare recipients are, on average, less supportive of welfare spending. But proximity to white recipients increases support for welfare spending among white respondents while proximity to black welfare recipients increases support for welfare spending among black respondents. Crucially, Luttmer shows that racial group loyalty is just as strong among high-income respondents as it is among low-income ones.

Building on Luttmer's work, Alesina and Glaeser (2004) demonstrate that social spending correlates with various measures of ethnic, linguistic, and religious fractionalization on a cross-national basis. Though their measures of fractionalization fail to capture this, Alesina and Glaeser's theoretical discussion clearly recognizes that the crucial issue is not fractionalization per se, but rather how racial or ethnic cleavages map onto the income distribution (cf. Selway 2011). "Significant numbers of minorities among the poor," they argue, means that, "the majority population can be roused against transferring money to people who are different from themselves".

More recently, Shayo's (2009) important contribution suggests that the concept of social affinity might usefully be extended to social classes defined by income. Positing that social identities are defined by self-categorization into groups and that there are multiple groups with which any given individual might identify, Shayo argues that individuals choose to identify with one or another group – say, their class or their nation – based on (a) perceived social distance to the prototypical member of each group, and (b) the relative status of the group in question. In our theoretical framework, individuals are enmeshed in social networks that are typically class-based, whether or not they in fact identify with their class. Members of the middle-income group must decide whether they prefer an alliance with the poor or with the affluent. Like Shayo, we posit that social distance constitutes an important consideration in the choice of alternative coalitions and suppose that income differentials are a reasonably good proxy for social distance, at least in the absence of cross-cutting ethnic or racial cleavages. It follows from these premises that we should expect middle-income voters to be more inclined to empathize with the poor – and to support parties that advocate pro-poor redistributive policies – when the income distance from the poor is small relative to the income distance from the affluent.

In our conceptualization, social affinity involves altruistic behaviour, but it is quite different from generalized altruism. If middle-income voters were motivated by generalized altruism, their sympathy for the poor would increase with the distance between their income and that of the poor. By contrast, proximity is the source of affinity in our theoretical framework. Put differently, social affinity involves what Fowler and Kam (2007) refer to as *parochial altruism*: altruism bounded by perceptions of common group membership or shared experience. Middle-income voters empathize with the poor (or affluent) when they perceive the poor (or affluent) as living lives similar to their own. In particular, we expect middle-income voters to empathize with the poor (or affluent) to the extent that they live in the same neighbourhoods, send their children to the same schools, and circulate within the same social networks. Having relatives who are poor is also likely to be a source of social affinity with the poor.

Arguably, mobility between income groups is an important component of (or condition for) affinity between income groups. A number of recent cross-national studies indicate that relative income mobility tends to decline with aggregate inequality. The obvious reason is that income gains or losses of a given size translate into larger movements across the income distribution, up or down, when the income distribution is more compressed. The probability of moving between any two positions in the income distribution is in part a function of the distance between the two positions. When the distance between the poor and the middle-income group is small, members of the middle-income group face a greater probability of becoming poor (or having children with low incomes) and this will, we hypothesize, reinforce their affinity with the poor. Conversely, prospects of upward mobility will reinforce middle-income affinity with the affluent when the distance between the middle and the affluent is small.

In future work, analysing individual preferences for redistribution, we hope to disentangle the effects of social affinity and self-interest informed by mobility prospects. However, we do not view social affinity and self-interest as competing explanations of individual preferences for redistribution. Rather, we wish to emphasize the potential complementarities of other-regarding and self-interested motivations. Social solidarity becomes an operative behavioural norm, we think, when individuals have some rational reason to suppose it might serve their own interests over the long run.

Our argument focuses on middle-income voters, but the underlying logic ought to apply to the poor and the affluent as well. When the distance to the middle is small, the poor should feel more affinity with the middle-income group and demand less redistribution. Similarly, the affluent should feel affinity with the middle-income group, and perhaps be less resistant to redistribution, when the distance between the middle and the affluent is small.

Our social-affinity hypothesis stands in sharp contrast to the social-rivalry hypothesis articulated by Corneo and Grüner (2002). These authors posit that middle-income voters oppose redistribution because they fear it will enable the poor to gain access to middle-class neighbourhoods and social networks, thereby undermining their own relative position in the status hierarchy. By this logic, proximity to the poor should undermine– rather than promote – support for redistribution among middle-income voters.

The status dimension of Shayo's (2009) theoretical model also points in the direction of social rivalry as an important factor behind individual preferences for redistribution. There is no middle class in the model that Shayo presents, but he briefly discusses such an extension. With respect to the poor, Shayo argues that redistribution improves their status, increasing their propensity to identify with their social class rather than their nation. Adding a middle class to his model, the implication would seem to be that greater proximity to the poor should reduce the value of being middle-class, rendering middle-class individuals more likely to identify with the nation and less likely to support redistribution.

In this paper, we test the social-affinity hypothesis against macro data and relate our core argument to previous macro-comparative studies of the relationship between inequality and redistribution. From a macro-comparative perspective, our key insight is that the combination of relatively small income differences in the lower half of the distribution and relatively large income differences in the upper half provides the most favourably conditions for redistributive politics. Conversely, the combination of relatively large income differences in the lower half of the distribution and relatively small differences in the upper half undermines support for redistribution among pivotal middle-income voters.

Like Kristov, Lindert, and McClelland (1992), we estimate models of redistribution with separate measures of income differentials in the two halves of the income distribution. We hypothesize that the 90-50 earnings ratio (i.e., the ratio of earnings in the 90th percentile to earnings in the 50th percentile) will be associated with more redistribution and that the 50-10 earnings ratio (i.e., the ratio of earnings in the 50th percentile to earnings in the 10th percentile) will be associated with less redistribution. Our argument implies that these measures of upper-and lower-half inequality matter jointly to middle-income support for redistribution. Conceiving social affinity with the poor as the inverse of social affinity with the affluent, we imagine that middle-income voters compare income distances in the two halves of the distribution in the process of choosing coalition partners. An increase of the 90-50 ratio will only have the predicted effect of moving middle-income voters towards greater support for redistribution insofar as it is not offset by a corresponding increase of the 50-10 ratio. At the same time, however, 90-50 and 50-10 ratios are closely correlated, across countries and also over time. To address this problem, we estimate models with a measure of how the two ratios are related to each other: the 90-10 ratio divided by the 50-10 ratio. This measure, which we refer to as skew, rises as dispersion in the upper half of the earnings distribution increases relative to dispersion in the lower half, and takes on a value of one whenever the 90-50 and 50-10 ratios are the same. We expect skew to be positively associated with redistribution.

Our approach draws on insights from recent research on racial and ethnic group solidarity and posits that social affinities are also based on income. We do not argue that income is a more important basis of social affinity than ethnicity. In our view, the relative importance of different sources of social affinity is an open empirical question. Relying on the stock of immigrants as the best available proxy for the ethnic concentration of minorities among the poor, our empirical analysis begins to address this question, but our primary objective here is to establish that income-based social affinity matters to the politics of redistribution.

EMPIRICAL SETUP

Our main empirical analysis consists of a series of models of redistribution (measured as the percentage change in Gini coefficients brought about by taxes and government transfers) and social spending (measured in percent of GDP). Redistribution is the theoretically relevant variable, but our data on redistribution is limited and entails potential complications. Estimating similar models with social spending as the dependent variable provides an important test of the robustness of our findings. In this section, we introduce the variables included in our models of redistribution and social spending, describe the data used to estimate these models, and specify the models themselves.

Main Variables of Interest

With data from the Luxembourg Income Study (LIS), we measure redistribution as the percentage change in Gini coefficients that we observe as we move from household income before taxes and transfers (gross market income) to household income after taxes and transfers (disposable income). In keeping with existing studies that use LIS data, our analysis is restricted to working-age households or, more precisely, households headed by someone between the ages of 25 and 59. This is because generous public pension systems reduce the incentive for individuals to accumulate savings. Since many retirees have no market income at all, studies of redistribution that include the retired population yield very high levels of market inequality, in a sense exaggerating the redistributive effects of public spending in countries with generous public pension systems.

Our LIS-based observations of redistribution were generated by Lane Kenworthy, initially for Kenworthy and Pontusson (2005). Kenworthy's updated dataset includes at least two observations of inequality measured in terms of both gross market income and disposable income for 16 OECD countries over the period 1969-2005, for a total of 90 country-year observations. For lack of data on earnings inequality, the dataset we use to estimate our redistribution models consists of 83 country-year observations drawn from 15 countries (with N=68 in models that include the lagged dependent variable).

Apart from its small size, two features of this dataset are potentially problematic. First, some countries are far better represented than others. With an average of 5.5 observations per country, the dataset includes two observations each for Belgium and Spain, but nine observations for the UK and ten for Canada. Second, the interval between observations of redistribution for a given country varies considerably. For most observations, the time since the previous observation ranges between three and six years (the average being 4.5), but we have nine instances of one or two years and, at other end of the spectrum, one instance of ten years between observations. This feature of the dataset raises concerns about our ability to capture true lag effects, as opposed to very noisy average effects.

We address the data limitations of our analysis of redistribution in two ways. Mindful of the potential influence of outliers, we report results based on our full dataset along with results obtained when we drop country-year observations that constitute outliers, with these identified as observations with standardized residuals greater than 1.5 standard deviations away from the mean. We also test the robustness of our redistribution results by analysing the determinants of social spending. To align the two analyses as closely as possible, the dependent variable in our second set of regression models is public social spending that is not targeted specifically to the elderly (i.e., total public social spending minus spending on pensions and services for the elderly), measured in percent of GDP. Across country-years for which we have observations of both redistribution among working-age households and non-elderly social spending, the correlation between the two is 0.86 (N=73). For the non-elderly population, then, social spending would appear to be a reasonable proxy for redistribution. The OECD Social Expenditures Database provides the data necessary to compute non-elderly social spending on an annual basis from 1980 onwards. For lack of data on earnings inequality, we end up with a dataset consisting of 329 country-year observations drawn from 18 countries (with N=311 in models that include the lagged dependent variable). Corroborating our redistribution results concerning the effects of the structure of inequality, our analysis of social spending should allay concerns about variable lag periods as well as the small size of the redistribution dataset.

Our measures of the structure of inequality are based on OECD data on gross earnings of full-time employees. While there are reasonable concerns about cross-national comparability, many studies have employed these data and the OECD has significantly improved data quality over multiple iterations. We use only the most recent version of the gross earnings data available (OECD 2007). The advantage of the OECD data, relative to other sources of data on market inequality, is that it provides separate measures of the upper and lower halves of the earnings distribution while also providing reasonably long time series of annual observations for the countries included in our analysis. Missing data still represent a constraint. Between available observations of earnings inequality, we have linearly interpolated missing observations. We have also extrapolated observations up to five years back when doing so allows us to include additional observations of redistribution.

Control Variables

In estimating the effects of earnings inequality on redistributive policy outcomes, we seek to control for other variables that have been identified as important determinants of redistribution. Our argument builds on studies that emphasize ethnic fragmentation as an obstacle to redistributive politics and posits that income is an important basis of social affinity in the absence of cross-cutting racial or ethnic cleavages. More specifically, our expectation that narrowing the gap between two income groups will generate greater affinity between them assumes that differences in the racial, ethnic, religious, and linguistic composition of the two groups remain constant.

From a theoretical point of view, it is important for us to control for the distribution of ethnic minorities across the income distribution, but here we run into serious problems of data and measurement. Most available indices of ethno-linguistic and religious fractionalization (e.g., Alesina et al. 2003) are not only time-invariant but also fail to capture the crucial extent to which minorities are concentrated among the poor (or perhaps, in a post-colonial setting, concentrated among the affluent). Recent articles by

Baldwin and Huber (2010) and Selway (2011) represent important advances in this domain. Yet both Baldwin and Huber's measure of between-group inequality and Selway's index of the "cross-cuttingness" of income and ethnic group membership remain time-invariant and several of the countries in our analysis are missing from their data.

In the absence of a better measure, we include a time-varying measure of the stock of immigrants in some of our empirical models of redistribution and social spending. Based on data collected by Rafaela Dancygier, this variable refers to the percentage of the population that is foreign-born for Australia, Canada, and the US, and the percentage of the population who are non-citizens for the other countries in our dataset. Following Alesina and Glaeser's (2004: 175-7) discussion of immigration as a threat to European welfare states, the assumption here is that immigrants are over-represented at the lower end of the income distribution. Data from Europeans Social Surveys provide some support for this assumption. Averaging across the four surveys conducted between 2002 and 2008, we observe that the percentage of foreign-born among the poor, defined as the bottom third of the income distribution of respondents, exceeds the percentage of foreign-born among the non-poor in all but two of the 13 European countries in our data (Italy and the UK). However, the extent to which immigrants are over-represented among the poor varies a great deal across these countries and this variation does not appear to be correlated with levels of immigration.

It is undoubtedly the case that some immigrants are high-income earners and that others manage to move up the income distribution over time. Quite plausibly, the immigrant populations of Australia, Canada, and the US are particularly heterogeneous from a socio-economic point of view. Moreover, as a proxy for the concentration of ethnic minorities among the poor, this variable completely misses the presence of native minorities among the poor, a prominent feature of American exceptionalism in the domain of social policy and redistributive politics.

At best, then, immigration represents a rough proxy for the concentration of minorities among the poor. In addition, the availability of data on immigration significantly reduces the number of country-year observations we can use to estimate our models. For both reasons, we begin by presenting our results without immigration and then add this variable.

An important recent focus in research on the political economy of redistribution is why countries with proportional representation (PR) tend to have more redistributive governments than countries with majoritarian electoral rules. While Persson and Tabellini (2000, 2003) argue that electoral rules affect the type of spending incumbent politicians choose, Persson, Roland, and Tabellini (2007) propose a model in which the effect of PR on government spending hinges on the greater probability of a coalition government under PR rules. Iversen and Soskice's (2006) alternative theory proceeds from the observation that since 1945 government participation by Left parties has been much more common in PR countries than in majoritarian countries. For Iversen and Soskice, the redistributive effects of electoral rules operate through government partisanship and the effect of electoral rules should be mediated entirely by government partisanship. In due course, we will introduce government partisanship into our analysis, but we leave this variable out for the time being on account of endogeneity concerns. To control for the electoral-systems effect, we include Gallagher's (1991) measure of proportionality. This index ranges from 0 (pure proportionality between vote and seat shares) to infinity as disproportionality increases. For ease of interpretation, we standardize the Gallagher index to vary between 0 and 1, and invert it so that larger values represent greater proportionality.

The varieties-of-capitalism literature implies that we need to control for national skill profiles. Iversen and Soskice (2001) argue that individuals with more specific skills are more likely to support social spending and show that vocational training share (VTS), measured by the share of an age cohort engaged in secondary and tertiary vocational training, is correlated with government spending on income transfers on a cross-national basis. In addition, Estevez-Abe, Iversen, and Soskice (2001: 169-78) show that VTS is associated with compression of earnings differentials on a cross-national basis, and Iversen (2005: 148-54) reports a strong positive effect of VTS on redistribution among working-age households. In short, skill specificity could be the source of any positive association between compression of the lower half of the earnings distribution and redistribution that we observe.

Iversen and his collaborators use VTS data from the period 1980-95. One of the two components of Iversen's VTS index – graduates of tertiary vocational programs as a percent of the tertiary age cohort – cannot be updated because UNESCO no longer publishes the requisite data. However, it is possible to construct continuous and consistent time series on the percentage of secondary-school students enrolled in vocational programs for the 15 countries in our analysis over the period 1980-2005.16 This will serve as our measure of vocational-training intensity in the analysis that follows. Aside from data availability, it is arguably a better measure than Iversen's in that it sidesteps the complicated question of the kinds of skills acquired through tertiary vocational training programs. It is certainly an appropriate control variable for our purposes, given that our primary concern here is to ensure that national skill profiles do not confound the relationship between 50-10 earnings ratios and redistribution. Unionization represents another potential source of spurious associations between bottom-end earnings compression and redistribution. Unions do not typically organize workers at the very bottom of the earnings distribution, but they do have a strong interest in setting a floor for competition in the labour market, and unionization tends to be associated with more compressed 50-10 ratios. Controlling for income and other relevant demographics, moreover, union members are more likely to both turn out and to support redistribution than non-union members (Pontusson and Kwon 2006). Thus we need to control for the effects of union density in order to test our hypothesis that bottom-end compression alters the preferences of middle-income voters.

Like many previous studies, we conceive voter turnout as an inverse proxy for income bias in voting. With higher turnout, poor citizens are more politically active relative to affluent citizens and, presumably, better represented by elected politicians. Hence we expect turnout to be associated with more redistribution.

More readily than any other variable, the unemployment rate serves to control for changes in the share of the working-age population that is eligible for redistributive social transfers. So long as unemployment insurance coverage and generosity remain unchanged, an increase in unemployment translates more or less automatically into greater redistribution (cf. Kenworthy and Pontusson 2005). We also control for female participation in the labour force since women are more likely to be part-time workers than men and therefore tend to have lower hourly wages. As the OECD data on relative earnings pertain to full-time employees, female labour-force participation may pick up effects of inequality – particularly low-end inequality – that are not captured by our measures of earnings inequality. Following Iversen and Rosenbluth (2006), among others, we expect female labour-force participation to be associated with more political support for redistributive social policies.

Working with a significantly larger dataset, we include three additional control variables in our models of social spending. First, these models take account of the fact that the dependent variable (non-elderly social spending) is expressed in percent of GDP by including GDP growth on the right-hand side of the regression equation. When the GDP denominator contracts, social spending automatically expands, but this does not mean that social policy has become more generous or redistributive. Secondly, our spending models include the percentage of the population above the age of 64. As a result of budget constraints, governments are likely to face a trade-off between spending on the elderly and non-elderly. All else equal, we expect population ageing to constrict the available room for non-elderly social spending to grow. Finally, the social spending models include a composite measure of (economic) globalization developed by Dreher (2006). Based on principal component analysis, Dreher's index includes capital mobility and trade, measuring both legal barriers and actual financial and trade flows. The effect of globalization has featured prominently in studies of social spending, with some scholars arguing that greater economic openness decreases spending by disciplining governments, others that openness increases government demands for compensatory social spending. While we have no particular theoretical priors with regard to this debate, it seems clear that our models of social spending should control for the effects of globalization.

MODEL SPECIFICATIONS

For each country *i* and year *t*, our statistical models of redistribution treat the level of redistribution (*Ri,t*) as a function of previous levels (*Ri,t-1*) and a set of policies and structural factors (*Pi,t*) that cause redistribution to deviate from the status quo. Since data on redistribution are unequally spaced, while values for the independent variables are annual, we follow Persson, Roland, and Tabellini (2007) in using a time-series cross-section model in which independent variables are averaged across the period since the previous observation of redistribution. Thus, if two observations of redistribution are five years apart (*t* and *t-5*), each independent variable is the average value for the five intervening years (*t-5* through *t-1*). Our models also include the lagged dependent variable to account for the status-quo level of redistribution and address potential problems raised by serial correlation. Ideally, our analysis should include country fixed-effects to account for unit-heterogeneity and its potential correlation with our variables of interest. Given the number of observations per country in our dataset, however, we cannot simultaneously include both the lagged dependent variable and country fixed effects (Nickell 1981). We are also hampered by the fact that some of the control variables in our model are slow-moving. Following Milanovic (2000), we therefore specify a set of fixed-effects models in which we include only measures of earnings inequality. These restricted models provide, we think, the most reasonable test of the effect of the structure of inequality on within-country variation in levels of redistribution.

We turn to models of non-elderly social spending in an effort to corroborate our redistribution results. Since we have a complete, annual series of social spending, variable lag periods no longer present a problem. We could simply employ one-year lags of our independent variables, but it seems unreasonable to suppose that the effects of earnings inequality and other independent variables would be so immediate. To capture more slow-moving causal processes and to approximate the specification of our redistribution models, our models instead measure all independent variables as five-year moving averages (the observation for each year being the average for the preceding five). Again, we report the results of estimating fixed-effects as well as random-effects specifications of the social spending models. Despite having a larger dataset for social spending, the limitations of our earnings inequality data mean that we end up including fewer than 10 observations for a handful of countries (Ireland, Italy, New Zealand, Norway, Spain, and Switzerland). As with redistribution, this renders the estimation of fully-specified fixed-effects models problematic. Thus, our fixed-effects models are again restricted to measures of earnings inequality, though in this case we continue to include GDP growth to address the denominator problem.

6

Understanding Social Change, Class and Caste System

UNDERSTANDING SOCIAL CHANGE

The transformation of culture (especially norms and values), behaviour, social institutions, and social structure over time refers to the transformation of culture, behaviour, social institutions, and social structure over time. The basic types of society: hunting and gathering, horticultural and pastoral, agricultural, industrial, and post-industrial. In looking at all of these societies, we have seen how they differ in such dimensions as size, technology, economy, inequality, and gender roles. In short, we have seen some of the ways in which societies change over time. Another way of saying this is that we have seen some of the ways in which societies change as they become more modern. To understand social change, then, we need to begin to understand what it means for a society to become more modern.

Modernization

The process and impact of becoming more modern. Modernization has been an important focus of sociology since its origins in the 19th century. Several dimensions and effects of modernization seem apparent (Nolan & Lenski, 2009).

First, as societies evolve, they become much larger and more *heterogeneous*. This means that people are more different from each other than when societies were much smaller, and it also means that they ordinarily cannot know each other nearly as well. Larger, more modern societies thus typically have weaker social bonds and a weaker sense of community than small societies and more of an emphasis on the needs of the individual.

We can begin to appreciate the differences between smaller and larger societies when we contrast a small college of 1,200 students with a large university of 40,000 students. Perhaps you had this contrast in mind when you were applying to college and had a preference for either a small or a large institution. In a small college, classes might average no more than 20 students; these students get to know each other well and to have a lot of interaction with the professor. In a large university, classes might hold 600 students or more, and everything is more impersonal. Large universities do have many advantages, but they probably do not have as strong a sense of community as is found at small colleges.

A second aspect of modernization is a loss of traditional ways of thinking. This allows a society to be creative and to abandon old ways that may no longer be appropriate, but it also means a weakening or even loss of the traditions that helped define the society and gave it a sense of identity.

A third aspect of modernization is the growth of individual freedom and autonomy. As societies grow, become more impersonal, and lose their traditions and sense of community, their norms become weaker, and individuals thus become freer to think for themselves and to behave in new ways. Although most of us would applaud this growth in individual freedom, it also means, as Émile Durkheim (1895/1962) recognized long ago, that people feel freer to *deviate* from society's norms and thus to commit deviance. If we want a society that values individual freedom, Durkheim said, we automatically must have a society with deviance.

Is modernization good or bad? This is a simplistic question about a very complex concept, but a quick answer is that it is both good and bad. We see evidence for both responses in the views of sociologists Ferdinand Tönnies, Max Weber, and Durkheim. *Culture and Society* discussed, Tönnies (1887/1963) said that modernization meant a shift from *Gemeinschaft* (small societies with strong social bonds) to *Gesellschaft* (large societies with weaker social bonds and more impersonal social relations). Tönnies lamented the loss of close social bonds and of a strong sense of community resulting from modernization.

Weber (1921/1978) was also concerned about modernization. The hallmarks of modernization, he thought, are rationalization, a loss of tradition, and the rise of impersonal bureaucracy. He despaired over the impersonal quality of rational thinking and bureaucratization, as he thought it was a dehumanizing influence.

Durkheim (1893/1933) took a less negative view of modernization. He certainly appreciated the social bonds and community feeling, which he called mechanical solidarity. Émile Durkheim's conception of the type of social bonds and community feeling in small, traditional societies resulting from their homogeneity., characteristic of small, traditional societies. However, he also thought that these societies stifled individual freedom and that social solidarity still exists in modern societies.

Beyond these abstract concepts of social bonding and sense of community, modern societies have certainly been a force for both good and bad in other ways. They have led to scientific discoveries that have saved lives, extended life spans, and made human existence much easier than imaginable in the distant past and even in the recent past. But they have also polluted the environment, engaged in wars that have killed tens of millions, and built up nuclear arsenals that, even with the demise of the Soviet Union, still threaten the planet. Modernization, then, is a double-edged sword. It has given us benefits too numerous to count, but it also has made human existence very precarious.

Sources of Social Change

We have seen that social change stems from natural forces and also from the intentional acts of groups of people. This section further examines these sources of social change.

Population Growth and Composition

Much of the discussion so far has talked about population growth as a major source of social change as societies evolved from older to modern times. Yet even in modern societies, changes in the size and composition of the population can have important effects for other aspects of a society. As just one example, the number of school-age children reached a high point in the late 1990s as the children of the post–World War II baby boom entered their school years. This swelling of the school-age population had at least three important consequences. First, new schools had to be built, modular classrooms and other structures had to be added to existing schools, and more teachers and other school personnel had to be hired (Leonard, 1998). Second, school boards and municipalities had to borrow dollars and/or raise taxes to pay for all of these expenses. Third, the construction industry, building supply centres, and other businesses profited from the building of new schools and related activities. The growth of this segment of our population thus had profound implications for many aspects of U.S. society even though it was unplanned and "natural." We explore population growth and change further in a later section.

Culture and Technology

Culture and technology are other sources of social change. Changes in culture can change technology; changes in technology can transform culture; and changes in both can alter other aspects of society.

Two examples from either end of the 20th century illustrate the complex relationship among culture, technology, and society. At the beginning of the century, the car was still a new invention, and automobiles slowly but surely grew in number, diversity, speed, and power. The car altered the social and physical landscape of the United States and other industrial nations as few other inventions have. Roads and highways were built; pollution increased; families began living farther from each other and from their workplaces; tens of thousands of people started dying annually in car accidents. These are just a few of the effects the invention of the car had, but they illustrate how changes in technology can affect so many other aspects of society.

At the end of the 20th century came the personal computer, whose development has also had an enormous impact that will not be fully understand for some years to come. Anyone old enough, such as many of your oldest professors, to remember having to type long manuscripts on a manual typewriter will easily attest to the difference computers have made for many aspects of our work lives. E-mail, the Internet, and smartphones have enabled instant communication and make the world a very small place, and tens of millions of people now use Facebook and other social media. A generation ago, students studying abroad or working in the Peace Corps overseas would send a letter back home, and it would take up to 2 weeks or more to arrive. It would take another week or 2 for them to hear back from their parents. Now even in poor parts of the world, access to computers and smartphones lets us communicate instantly with people across the planet.

As the world becomes a smaller place, it becomes possible for different cultures to have more contact with each other. This contact, too, leads to social change to the extent that one culture adopts some of the norms, values, and other aspects of another culture. Anyone visiting a poor nation and seeing Coke, Pepsi, and other popular U.S. products in vending machines and stores in various cities will have a *culture shock* that reminds us instantly of the influence of one culture on another. For better or worse, this impact means that the world's diverse cultures are increasingly giving way to a more uniform *global culture.*

This process has been happening for more than a century. The rise of newspapers, the development of trains and railroads, and the invention of the telegraph, telephone, and, later, radio and television allowed cultures in different parts of the world to communicate with each other in ways not previously possible. Affordable jet transportation, cell phones, the Internet, and other modern technology have taken such communication a gigantic step further.

Many observers fear that the world is becoming "Westernized" as Coke, Pepsi, McDonald's, and other products and companies invade other cultures. Others say that Westernization is a good thing, because these products, but especially more important ones like refrigerators and computers, do make people's lives easier and therefore better. Still other observers say the impact of Westernization has been exaggerated. Both within the United States and across the world, these observers say, many cultures continue to thrive, and people continue to hold on to their ethnic identities.

Social Conflict

Change also results from social conflict, including wars, ethnic conflict, efforts by social movements to change society, and efforts by their opponents to maintain the status quo. The immediate impact that wars have on societies is obvious, as the deaths of countless numbers of soldiers and civilians over the ages have affected not only the lives of their loved ones but also the course of whole nations. To take just one of many examples, the defeat of Germany in World War I led to a worsening economy during the next decade that in turn helped fuel the rise of Hitler. In a less familiar example, the deaths of so many soldiers during the American Civil War left many wives and mothers without their family's major breadwinner. Many of these women thus had to turn to prostitution to earn an income, helping to fuel a rise in prostitution after the war (Marks, 1990).

POPULATION

We have commented that population growth is an important source of other changes in society. A generation ago, population growth was a major issue in the United States and some other nations. *Zero population growth*, or ZPG, was a slogan often heard. There was much concern over the rapidly growing population in the United States and, especially, around the world, and there was fear that our "small planet" could not support massive increases in the number of people (Ehrlich, 1969). Some of the most dire predictions of the time warned of serious food shortages by the end of the century.

Those predictions did not come to pass, and concern over population growth has faded as the world's resources seem to be standing up to population growth. Widespread hunger in Africa and other regions does exist, with hundreds of millions of people suffering from hunger and malnutrition, but many experts attribute this problem not to overpopulation and lack of food but rather to problems in distributing the sufficient amount of food that actually does exist to people in poor nations.

Sociology Making a Difference

A popular belief is that world hunger exists because there is too little food to feed too many people in poor nations in Africa, Asia, and elsewhere. Sociologists Stephen J. Scanlan, J. Craig Jenkins, and Lindsey Peterson (2010) call this belief the "scarcity fallacy." According to these authors, "The conventional wisdom is that world hunger exists primarily because of natural disasters, population pressure, and shortfalls in food production". However, this conventional wisdom is mistaken, as world hunger stems not from a shortage of food but from the inability to deliver what is actually a sufficient amount of food to the world's poor. As Scanlan and colleagues note,

A good deal of thinking and research in sociology suggests that world hunger has less to do with the shortage of food than with a shortage of *affordable* or *accessible* food. Sociologists have found that social inequalities, distribution systems, and other economic and political factors create barriers to food access.

This sociological view has important implications for how the world should try to reduce global hunger, say these authors. International organizations such as the World Bank and several United Nations agencies have long believed that hunger is due to food scarcity, and this belief underlies the typical approaches to reducing world hunger that focus on increasing food supplies with new technologies and developing more efficient methods of delivering food. But if food scarcity is not a problem, then other approaches are necessary.

Scanlan and colleagues argue that food scarcity is, in fact, not the problem that international agencies and most people believe it to be:

The bigger problem with emphasizing food supply as the problem, however, is that scarcity is largely a myth. On a per capita basis, food is more plentiful today than any other time in human history....[E]ven in times of localized production shortfalls or regional famines there has long been a global food surplus.

If the problem is not a lack of food, then what is the problem? Scanlan and colleagues argue that the real problem is a lack of access to food and a lack of equitable distribution of food: "Rather than food scarcity, then, we should focus our attention on the persistent inequalities that often accompany the growth in food supply".

What are these inequalities? Recognizing that hunger is especially concentrated in the poorest nations, the authors note that these nations lack the funds to import the abundant food that does exist. These nations' poverty, then, is one inequality that leads to world hunger, but gender and ethnic inequalities are also responsible. For example, women around the world are more likely than men to suffer from hunger, and hunger is more common in nations with greater rates of gender inequality (as measured by gender differences in education and income, among other criteria). Hunger is also more common among ethnic minorities not only in poor nations but also in wealthier nations. In findings from their own research, these sociologists add, hunger lessens when nations democratize, when political rights are protected, and when gender and ethnic inequality is reduced.

If inequality underlies world hunger, they add, then efforts to reduce world hunger will succeed only to the extent that they recognize the importance of inequality in this regard: "To get at inequality, policy must give attention to democratic governance and human rights, fixing the politics of food aid, and tending to the challenges posed by the global economy". For this to happen, they say, food must be upheld as a "fundamental human right." More generally, world hunger cannot be effectively reduced unless and until ethnic and gender inequality is reduced. Scanlan and colleagues conclude.

The challenge, in short, is to create a more equitable and just society in which food access is ensured for all. Food scarcity matters. However, it is rooted in social conditions and institutional dynamics that must be the focus of any policy innovations that might make a real difference.

In calling attention to the myth of food scarcity and the inequalities that contribute to world hunger, Scanlan and colleagues point to better strategies for addressing this significant international problem. Once again, sociology is making a difference.

Concern over population growth also decreased because of criticism by people of color that ZPG was directed largely at their ranks and smacked of racism. The call for population control, they said, was a disguised call for controlling the growth of their own populations and thus reducing their influence (Kuumba, 1993).

Still another reason for the reduced concern over population growth is that birth rates in many industrial nations have slowed considerably. Some nations are even experiencing population declines, while several more are projected to have population declines by 2050. For a country to maintain its population, the average woman needs to have 2.1 children, the *replacement level* for population stability. But several industrial nations, not including the United States, are far below this level. Increased birth control is one reason for their lower fertility rates, but so are the decisions by women to stay in school longer and then to go to work right after their schooling ends and not having their first child until somewhat later.

Ironically, these nations' population declines have begun to concern demographers and policy makers (Shorto, 2008). Because people in many industrial nations are living longer while the birth rate drops, these nations are increasingly having a greater proportion of older people and a smaller proportion of younger people. In several European nations, there are more people 61 or older than 19 or younger. As this trend continues, it will become increasingly difficult to take care of the health and income needs of so many older persons, and there may be too few younger people to fill the many jobs and provide the many services that an industrial society demands. The smaller labour force may also mean that governments will have fewer income tax dollars to provide these services.

To deal with these problems, several governments have initiated *pronatalist* policies aimed at encouraging women to have more children. In particular, they provide generous child-care subsidies, tax incentives, and flexible work schedules designed to make it easier to bear and raise children, and some even provide couples outright cash payments when they have an additional child. Russia in some cases provides the equivalent of about $9,000 for each child beyond the first, while Spain provides 2,500 euros (equivalent to about $3,400) for each child (Haub, 2009).

Demography and Demographic Concepts

As all of these issues indicate, changes in the size and composition of population have important implications for other social changes. The study of population is so significant that it occupies a special subfield within sociology called demography. The study of population growth and changes in population composition.. To be more precise, demography is the study of changes in the size and composition of population. It encompasses several concepts: fertility and birth rates, mortality and death rates, and migration (Weeks, 2008). Let's look at each of these briefly.

Fertility and Birth Rates

The number of live births. Demographers use several measures of fertility. The number of live births for every 1,000 people in a population in a given year., or the number of live births for every 1,000 people in a population in a given year. To determine the crude birth rate, the number of live births in a year is divided by the population size, and this result is then multiplied by 1,000. For example, in 2008 the United States had a population of about 304 million and 4,251,095 births. Dividing the latter figure by the former figure gives us 0.0140 rounded off. We then multiply this quotient by 1,000 to yield a crude birth rate of 14.0 births per 1,000 population (U.S. Census Bureau, 2010). We call this a "crude" birth rate because the denominator, population size, consists of the total population, not just the number of women or even the number of women of childbearing age (commonly considered 15–44).

The number of live births per 1,000 women aged 15–44. (also just called the *fertility rate* or *birth rate*), or the number of live births per 1,000 women aged 15–44 (i.e., of childbearing age). This is calculated in a manner similar to that for the crude fertility rate, but in this case the number of births is divided by the number of women aged 15–44 before multiplying by 1,000. The U.S. general fertility rate for 2007 was about 69.5 (i.e., 69.5 births per 1,000 women aged 15–44).

The number of children an average woman is expected to have in her lifetime, sometimes expressed as the number of children an average 1,000 women are expected to have in their lifetimes., or the number of children an average woman is expected to have in her lifetime. This measure often appears in the news media and is more easily understood by the public than either of the first two measures. In 2007, the U.S. total fertility rate was 2.1. Sometimes the total fertility rate is expressed as the average number of births that an average group of 1,000 women would be expected to have. In this case, the average number of children that one woman is expected to have is simply multiplied by 1,000. Using this latter calculation, the U.S. total fertility rate in 2007 was 2,100 (i.e., an average group of 1,000 women would be expected to have, in their lifetimes, 2,100 children).

Mortality and Death Rates

The number of deaths for every 1,000 people in a population in a given year., the number of deaths for every 1,000 people in a population in a given year. To determine the crude death rate, the number of deaths is divided by the population size, and this result is then multiplied by 1,000. In 2006 the United States had slightly more than 2.4 million deaths for a crude death rate of 8.1 deaths for every 1,000 persons. We call this a "crude" death rate because the denominator, population size, consists of the total population and does not take its age distribution into account. All things equal, a society with a higher proportion of older people should have a higher crude death rate. Demographers often calculate *age-adjusted* death rates that adjust for a population's age distribution.

Migration

The movement of people into and out of specific regions. Since the dawn of human history, people have migrated in search of a better life, and many have been forced to migrate by ethnic conflict or the slave trade. Several classifications of migration exist. When people move into a region, we call it *in-migration*, or *immigration*; when they move out of a region, we call it *out-migration*, or *emigration*. The *in-migration rate* is the number of people moving into a region for every 1,000 people in the region, while the *out-migration rate* is the number of people moving from the region for every 1,000 people. The difference between the two is the *net migration rate* (in-migration minus out-migration).

Migration can also be either domestic or international in scope. *Domestic migration* happens within a country's national borders, as when retired people from the northeastern United States move to Florida or the Southwest. *International migration* happens across national borders. When international immigration is heavy, as it has been into the United States and Western Europe in the last few decades, the effect on population growth and other aspects of national life can be significant. Domestic migration can also have a large impact. The great migration of African Americans from the South into northern cities during the first half of the 20th century changed many aspects of those cities' lives (Berlin, 2010). Meanwhile, the movement during the past few decades of northerners into the South and Southwest also had quite an impact: the housing market initially exploded, for example, and traffic increased.

SOCIAL CLASS

Few concepts are more contested in sociological theory than the concept of "class." In contemporary sociology there are scholars who assert that "class as a concept is ceasing to do any useful work in sociology" (Pahl, 1989) or even more stridently proclaim "the death of class". Yet, at the same time, there are also sociologists who write books with titles such as Bringing Class Back In, Reworking Class (Hall, 1997), Repositioning Class (Marshall 1997), and Class Counts (Wright, 1997). In some theoretical traditions in sociology, most notably Marxism, class figures at the very core of the theoretical structure; in others, especially the tradition identified with Durkheim, only pale shadows of class appear.

In what follows we will first examine in broad strokes the different ways in which the word class is used in sociological theory. This will be followed by a more fine-grained exploration of the differences in the concept of class in the two most important traditions of class analysis, the Weberian and the Marxist.

Varieties of Class Concepts

Many discussions of the concept of class confuse the terminological problem of how the word class is used within social theory with theoretical disputes about the proper definition and elaboration of the concept of class. While all uses of the word class in social theory invoke in one way or another the problem of understanding systems of economic inequality, different uses of the word are imbedded in very different theoretical agendas involving different kinds of questions and thus different sorts of concepts. One way of sorting out these alternative meanings is to examine what might be termed the anchoring questions within different agendas of class analysis. These are the questions that define the theoretical work the concept of class attempts to do. Five such anchoring questions in which the word "class" figures centrally in the answers are particularly important.

Class as Subjective location. First, the word "class" sometimes figures in the answer to the question: "How do people, individually and collectively, locate themselves and others within a social structure of inequality?" Class is one of the possible answers to this question. In this case the concept would be defined something like this: "Classes are social categories sharing subjectively-salient attributes used by people to rank those categories within a system of economic stratification". With this definition of class, the actual content of these evaluative attributes will vary considerably across time and place. In some contexts, class-as-subjective-classification will revolve around life styles, in others around occupations, and in still others around income levels. Sometimes the economic content of the subjective classification system is quite direct – as in income levels; in other contexts, it is more indirect, as in expressions such as "the respectable classes", the "dangerous classes". The number of classes will also vary contextually depending upon how the actors in a social situation themselves define class distinctions. Class is not defined by a set of objective properties of a person's social situation, but by the shared subjective understandings of people about rankings within social inequality. Class, in this sense of the word, would be contrasted to other forms of salient evaluation – religion, ethnicity, gender, occupation, etc. – which may have economic dimensions but which are not 2 centrally defined in economic terms.

Class as objective position within distributions. Second, class is often central to the question, "How are people objectively located in distributions of material inequality." In this case, class is defined in terms of material standards of living, usually indexed by income or, possibly, wealth. Class, in this agenda, is a gradational concept; the standard image is of rungs on a ladder, and the names for locations are accordingly such things as upper class, upper middle class, middle class, lower middle class, lower class, under class. This is the concept of class that figures most prominently in popular discourse, at least in countries like the United States without a strong working-class political tradition. When American politicians call for "middle class tax cuts" what they characteristically mean is tax cuts for people in the middle of the income distribution. Subjective aspects of the location of people within systems of stratification may still be important in sociological investigations using this concept of class, but the word class itself is being used to capture objective properties of economic inequality, not simply the subjective classifications. Class, in this context, is contrasted with other ways that people are objectively located within social structures, for example, by their citizenship status, their power, or their subjection to institutionalized forms of ascriptive discrimination.

Class as the relational explanation of economic life chance. Third, class may be offered as part of the answer to the question: "What explains inequalities in economically-defined life chances and material standards of living of individuals and families?" This is a more complex and demanding question than the first two, for here the issue is not simply descriptively locating people within some kind of system of stratification — either subjectively or objectively — but identifying certain causal mechanisms that help determine salient features of that system. When class is used to explain inequality, typically, the concept is not defined primarily by subjectively-salient attributes of a social location but rather by the relationship of people to income-generating resources or assets of various sorts. Class thus becomes a relational, rather than simply gradational concept. This concept of class is characteristic of both the Weberian and Marxist traditions of social theory. Class, in this usage, is contrasted to the many other determinants of a person's life chances – for example, geographical location, forms of discrimination anchored in ascriptive characteristics like race or gender, or genetic endowments. Location, discrimination, and genetic endowments may, of course, still figure in the analysis of class – they may, for example, play an important role in explaining why different sorts of people end up in different classes – but the definition of class as such centres how people are linked to those income-generating assets.

Class as a dimension of historical variation in systems of inequality. Fourth, class figures in answers to the question, "How should we characterize and explain the variations across history in the social organization of inequalities?" This question implies the need for a macro-level concept, rather than simply a micro-level concept capturing the causal processes of individual lives; and it requires a concept that allows for macro-level variations across time and place. This question is also important in both the Marxist and Weberian traditions, but as we will see later, here the two traditions have quite different answers. Within the Marxist tradition, the most salient aspect of historical variation in inequality is the ways in which economic systems vary in the manner in which an economic surplus is produced and appropriated, and classes are therefore defined with respect to the mechanisms of surplus extraction. For Weber, in contrast, the central problem of historical variation is the degree of rationalization of different dimensions of inequality. This underwrites a conceptual space in which on the one hand class and status are contrasted as distinct forms of inequality, and an the other hand class is contrasted with non-rationalized ways through which individual life-chances are shaped. Class as a foundation of economic oppression and exploitation. Finally, class plays a central role in answering the question, "What sorts of transformations are needed to eliminate economic oppression and exploitation within capitalist societies?" This is the most contentious question for it implies not simply an explanatory agenda about the mechanisms that generate economic inequalities, but a normative judgment about those inequalities – they are forms of oppression and exploitation – and a normative vision of the transformation of those inequalities. This is the distinctively Marxist question and it suggests a concept of class laden with normative content. It supports a concept of class which is not simply defined in terms of the social relations to economic resources, but which also figures centrally in a political project of emancipatory social change.

Different theoretical approaches to class analysis build their concepts of class to help answer different clusters of these questions. The array of central questions linked to different approaches to class analysis. Weber's work revolves around the third and fourth questions, with the fourth question concerning forms of historical variation in social organization of inequalities providing the anchor for his understanding of class. The narrower question about explaining individual life chances gets its specific meaning from its relationship to this broader historical question. Michael Mann's work on class, especially in his multivolume study of The Sources of Social Power is, like Weber's, also centered on the four question.. John Goldthorpe's class analysis centres firmly on the third question. While his work is often characterized as having a Weberian inflection, his categories are elaborated strictly in terms of the requirements of describing and explaining economic life chances, not long-term historical variations in systems of inequality. For Pierre Bourdieu, class analysis is anchored in a more open-ended version of the third question. Where he differs from Weber and other Weber-inspired class analysts is in expanding the idea of life-chances to include a variety of non-economic aspects of opportunity (e.g. cultural opportunities of various sorts) and expanding the kinds of resources relevant to explaining those life-chances from narrowly economic resources to a range of cultural and social resources (called "cultural capital" and "social capital"). "Class" for Bourdieu, therefore, is a much more expansive concept, covering all inequalities in opportunities (life chances) that can be attributed to socially-determined inequalities of resources of whatever sort. Finally, class analysis in the Marxist tradition is anchored in the fifth question concerning the challenge to systems of economic oppression and exploitation. The questions about historical variation and individual life chances are also important, but they are posed within the parameters of the problem of emancipatory transformations.

In the rest of this essay I will examine in some detail how these questions are played out in the Weberian and Marxist traditions, the two most important traditions of class analysis in sociological theory. The concepts of class in these two theoretical traditions share much in common: they both reject simple gradational definitions of class; they are both anchored in the social relations which link people to economic resources of various sorts; they both see these social relations as affecting the material interests of actors, and, accordingly, they see class relations as the potential basis for solidarities and conflict. Yet, they also differ in certain fundamental ways. The core of the difference is captured by the favorite buzz-words of each theoretical tradition: life-chances for Weberians, and exploitation for Marxists. This difference, in turn, reflects the location of class analysis within their broader theoretical agendas.

Class as Market-determined Life Chances

What has become the Weber-inspired tradition of class analysis is largely based on Weber's few explicit, but fragmentary, conceptual analyses of class in Economy and Society ([1924] 1978). Weber writes: We may speak of a "class" when (1) a number of people have in common a specific causal component of their life chances, insofar as (2) this component is represented exclusively by economic interests in the possession of goods and opportunities for income, and (3) is represented under the conditions of the commodity or labour markets. This is "class situation."

It is the most elemental economic fact that the way in which the disposition over material property is distributed among a plurality of people, meeting competitively in the market for the purpose of exchange, in itself creates specific life chances....

But always this is the generic connotation of the concept of class: that the kind of chance in the market is the decisive moment which presents a common condition for the individual's fate. Class situation is, in this sense, ultimately market situation.

In short, the kind and quantity of resources you own affects your opportunities for income in market exchanges. "Opportunity" is a description of the feasible set individuals face, the trade-offs they encounter in deciding what to do. Owning means of production (the capitalist class) gives a person different alternatives from owning skills and credentials (the "middle" class), and both of these are different from simply owning unskilled labour power (the working class). Furthermore, in a market economy, access to market-derived income affects the broader array of life experiences and opportunities for oneself and one's children. The study of the life-chances of children based on parent's market capacity, is thus an integral part of the Weberian agenda of class analysis.

This definition of class in terms of market-determined life chances is clearly linked to the third question posed above: "What explains inequalities in economically-defined life chances and material standards of living?" Weber's answer is: in capitalist societies the material resources one brings to market exchanges explain such inequalities in life chances. But even more deeply, Weber's conceptualization of class is anchored in the fourth question, the question of how to characterize and explain historical variation in the social organization of inequality. Two issues are especially salient here: first, the historical variation in the articulation of class and status, and second, the broad historical problem in understanding the rationalization of social processes.

Class is part of a broader multidimensional schema of stratification in Weber in which the most central contrast is between "class" and "status". Status groups are defined within the sphere of communal interaction (or what Weber calls the "social order") and always imply some level of identity in the sense of some recognized "positive or negative social estimation of honor" (Weber [1924] 1978:932). A status group cannot exist without its members being in some way conscious of being members of the group: "In contrast to classes, Stände (status groups) are normally groups".

This conceptual contrast between class and status for Weber is not primarily a question of the motives of actors: It is not that status groups are derived from purely symbolic motives and class categories are derived from material interests. Although people care about status categories in part because of their importance for symbolic ideal interests, class positions also entail such symbolic interests, and both status and class are implicated in the pursuit of material interests. As Weber ([1924] 1978: 935) writes, "material monopolies provide the most effective motives for the exclusiveness of a status group". Rather than motives, the central contrast between class and status is the nature of the mechanisms through which class and status shape inequalities of the material and symbolic conditions people's lives. Class affects material well-being directly through the kinds of economic assets people bring to market exchanges. Status affects material well-being indirectly, through the ways that categories of social honor underwrite various coercive mechanisms that, in Weber's ([1924] 1978: 935) words, "go hand in hand with the monopolization of ideal and material goods or opportunities".

The contrast between class and status provide one of the axes of Weber's analysis of historical variation in systems of inequality. Weber ([1924] 1978: 938) writes: When the bases of the acquisition and distribution of goods are relatively stable, stratification by status is favoured. Every technological repercussion and economic transformation threatens stratification by status and pushes the class situation into the foreground. Epochs and countries in which the naked class situation is of predominant significance are regularly the periods of technical and economic transformations. One of the central reasons why capitalist societies are societies within which class becomes the predominant basis of stratification is precisely because capitalism fosters continual "technical and economic transformation."

Weber's concept of class is also closely linked to his theoretical preoccupation with the problem of historical variation in the process of rationalization of social life. Following Levine's (1985:210) decomposition of Weber's complex conceptual inventory of forms of rationalization, the problem of class for Weber is primarily situated within one particular form of rationalization: the objective instrumental rationalization of social order. In all societies the ways people gain access to and use material resources is governed by rules that are objectively embodied in the institutional settings within which they live. When the rules allocate resources to people on the basis of ascriptive characteristics, and when the use of those material resources is governed by tradition rather than the result of a calculative weighing of alternatives, then economic interactions take place under nonrationalized conditions. When those rules enable people to make precise calculations about alternative uses of those resources and discipline people to use those resources in more rather than less efficient ways on the basis of those calculations, then those rules can be described as "rationalized." This occurs, in Weber's analysis, when market relations have the most pervasive influence on economic interactions (i.e., in fully developed capitalism). His definition of classes in terms of the economic opportunities people face in the market, then, is simultaneously a definition of classes in terms of rationalized economic interactions. Class, in these terms, assumes its central sociological meaning to Weber as a description of the way people are related to the material conditions of life under conditions in which their economic interactions are regulated in a maximally rationalized manner. Weber is, fundamentally, less interested in the problem of the material deprivations and advantages of different categories of people as such, or in the collective struggles that might spring from those advantages and disadvantages, than he is in the underlying normative order and cognitive practices – instrumental rationality – that are embodied in the social interactions that generates these life chances. "Class," in these terms, is part of the answer to a broad question about historical variations in the degree and forms of rationalization of social life in general, and the social organization of inequality in particular.

The Marxist Concept: Class as Exploitation

The pivotal question that anchors the Marxist conceptualization of class is the question of human emancipation: "What sorts of transformations are needed to eliminate economic oppression and exploitation within capitalist societies?" The starting point for Marxist class analysis is a stark observation: The world in which we live involves a juxtaposition of extraordinary prosperity and enhanced potentials for human creativity and fulfilment along with continuing human misery and thwarted lives. The central task of the theory is to demonstrate first, that poverty in the midst of plenty is not somehow an inevitable consequence of the laws of nature, but the result of the specific design of our social institutions, and second, that these institutions can be transformed in such a way as to eliminate such socially unnecessary suffering. The concept of class, then, in the first instance is meant to help answer this normatively laden question.

The specific strategy in the Marxist tradition for answering the normative question leads directly to the question about historical variation. The normative question asks what needs transforming for human emancipation to occur. The theory of history in Marx – generally called "historical materialism" – lays out an account of the historical dynamics that make such transformations possible, and in the more deterministic version of the theory, inevitable. Again, the concept of class figures centrally in this theory of historical development.

The most distinctive feature of the concept of class elaborated within Marxism to contribute to the answer of these two questions is the idea of exploitation. Marx shares with Weber the central idea that classes should be defined in terms of the social relations that link people to the central resources that are economically relevant to production. And, as with Weber, Marx sees these relations as having a systematic impact on the material well being of people — both "exploitation" and "life chances" identify inequalities in material well-being that are generated by inequalities in access to resources of various sorts. Thus both of these concepts point to conflicts of interest over the distribution of the assets themselves. What exploitation adds to this is a claim that conflicts of interest between classes are generated not simply by what people have, but also by what people do with what they have. The concept of exploitation, therefore, points our attention to conflicts within production, not simply conflicts in the market.

Exploitation is a complex and challenging concept. In classical Marxism this concept was elaborated in terms of a specific conceptual framework for understanding capitalist economies, the "labour theory of value." In terms of sociological theory and research, however, the labour theory of value has never figured very prominently, even among sociologists working in the Marxist tradition. And in any case, the concept of exploitation and its relevance for class analysis does not depend on the labour theory of value.

The concept of exploitation designates a particular form of interdependence of the material interests of people, namely a situation that satisfies three criteria:

(1) The inverse interdependent welfare principle: the material welfare of exploiters causally depends upon the material deprivations of the exploited.

(2) The exclusion principle: this inverse interdependence of welfares of exploiters and exploited depends upon the exclusion of the exploited from access to certain productive resources.

(3) The appropriation principle: Exclusion generates material advantage to exploiters because it enables them to appropriate the labour effort of the exploited.

Exploitation is thus a diagnosis of the process through which the inequalities in incomes are generated by inequalities in rights and powers over productive resources: the inequalities occur, in part at least, through the ways in which exploiters, by virtue of their exclusionary rights and powers over resources, are able to appropriate surplus generated by the effort of the exploited. If the first two of these principles are present, but not the third, economic oppression may exist, but not exploitation. The crucial difference is that in nonexploitative economic oppression, the privileged social category does not itself need the excluded category. While their welfare does depend upon exclusion, there is no on-going interdependence of their activities. In the case of exploitation, the exploiters actively need the exploited: exploiters depend upon the effort of the exploited for their own welfare.

This conceptualization of exploitation underwrites an essentially polarized conception of class relations in which, in capitalist societies, the two fundamental classes are capitalists and workers. Capitalists, by virtue of their ownership and control of the means of production, are able to appropriate the laboring effort of workers embodied in the surplus produced through the use of those means of production. The Marxist tradition of class analysis, however, also contains a variety of strategies for elaborating more concrete class concepts which allow for much more complex maps of class structures in which managers, professionals and the self-employed, are structurally differentiated from capitalists and workers. Wright (1985, 1997), for example, argues that managers in capitalist firms constitute a type of "contradictory location within class relations" in the sense having the relational properties of both capitalists and workers.

The exploitation-centered concept of class provides a framework for linking the micro-level question about explaining individual material conditions and interests with the macro-level question about historical variation and the normative question about emancipatory transformation. What needs changing in capitalism is a system of property relations that confers power on capitalists and enables them to exploit and oppress others. This social organization of class relations is not an expression of a natural law, but is one form in a systematic pattern of historical variation. And the life experiences and interests of individuals living within these relations generate patterns of conflict that have the potential of pushing these historical variations in ways that accomplishes the emancipatory transformation.

The Two Traditions Compared

The contrast between Marxist and Weberian frameworks of class analysis.

Both Marxist and Weberian class analysis differ sharply from simple gradational accounts of class in which class is itself directly identified within inequalities in income since both begin with the problem of the social relations that determine the access of people to economic resources. In a sense, therefore, Marxist and Weberian definitions of class in capitalist society share much the same operational criteria for class structure within capitalist societies.

Where they differ is in the theoretical elaboration and specification of the implications of this common set of criteria: the Marxist model sees two causal paths being systematically generated by these relations – one operating through market exchanges and the other through the process of production itself – whereas the Weberian model traces only one causal path, and the Marxist model elaborates the mechanisms of these causal paths in terms of exploitation as well as bargaining capacity within exchange whereas the Weberian model only deals with the latter of these.

In a sense, then, the Weberian strategy of class analysis is contained within the Marxist model.

While the Marxist concept of class may be particularly suited to the distinctively Marxist question about potential emancipatory transformations, is it still sociologically useful if one rejects that question?

There are a number of reasons why elaborating the concept of class in terms of exploitation has theoretical pay-offs beyond the specific normative agenda of Marxist class analysis itself:

1. Linking exchange and production. The Marxist logic of class analysis affirms the intimate link between the way in which social relations are organized within exchange and within production. This is a substantive, not definitional, point: the social relations which organize the rights and powers of individuals with respect to productive resources systematically shapes their location

both within exchange relations and within the process of production itself.

2. Conflict. One of the standard claims about Marxist class analysis that it foregrounds conflict within class relations. Indeed, a conventional way of describing Marxism in sociological textbooks is to see it as a variety of "conflict theory." This characterization, however, is not quite precise enough, for conflict is certainly a prominent feature of Weberian views of class as well. The distinctive feature of the Marxist account of class relations in these terms is not simply that it gives prominence to class conflict, but that it understands conflict as generated by inherent properties of those relations rather than simply contingent factors.
3. Power. At the very core of the Marxist construction of class analysis is not simply the claim that class relations generate deeply antagonistic interests, but that they also give people in subordinate class locations forms of power with which to struggle for their interests. Since exploitation rests on the extraction of labour effort, and since people always retain some measure of control over their own effort, they always confront their exploiters with capacities to resist exploitation. This is a crucial form of power reflected in the complex counter-strat[illegible] the exploiting classes are forced to adopt th[illegible], surveillance, elaboration of instruments of supervi[illegible] monitoring, and sanctioning.
4. Coercion and consent. M[illegible]ist class analysis contains the rudiments of w[illegible] might be termed an endogenous theory of the [illegible]rmation of consent. The argument is basicall[illegible]is: The extraction of labour effort in systems of [illegible]ploitation is costly for exploiting classes because of the inherent capacity of people to resist their own exploitation. Purely coercively backed systems of exploitation will often tend to be sub-optimal since under many conditions it is too easy for workers to wit[illegible] diligent performance of labour eff[illegible] will therefore hav[illegible] those costs. [illegible]

costs of extracting labour effort is to do things which elicit the active consent of the exploited. These range from the development of internal labour markets which strengthen the identification and loyalty of workers to the firms in which they work to the support for ideological positions which proclaim the practical and moral desirability of capitalist institutions. Such consent-producing practices, however, also have costs attached to them, and thus systems of exploitation can be seen as always involving trade-offs between coercion and consent as mechanisms for extracting labour effort.

5. Historical/comparative analysis. As originally conceived, Marxist class analysis was an integral part of a sweeping theory of the epochal structure and historical trajectory of social change. But even if one rejects historical materialism, the Marxist exploitation-centered strategy of class analysis still provides a rich menu of concepts for historical and comparative analysis. Different kinds of class relations are defined by the specific mechanisms through which exploitation is accomplished, and these differences in turn imply different problems faced by exploiting classes for the reproduction of their class advantage and different opportunities for exploited classes to resist. Variations in these mechanisms and the specific ways in which they are combined in concrete societies provide an analytically powerful road map for comparative research. Weber's class concept also figures in an account of historical variation, and one of its strengths is the way in which his conceptual menu draws attention to the interplay of class and status and to historical variations in the forms of rationality governing life-chances. These are not issues brought into focus by the Marxist concept of class. On the other hand, the Weberian concept, by marginalizing the problem of exploitation, fails to bring to centre stage the historical variability in forms of conflict linked to the central mechanisms of extraction and control over the social surplus.

CASTE SYSTEM

Sikhism and Caste System

A total rejection of the caste system is a typical feature of the Sikh tradition. Sikhism in fact originated as a voice of protest against the many prevalent ills of contemporary Indian society. The caste system was the most damaging and debilitating of them. It completely negated the humanitarian and egalitarian principles, fundamental to the Sikh creed. Guru Nanak, founder of Sikhism, and his nine spiritual successors strongly attacked the system. The advent of Sikhism in the midst of caste rigidities and superstitions was truly a radical beginning.

Caste, lexically defined as "a hereditary social group comprising persons of the same ethnic stock, social rank, occupation and more or less distinctive mores" is a characteristic common to all societies the world over, and hardly shows anything more than social differentiations that have developed in varying degrees of discrimination or exclusiveness. In the Punjab, for instance, caste (jat or zat) signifies only an ethnic group gotra (family, line, sept or class) just like the MacDonalds, Montagues, Montmorencies, etc, in England, It is only when it develops into a system with its rigid stratification and permanent division of social status based on birth alone, as it did in India, that caste becomes a curse.

A system is qualitatively different from a casual or unintentional assortment of factors or forces. It is what distinguishes philosophy, religion or science from an unintegrated mass of doctrines and tenets. It is what distinguishes an army from a rabble, as it involves organization, arrangement, method and considered principles of procedure. Above all, a system presumes a direction, a plan, a purpose, an objective towards the fulfilment of which the functioning of the different parts of the system is oriented, coordinated and harmonized. Moreover, a system has its own cumulative power, thrust, momentum not easy to stem, and grip, hold and shackle almost impossible to unfetter. The caste system that developed in India over the millennia possessed all these ingredients and characteristics. And more, it was given the garb of religion, the

Varnasrma Dharma, signifying divine origin or sanction for it. That social distinctions existed, as in other primitive societies, in pre-Aryan India is evidenced by the ruins of the Indus Valley civilization, but whether these were characterized by permanent divisions based on birth we do not know. The caste system in the Hindu society as generally understood definitely developed after the advent of the Aryans. Whether a four-fold division into occupational groups was historical necessity for the invaders is irrelevant here. The fact is that among the sacerdotal groups, the Brahmans, came to possess real power in matters social as well as religious and became, besides being the sole interpreters of religious texts, exclusive authors and arbiters of the social code. They divided society into castes and sub-castes meticulously arranged in a hierarchical social pyramid in which the social grade of each group and individual was fixed permanently by birth.

Each layer in the pyramid was superior in caste status (virtually in social status) to all the layers below it, and lower in caste status to all the others above it, irrespective of their political power and economic position. Even the Brahmans at the top of the pyramid and the untouchables at its bottom were graded among their own ranks. The privileges, disabilities, obligations, and duties, i.e. practically all aspects of social behaviour, of each sub-caste by fixed rules and codes were formulated by Brahmans particularly by Manu who claimed direct descent from Brahma, the creator of universe. These sub-castes were, by and large, endogamous groups, and they worked sedulously to isolate themselves from each other in other social matters too. Mutual exclusiveness was caused predominantly not by social, but by ritualistic factors. Such factors as personal endowments, wealth, political power, colour and racial prejudices, and even taboos, which determined the hierarchical set-ups in other societies, were not the final determinants in the Indian caste system, though these did contribute to its development. Although individuals, groups and sub-castes were in the grip of a continuously downward process, there was practically no upward social mobility.

Caste system of the Varnasrama had its own intricacies. Its constituents were interdependent and interlocked, both horizontally and vertically, in a self-perpetuating social fabric. Within the sub-caste, each constituent of the system (hereditary functionalism, social and ritualistic taboos, pollution, religion, etc.) tied its own caste-knot around the individual.

The fundamental assumption of the caste ideology is that men are not equal, but are forever unequal. Permanent human inequality is the officially declared Brahmanical ideology, and this forms the basis of the Hindu social order. God Himself is the author of this inequality. The Veda was declared by Manu to be the direct revelation of God, and it is a Rig Vedic hymn, Purusa Sukta, which forms the source for the caste ideology. It says that God created Brahmans from His head, Ksatriyas from His arms, Vaisyas from His legs and Sudras from His feet. Even the Dharma Sastra of Manu is said to be the inspired word of the Vedas, almost of equal authority with them. Manu did not rest content with establishing the divine authority of the Vedas. His object thereby was to sanctify the caste system and the position of the Brahmans. He declared that the teaching of a Brahman is authoritative for 'man' because the Veda is the foundation for that (Manu, XI. 85).

THE CASTE SYSTEM IN INDIA

India's caste system : India has a hierarchical caste system in the society. Within Indian culture, whether in the north or the south, Hindu or Muslim, urban or village, virtually all things, people, and groups of people are ranked according to various essential qualities. If one is attuned to the theme of hierarchy in India, one can discern it everywhere. Although India is a political democracy, in daily life there is little advocacy of or adherence to notions of equality.

Castes systems in India and caste like groups—those quintessential groups with which almost all Indians are associated—are ranked. Within most villages or towns, everyone knows the relative rankings of each locally represented caste, and people's behaviour toward one another is constantly shaped by this knowledge. Between the extremes of the very high and very low castes, however, there is sometimes disagreement on the exact relative ranking of castes clustered in the middle. Castes system in India are primarily associated with Hinduism but also exist among other Indian religious groups. Muslims sometimes expressly deny that they have castes—they state that all Muslims are brothers under God—but observation of Muslim life in various parts of India reveals the existence of castelike groups and clear concern with social hierarchy. Among Indian Christians, too, differences in caste are acknowledged and maintained.

Throughout India, individuals are also ranked according to their wealth and power. For example, there are "big men" (*bare admi*, in Hindi) and "little men" (*chhote admi*) everywhere. "Big men" sit confidently on chairs, while "little men" come before them to make requests, either standing or crouching down on their haunches, certainly not presuming to sit beside a man of high status as an equal. Even men of nearly equal status who might share a string cot to sit on take their places carefully—the higher-ranking man at the head of the cot, the lower-ranking man at the foot.

Within families and kinship groupings, there are many distinctions of hierarchy. Men outrank women of the same or similar age, and senior relatives outrank junior relatives. Several other kinship relations involve formal respect. For example, in northern India, a daughter-in-law of a household shows deference to a daughter of a household. Even among young siblings in a household, there is constant acknowledgment of age differences: younger siblings never address an older sibling by name, but rather by respectful terms for elder brother or elder sister. However, an older sibling may address the younger by name. Even in a business or academic setting, where colleagues may not openly espouse traditional observance of caste or class ranking behaviour, they may set up fictive kinship relations, addressing one another by kinship terms reflecting family or village-style hierarchy. For example, a younger colleague might respectfully address an older colleague as *chachaji* (respected father's younger brother), gracefully acknowledging the superior position of the older colleague.

Purity and Pollution

Many status differences in Indian society are expressed in terms of ritual purity and pollution. Notions of purity and pollution are extremely complex and vary greatly among different castes, religious groups, and regions. However, broadly speaking, high status is associated with purity and low status with pollution. Some kinds of purity are inherent, or inborn; for example, gold is purer than copper by its very nature, and, similarly, a member of a high-ranking Brahman, or priestly, caste is born with more inherent purity than a member of a low-ranking Sweeper (Mehtar, in Hindi) caste. Unless the Brahman defiles himself in some extraordinary way, throughout his life he will always be purer than a Sweeper. Other kinds of purity are more transitory—a Brahman who has just taken a bath is more ritually pure than a Brahman who has not bathed for a day. This situation could easily reverse itself temporarily, depending on bath schedules, participation in polluting activities, or contact with temporarily polluting substances.

Purity is associated with ritual cleanliness—daily bathing in flowing water, dressing in properly laundered clothes of approved materials, eating only the foods appropriate for one's caste, refraining from physical contact with people of lower rank, and avoiding involvement with ritually impure substances. The latter include body wastes and excretions, most especially those of another adult person. Contact with the products of death or violence are typically polluting and threatening to ritual purity.

During her menstrual period, a woman is considered polluted and refrains from cooking, worshiping, or touching anyone older than an infant. In much of the south, a woman spends this time "sitting outside," resting in an isolated room or shed. During her period, a Muslim woman does not touch the Quran. At the end of the period, purity is restored with a complete bath. Pollution also attaches to birth, both for the mother and the infant's close kin, and to death, for close relatives of the deceased.

Members of the highest priestly castes, the Brahmans, are generally vegetarians (although some Bengali and Maharashtrian Brahmans eat fish) and avoid eating meat, the product of violence and death. High-ranking Warrior castes (Kshatriyas), however, typically consume nonvegetarian diets, considered appropriate for their traditions of valor and physical strength.

A Brahman born of proper Brahman parents retains his inherent purity if he bathes and dresses himself properly, adheres to a vegetarian diet, eats meals prepared only by persons of appropriate rank, and keeps his person away from the bodily exuviae of others (except for necessary contact with the secretions of family infants and small children). If a Brahman happens to come into bodily contact with a polluting substance, he can remove this pollution by bathing and changing his clothing. However, if he were to eat meat or commit other transgressions of the rigid dietary codes of his particular caste, he would be considered more deeply polluted and would have to undergo various purifying rites and payment of fines imposed by his caste council in order to restore his inherent purity.

In sharp contrast to the purity of a Brahman, a Sweeper born of Sweeper parents is considered to be born inherently polluted. The touch of his body is polluting to those higher on the caste hierarchy than he, and they will shrink from his touch, whether or not he has bathed recently. Sweepers are associated with the traditional occupation of cleaning human feces from latrines and sweeping public lanes of all kinds of dirt. Traditionally, Sweepers remove these polluting materials in baskets carried atop the head and dumped out in a garbage pile at the edge of the village or neighbourhood. The involvement of Sweepers with such filth accords with their low-status position at the bottom of the Hindu caste hierarchy, even as their services allow high-status people, such as Brahmans, to maintain their ritual purity.

Members of the Leatherworker (Chamar) caste are ascribed a very low status consonant with their association with the caste occupation of skinning dead animals and tanning the leather. Butchers (Khatiks, in Hindi), who kill and cut up the bodies of animals, also rank low on the caste hierarchy because of their association with violence and death. However, castes associated with ruling and warfare—and the killing and deaths of human beings—are typically accorded high rank on the caste hierarchy. In these instances, political power and wealth outrank association with violence as the key determinant of caste rank.

Maintenance of purity is associated with the intake of food and drink, not only in terms of the nature of the food itself, but also in terms of who has prepared it or touched it. This requirement is especially true for Hindus, but other religious groups hold to these principles to varying degrees. Generally, a person risks pollution—and lowering his own status—if he accepts beverages or cooked foods from the hands of people of lower caste status than his own. His status will remain intact if he accepts food or beverages from people of higher caste rank. Usually, for an observant Hindu of any but the very lowest castes to accept cooked food from a Muslim or Christian is regarded as highly polluting.

In a clear example of pollution associated with dining, a Brahman who consumed a drink of water and a meal of wheat bread with boiled vegetables from the hands of a Sweeper would immediately become polluted and could expect social rejection by his caste fellows. From that moment, fellow Brahmans following traditional pollution rules would refuse food touched by him and would abstain from the usual social interaction with him. He would not be welcome inside Brahman homes—most especially in the ritually pure kitchens—nor would he or his close relatives be considered eligible marriage partners for other Brahmans. Generally, the acceptance of water and ordinary foods cooked in water from members of lower-ranking castes incurs the greatest pollution. In North India, such foods are known as *kaccha khana*, as contrasted with fine foods cooked in butter or oils, which are known as *pakka khana*. Fine foods can be accepted from members of a few castes slightly lower than one's own. Local hierarchies differ on the specific details of these rules.

Completely raw foods, such as uncooked grains, fresh unpeeled bananas, mangoes, and uncooked vegetables can be accepted by anyone from anyone else, regardless of relative status. Toasted or parched foods, such as roasted peanuts, can also be accepted from anyone without ritual or social repercussions. (Thus, a Brahman may accept gifts of grain from lower-caste patrons for eventual preparation by members of his own caste, or he may purchase and consume roasted peanuts or tangerines from street vendors of unknown caste without worry.) Water served from an earthen pot may be accepted only from the hands of someone of higher or equal caste ranking, but water served from a brass pot may be accepted even from someone slightly lower on the caste scale. Exceptions to this rule are members of the Waterbearer (Bhoi, in Hindi) caste, who are employed to carry water from wells to the homes of the prosperous and from whose hands members of all castes may drink water without becoming polluted, even though Waterbearers are not ranked high on the caste scale.

These and a great many other traditional rules pertaining to purity and pollution constantly impinge upon interaction between people of different castes and ranks in India. Although to the non-Indian these rules may seem irrational and bizarre, to most of the people of India they are a ubiquitous and accepted part of life.

Thinking about and following purity and pollution rules make it necessary for people to be constantly aware of differences in status. With every drink of water, with every meal, and with every contact with another person, people must ratify the social hierarchy of which they are a part and within which their every act is carried out. The fact that expressions of social status are intricately bound up with events that happen to everyone every day—eating, drinking, bathing, touching, talking—and that transgressions of these rules, whether deliberate or accidental, are seen as having immediately polluting effects on the person of the transgressor, means that every ordinary act of human life serves as a constant reminder of the importance of hierarchy in Indian society.

There are many Indians, particularly among the educated urban elite, who do not follow traditional purity and pollution practices. Dining in each others' homes and in restaurants is common among well-educated people of diverse backgrounds, particularly when they belong to the same economic class. For these people, guarding the family's earthen water pot from inadvertent touch by a low-ranking servant is not the concern it is for a more traditional villager. However, even among those people whose words and actions denigrate traditional purity rules, there is often a reluctance to completely abolish consciousness of purity and pollution from their thinking. It is surely rare for a Sweeper, however well-educated, to invite a Brahman to dinner in his home and have his invitation unselfconsciously accepted. It is less rare, however, for educated urban colleagues of vastly different caste and religious heritage to enjoy a cup of tea together. Some high-caste liberals pride themselves on being free of "casteism" and seek to accept food from the hands of very low-caste people, or even deliberately set out to marry someone from a significantly lower caste or a different religion. Thus, even as they deny it, these progressives affirm the continuing significance of traditional rules of purity, pollution, and hierarchy in Indian caste system.. 1995 data. India's caste system. Courtesy Library of Congress.

SOCIAL MOBILITY

When studying social classes, the question naturally arises: Is it possible for people to move within a society's stratification system? In other words, is there some possibility of social mobility, or progression from one social level to another? *Yes*, but the degree to which this is possible varies considerably from society to society. On the one hand, in a closed society with a caste system, mobility can be difficult or impossible. Social position in a caste system is decided by assignment rather than attainment. This means people are either born into or marry within their family's caste; changing caste systems is very rare. An example of the rigid segregation of caste systems occurs today in India, where people born into the lowest caste (the "untouchables") and can never become members of a higher caste. South Africa also has a caste system.

On the other hand, in an open society with a class system, mobility is possible. The positions in this stratification system depend more on achieved status, like education, than on ascribed status, like gender. For example, the United States' social stratification is of this type, meaning movement between social strata is easier and occurs more frequently.

Patterns of Social Mobility

Several patterns of social mobility are possible:

- Horizontal mobility involves moving within the same status category. An example of this is a nurse who leaves one hospital to take a position as a nurse at another hospital.

- Vertical mobility, in contrast, involves moving from one social level to another. A promotion in rank in the Army is an example of upward mobility, while a demotion in rank is downward mobility.
- Intragenerational mobility, also termed career mobility, refers to a change in an individual's social standing, especially in the workforce, such as occurs when an individual works his way up the corporate ladder.
- Intergenerational mobility refers to a change in social standing across generations, such as occurs when a person from a lower-class family graduates from medical school.

Sociologists in the United States have been particularly interested in this latter form of mobility, as it seems to characterize the "American Dream" of opportunity and "rags to riches" possibilities.

Structural Mobility and Individual Mobility

Major upheavals and changes in society can enhance large numbers of people's opportunities to move up the social ladder at the same time. This form of mobility is termed structural mobility. Industrialization, increases in education, and post-industrial computerization have allowed large groups of Americans since 1900 to improve their social status and find higher-level jobs than did their parents. Nevertheless, not everyone moves into higher-status positions. Individual characteristics—such as race, ethnicity, gender, religion, level of education, occupation, place of residence, health, and so on—determine individual mobility. In the United States, being a member of a racial minority, female, or a disabled person have traditionally limited the opportunities for upward mobility.

7

Stratification of Caste System

HINDU SOCIAL ORDER AND THE HUMAN RIGHTS OF DALITS

Social scientists have inquired into whether the religious and societal notions (or ideologies) of behaviour in different societies confirm or come in conflict with the secular and universalistic approach to human rights. They have tried to identify the (religious and social) codes of behaviour that conflicted with or supported the universal rights. Some have considered the UN human rights framework to be the particular expression of secular humanists against which other religious and social traditions are examined and compared.

We will discuss how the Hindu social order (particularly its main pillar, the caste system and untouchability) in its classical form comes in direct conflict with the universal human rights framework. And how the continuation of the practice of caste system and untouchability in modified forms leads to the ubiquitous violations of human rights, particularly of the dalits. Despite the legal provisions, since the caste system and the institution of untouchability continue to govern the social behaviour of high caste Hindus it makes the enforcement of human rights difficult, if not impossible.

The drafting of the Indian Constitution in late 1947-48 coincided with the UN Declaration on Human Rights in 1948. The section of the Constitution on "Fundamental Rights" and the "Directive Principles" emulates the UN Declaration. The provision in the Constitution reads: *[It is solemnly resolved] to secure to all citizens Justice: Social, Economic and Political, Liberty of thought, expression, belief, faith and worship. And equality of status and of opportunity, and to promote among them all fraternity, assuring the dignity of individual and unity.*

The Constitution also states that: *The state shall not discriminate against any citizen on grounds of religion, race, caste, place and birth or any form.* In the Directive Principles it is added that *The State shall promote with special care the educational and economic interest of the scheduled castes / tribes and shall protect them from social injustice and all forms of exploitation.* In accordance with these Constitutional provisions a number of measures have been initiated by the government for providing protection to untouchables (Scheduled Castes or SCs). These measures are both protective and developmental. In the 'protective' sphere untouchability was legally abolished and its practice in any form forebidden by the Protection of Civil Rights (Anti-Untouchability) Act of 1955.

Nearly two decades later, protections for SCs were reviewed to make them more stringent and effective in the Bonded Labour (Abolition) Act 1976. In 1989, the Government enacted yet another Act, namely the Scheduled Castes and Tribes (Prevention of Atrocities) Act in order to prevent atrocities against SC/STs. The need for this additional Act was felt because under the circumstances, PCR 1955 and normal provisions of the Indian Penal Code had been found to be inadequate to provide safeguards to SC/ST against several crimes. In the economic, educational and political spheres provisions have been made through the reservation and representation to improve their access and participation. The provision of political reservation in various bodies, reservation in government services, admission to educational institutions and in several other areas are some of the promotional measures under this category. It must be mentioned that discrimination in private sphere-social or economic-is not covered by this legislation.

Human Rights Under Hindu Social Order

The Hindu social order, particularly its main pillars: the caste system and untouchability, presents a unique case. As a system of social, economic and religious governance it is founded not on the principle of liberty (or freedom), equality and fraternity-the values which formed the basis of universal human rights-but on the principle of inequality in every sphere of life. In Ambedkar's view, the doctrine of inequality is the core and heart of the Hindu social order. It leaves no difference between legal philosophy (and law) and moral philosophy (morality). (Ambedkar 1987 first published, Deepak Lal, 1988). The three unique features of the caste system need to be understood.

In the social sphere the caste system involves (a) division of people in social groups (castes). The social, religious, cultural and economic rights of members of the castes are predetermined in advance by birth into that caste and are hereditary (b) an unequal distribution of these rights across caste groups (c) provision of a mechanism of social and economic ostracism calculated to ensure rigid adherence to the system and justification of the social system by the philosophy of Hinduism. In the sphere of economic rights, the Hindu social order also lays down a scheme of distribution, namely (a) it fixes the occupations for each caste by birth and its hereditary continuation; (b) unequal distribution of these economic rights related to property, trade, employment, wages, education etc., among the caste groups; and (c) hierarchy of occupation based on social stigma.

These features imply that the Hindu social order is based on three interrelated elements, namely predetermination of social, religious and economic rights of each caste based on birth; the unequal and hierarchical (graded) division of these rights among the castes; and provision of strong social, religious and economic ostracism supported by social and religious ideology to maintain the Hindu social order.

In this framework the concept of "human rights" under the Hindu social system takes on a specific meaning. Unlike other human societies, the Hindu social order in its classical form does not recognize the individual and his distinctiveness as the centre of the social purpose. The unit of the Hindu society is not the individual. Even the family is not regarded as a unit of society except for the purposes of marriages and inheritance

(Ambedkar 1987, first published). The primary unit of society is caste. There is no room for individual merit and the consideration of individual justice. Rights that an individual has are not due to him personally; it is due to him because he belongs to a particular caste. Similarly, if an individual suffers from a lack of rights, it is not because he deserves it by his conduct. The disability is imposed upon the caste and as a member of the caste that is his lot.

The other implication is that, the caste system also involves the principle of rank and gradation, in so far as the rights increase in ascending order from untouchable to Brahmin. It is a hierarchically interlinked system. In this framework castes are artfully interlinked with each other in a manner such that the right and privileges of higher castes become the disabilities of the lower castes, particularly the untouchables. In this sense, in Ambedakar's view the caste in a single number cannot exist. Caste can exist only in plural number. There cannot be such a thing as caste as a singular phenomenon. So one has to look at the castes as a system, where each is interlinked with other in unequal measures of social, religious, economic relations and rights.

This hierarchically interlinked character of the caste system implies a concept of "human rights" and "humanhood" which is different and unique. In this particular order of hierarchy the Brahmins are not only placed at the top but are considered to be "superior social beings" worthy of special rights and privileges. At the bottom, the untouchables are treated as "sub-human beings or lesser human beings" considered unworthy of many rights.

Untouchables are considered as inferior social beings and therefore not entitled to any individual rights i.e., civic, religious, political and economic. In fact, the disabilities are so severe that they are physically and socially isolated and excluded from the rest of the Hindu society. Isolation and exclusion of untouchables is a unique feature of the Hindu social order. Classes or social groups are common to all societies, but as long as the classes or social groups do not practice isolation and exclusiveness they are only non-social in their relations towards one another. "Isolation and exclusiveness" makes them anti-social and inimical to one another. (Ambedkar, first published 1987).

The Evidence

The annual reports of the Commission for Scheduled Caste and Schedule Tribe provide the data on the registered cases of untouchability and atrocities against the Scheduled Castes. That average number of cases registered under Anti Untouchability Act (or Human Right Act) were 480 during the 1950s, 1903 during the 1960s, 3240 during the 1970s, 3875 during the 1980s and 1672 during the first half of the 1990s. That during the nine year period between 1981-86 and 1995-97 a total of two lakhs cases of atrocities on the SC were registered, which means on an average three thousand cases of atrocities were committed on them annually.

The break-up of the atrocities for the year 1997 shows 504 cases of murder, 3452 of grievous hurt, 384 of arson, 1002 of rape and 12149 cases of other offences. The data for the period between 1981 and 1997 showed that on an average annually about 508 SC persons were murdered, about 2343 hurt, 847 subjected to arson, 754 became victims of physical violence and about 12,000 were subjected to other offences.

Four Regional Cases

Generally, cases which are registered with the police are of a severe nature and attract public attention. A large number of cases however remain unreported. The studies based on village surveys bring out the actual magnitude of the practice of untouchability and atrocities. From the massive literature on the practice of untouchability and atrocities, four regional studies are presented here; from Karnataka (1973-74 and 1991) and Andhra Pradesh (1977) in the south, Orissa (1987-88) in the east and Gujarat (1971 and 1996) in the west.

Discrimination & Deprivation

Very few empirical studies have tried to study the phenomenon of economic discrimination. Banerjee and Knight (1991) and also Deshi and Singh (1995) have brought out the significant presence of caste and untouchability-based economic discrimination in urban job markets. Banerjee and Knight

(1991) in their study of the Delhi urban job market during 1975-76 observed that "use of the standard methodology showed that there is indeed discrimination by caste. Discrimination appears to operate at least in part through traditional mechanism, with untouchables disproportionately represented in poorly-paid" dead-end jobs.

Among the regional studies considered earlier, the studies from Andhra Pradesh and Karnataka also provide evidence of economic discrimination in occupation, employment, wages and loans, and other economic spheres. The study from Andhra Pradesh (Venkateswarlu 1990) indicates that when untouchables wanted to switch over from their traditional occupation in the rural area to some other occupation, they were abused or beaten. The Karnataka study (Khan 1995) revealed that nearly 85 per cent of the respondents continue with their traditional occupation and only 15 per cent could make a switch. In the urban areas, however, 56 per cent expressed a shift from the traditional occupation. The Orissa study for 1987-88 (Tripathy 1994) observed nearly 96 per cent of respondents in one village and all the formerly untouchable respondents in the second village were discriminated against in wage payments. 28 per cent in one village and 20 per cent in another faced discrimination in the share of rent. Discrimination in interest rates changed by the moneylender was found in both villages.

We will add to these studies by looking at some complementary data, and putting some similar or related questions: How far do the traditional customary restrictions related to ownership of sources of income imposed on the low-caste untouchable continue? Has their access to agricultural land and capital in rural and urban areas improved? We have selected data on the comparative situation of the Scheduled Castes (SC) and others in rural and urban areas in the late 1980s and early 1990s. Some sources also go back to the 1960s, 1970s and early 1980s.

Lack of Access to Agricultural Land and Capital

About three-fourths of the SCs live in rural areas, where the main sources of income are either cultivation of agricultural land, wage labour or some kind of non-farm self-employment. Access to agricultural land for cultivation and capital for undertaking non-farm self-employment is critical. In 1993-94 only one-fifth of all SC households cultivated land as (independent) self-employment workers whereas among the others (i.e. non-SC/ST) the percentage was more than twice this rate. The percentage of those employed in some kind of non-farm self-employment activities, which indicate access to capital, was very low among the Scheduled Castes. Taking both farm and (rural) non-farm self-employment, about one-fourth of SC household seem to be engaged in self-employment activities as compared to more than half for others, in rural area. (Thorat, 2001)

In urban areas the disparity in the access to capital is well reflected in the lower proportion of self-employed workers among the Scheduled Castes. The lower proportion of SC as self-employed in agriculture, in non-farm sector in rural area and in urban area as compared to others, revealed the continuation of lack of access ownership of agricultural land and capital. The limited access is both due to the historical legacy associated with the restrictions of caste system to require means of income by the untouchables and ongoing discrimination in land market and capital market and other related economic spheres. (Thorat, 2001)

Inadequate access to agricultural land and capital (for self-employment activities) leaves no option to SC workers except to resort to manual wage labour, consequently it leads to enormously high level of (manual) wage labour among the SCs, nearly sixty per cent as compared to only one-third for others. In urban areas also disparities in the incidence of wage labour are evident. The proportion of casual labour among the SCs is around one-third as against only 10 per cent among the others. (Thorat, 1999).

Since more than sixty per cent of the SC workers in rural areas and more than one third in urban areas depend on wage employment, their earnings are determined by the level of employment and wage rates. It seems most possible that the SC workers suffer from discrimination in employment. The unemployment rate of SCs is much higher than that of other workers and they suffer from high under-employment as compared to others in Indian society. Higher unemployment rate of SC workers (which is twice that of others) indicates a possible existence of caste-based discrimination against SC workers in hiring. In the earlier section we presented evidence of discrimination against SCs in occupation, employment and wages.

With higher incidence of wage labour associated with high rate of under-employment the SCs would suffer from low income and consumption and a resultant greater level of poverty. This is reflected in the proportion of persons falling below a critical minimum level of consumption expenditure, what is called the poverty line. In 1993-94 about half of SC households were below the poverty line in rural areas as compared to only less than one-third for the general population. The poverty level among the SCs was thus high compared to others. What is striking is the variation in poverty ratio among wage labour across occupation group. The incidence of poverty was about sixty per cent among agricultural labourers, and forty per cent in non-agricultural labour. The level was relatively low for persons engaged in self-employed activities in agriculture (37.71 per cent) and in the non-agricultural sector (38.19 per cent). For each of these occupation groups, however, the proportion of SC household was much higher than their counterparts among the non-SC/ST group.

In urban areas about half of the SCs were below the poverty line in 1993-94, as compared to only one-third among the Others. Further, the incidence was astonishingly high among the casual labour as nearly two third were poor. The disparities in the level of urban poverty between the two social groups were relatively higher in the case of self-employment and regular salaried and wageworkers but less in the case of casual labour. This indicates that by the early 1990s still half of the SC population was below the poverty line both in rural and urban areas. The 1993-94 figures revealed that the SCs were at least twenty-five years behind the other group in terms of level of poverty.

This macro-level comparative account of the economic position of the formerly untouchable and upper-caste persons covering relevant economic indicators provides convincing evidence of the continuing economic inequalities associated with caste. It is thus beyond doubt that the historical impact of traditional caste-based restrictions on the ownership of property, employment and occupation are still visible in significant measure, the access of the formerly untouchables to income-earning capital assets and employment is limited, and their segregation into manual labour is overwhelmingly high. The two prime economic attributes of the caste system thus seem to be present in sizeable measure, even today.

Decisive Reasons for Continuity

. In the end the question is: why do the higher castes continue to practice untouchability, and discrimination in social, cultural, religious, political and economic spheres. And why do they resort to physical and other violence when the untouchables try to gain lawful access to human rights and equal participation in social, political, cultural, religious and economic sphere of community life? The reasons for widespread practice of untouchability, discrimination and atrocities as well as violent reaction by the higher castes are to be found in their continuing belief and faith in the sanctity of the institution of caste and in untouchability. The traditional Hindu social order continues to govern the thought process and behaviour of the large majority of Hindus in rural areas.

The provisions in the Constitution and law are secular and equal but the customary rules of the caste system and the institution of untouchability are based on the principle of inequality in social, economic, cultural and religious sphere. This obviously brings a conflict between what is contained in the constitution and law, and what is contained in the traditional customary rules, norm, and values of the caste system and untouchability. People continued to follow the latter because it provides immense privilege and serves their social, political and economic interests. And when the dalits try to get equal access and 'assert' their rights, it often invites the wrath of higher caste persons in the form of atrocities and physical violence. About the reasons for the atrocities on the SC/ST the Report of the Commission of the SC/ST 998 observed,

"Some of the major causes of atrocities and other offences against Scheduled Castes and Scheduled Tribes are related to issues of land and property, access to water, wage payments, indebtedness and bonded or forced labour. Issues of human dignity, including compulsion to perform distasteful tasks traditionally forced on Scheduled Castes, and molestation and exploitation of dalit women are also involved. Caste related tension is exacerbated by economic factors, which contribute to violence. It is the assertion of their rights, be they economic, social or political, by the Scheduled Castes and Scheduled Tribes and their development, which often invite the wrath of the vested interests. Disputes during elections, animosity due to reservation, jealousy due to increasing economic prosperity, violence related to the process of taking possession and retaining Government allotted land, tension due to refusal of SCs to perform tasks such as disposal of dead cattle or cutting umbilical cord, are manifestations of the resentment of the high caste against increasing awareness among Scheduled Castes, assertion and prosperity among the SCs. Like land, water is another sensitive issue. Accessibility of drinking water and water for irrigation and disposal of water removed from water logged areas become issues that can trigger off atrocities on SCs. Castiest favor during religious and social ceremonies, disputes arising during sowing and harvesting operations, and removal of crops from the granary after harvesting, have also been known to cause tension. Increasing awareness and empowerment of SCs, manifested in resistance to suppression, also result in clashes".

The official evidence and the regional studies based on primary data revealed that in rural India in several spheres, if not in all spheres, the social behaviour of high caste Hindus is still governed by the norms and codes of the traditional caste system, although there are changes in some spheres of social relations. The settlements of the untouchables in rural areas are away from the high-caste locality, endogamy (which is the backbone of the caste system) continues, entries for the untouchables in private houses and temples in rural areas are limited, and common sharing of tea and food is also extremely limited. Pressures and restrictions on voting and political participation also prevail. The restriction on the change of occupation and discrimination in employment, wage rate, share of rent, rate of interest charged and in sale of items from shops owned by the untouchables is still observed in some degree in the rural areas, where three-fourths of the untouchables live.

This goes to shows that the enforcement and practice of universal human rights in society is not conditioned by the formal supportive legal framework (such as the Constitution and other laws) alone. Often, cultural, social, religious and economics notions make the enforcement and practice of human rights difficult. Non-formal institutions; social, religious as well as economic, involve a framework of social behaviour of their own, which may not be in consonance with the principles enunciated by the United Nations, or the Constitution of a nation in which case different sets of values may result in conflicts. It implies that unless inequalities imbedded in the social, economics and cultural structure of the Hindu society are addressed, the legal measures will make little difference in providing access to human rights to the dalits in India.

INDIAN MUSLIMS: STRUCTURE AND SOCIAL JUSTICE ISSUES IN DEVELOPING INDIA

Voluntary organisation has a major, vital and crucial role in the empowerment of a community and country at large, in the world of competitiveness, channelization of the state affirmative actions, monitoring of the disbursement of the welfare funds and constant interaction with the welfare agencies are the key factors on which every responsible community focuses its attention. Muslim community is much backward in comparison to others and in fact it has fewer numbers of NGOs working for empowerment of the community while community is already facing the middle class intellectual's socio development activists after the crucial division of India in 1947.

Samaj Kalyan Evam Vikas Adhyayan Kendra (SEVAK) duly registered with aim and object, working is to study, surveying, implementation work for total development, social justice, co-existence, peace and national interest issues work for Muslim minorities since 1989 in UP State a major highest Muslim populated province with Uttarakhand 3.17 crore people having 18 per cent population out of 17.46 crore, in the specific district consisting more than 60 per cent Muslim, OBC/Dalit Muslims. Socio-economic educational status along with the study and monitoring of declared minority welfare government programmes after and before independence as case study regarding the socio-economic and educational backwardness of Muslims.

SEVAK completed Muslim minority survey on structure of Muslims in India with Social Justice Values after Independence by one to one and one to group discussions in weaker sections OBC and Dalit Muslims regarding the government development programmes, implementation in Muslim, OBCs, and their role in building the developing agenda in UP and India. It was told that Muslims are not getting the benefits of government as OBC reservations, mostly benefits of education, employment, social justice and empowerment goes to Hindu OBCs in 70 castes due to their strength, power and politics game, while Dalit Muslims are also included in OBC and in fact Dalit Muslims are not included in Scheduled Caste Presidential Order 1950. The Mahigeer/Chirimar are also not included in ST list respectively provision given in Article 341 and 342 of the Constitution.

It is a fact that social structure of Muslims in India are more than 80 per cent converted Hindu Dalits and directly affected with Hindu castes. Indian Muslim caste base detail of their social profile has shown in Census of India 1901 that 133 social groups are Muslim and society in India are divided in four major upper and lower group one ASHRAF are related origin to out of India and ARABIA, PERSIA, TURKISTAN and AFGHANISTAN, they are Sayed Sheikh Mughal, Pathan. IInd AJLAF converted Hindu backwards castes of artisans and traditional workers, while upper caste Hindu converted known as NAV-MUSLIM. Rest converted ARZAL lowest castes, such as Sweepers, Halalchor, Bakkha Banjara, Lal Beg Bedia, etc.

As case study for 13 crore Muslims' contribution and participation in developing India for developed India journey British Government and diplomats were aware that casteism Warna system of Indian society cannot abolish easily despite the religion conversion from any religion and it will be a problem for the developed India after independence. So minority and their socio economic development packages were introduced in Round Table conference and other acts. The Muslim Zamindars, socio-economic activists Congress leaders were invited for reports and discussion, Dr BR Ambedkar took a leading part for upliftment guarantee and reservation facility for the socio-economic backward group, castes of Indian society.

That such policy to attract Muslims with the democratic governments is responsible for the present burning problem terrorism and issues of Muslim minority. Because of that no effort has been made after independence by state and central governments since 1950 to share the social justice, equality norms to Muslim of Indian origin for at least coverted Muslims. 80 per cent population, mostly from Indian Hindu Dalits and backwards Indian society. Overall it is also remarkable fact that greater India was ruled by Muslims and Britishers over thousands of years. But after the conversion in Islam, compilent effective efforts for their social justice and welfare were not implemented by King Raja Nawab Zamindars, even British governor generals. Before independence a term for Indian minority and social justice for socio-economic educational development was raised in Round Table Conference and British Charter – 1935, also as a key package for developing India. But unfortunately due to division of India at the time of independence, constituting Muslim country PAKISTAN and related communalism between Hindus and major minorities Mislims, the facilities of Dalit reservation under Article 341 of Indian Constitution was implemented only for Hindu Dalits by a presidential order for Scheduled Castes-1950. Voluntary organisation worked as case study thinks that such a unconstitutional order provisions are against the provision of equal opportunity and rights for all citizens major provision given under Article 14, 15, 16, 17, 21 and 25 of the Constitution of India.

The activists of voluntary organisation thinks that Dr Ambedkar made efforts for the social justice campaign not for particular religion and community, made the struggle for all Dalits of India, but Hindu hardcores left all the Minorities Dalit, having a remarkable fact that Muslim and Christian are more than 80 per cent population is converted from Dalit Hindus, but they are not included in 1950 ordinance of President Dr Rajendra Prasad. It is observed that such a unconstitutional mistake was monitored in 1956 when an amendment bill in Presidential Order – 1950 for Article 341 was introduced and passed to include Dalit Sikh and after one more very small minority NAV-BUDDHISTS were also included in Article 341 in 1990 by an amendment in Parliament. But in lack of socio-economic agenda in Muslims and Christians it is yet in waiting whose population is 13.8 crore and 2.4 crore respectively but Sikh were included in the population only 78.46 lakh – 1956 and Buddhist on 64.76 lakh population.

Samaj Kalyan Vikas Adhyayan Kendra are one of the few voluntary notable organisations working for the innovative of Minority development emphasise that we can get success to control the terrorism in India by social justice campaign and thus it is very important to lift religious ban in social justice campaign under Article 341 for Indian Dalits, specially the same traditional classes and castes of Hindus found in rest minorities.

Organisation emphasises that it is the moral duty of government to consider the reservation policy for Dalit and OBC Muslim minority in their prescribed quota. It is also observed that Muslim mostly castes are introduced in OBC group, but they are not getting the benefit due to already heavy burden of other Hindus, OBCs, Muslim OBCs, except Dalit caste are entitled the 9 per cent separate reservation within 27 per cent reservation of OBCs in UP as social justice campaign in UP to saturate the development and social justice strategy in Muslim minority.

During the case study Muslim minority headed districts of UP, Pilibhit, Bareilly, Rampur, Meerut, Moradabad, Sitapur, Lakhimpur, Badaun, Haridwar, Deharadun more than 15 per cent population were enlisted to study the socio-economic educational status of Muslim and their role in development strategy and other state Andhra Pradesh social worker form Guntur, Assam, Barapeta, Bihar, Muzzafarpur, Kishanganj, Delhi, Seelampur, Karnataka, Beeder, West Bengal, Malda, met in different workshop seminar INSAF CONFRENCE in between year 2000-05 at Delhi, Lucknow, Patna city to include Dalit Muslim under Article-341 for social justice. A favourable environment was already made recommendation by Bihar state government on 31st December 2000 to GOI Ministry of Social Justice and Empowerment for include Dalit Muslim in Article 341 Dr Raghuwansh Prasad MP introduced a private Third Constitution Schedule Castes Order Amendment Bill 2000 on 17 May 2000 to include 26 Muslim castes in Schedule Castes President Order and debate took place first time on 26-12-1999 in Parliament by Dr Raghuwansh Prasad and other in 13th Parliament last period a effective Parliament debate was performed on December 18, 2003 on issue to include the Dalit Muslim and Dalit Christian in proper social class of Schedule Caste and Tribes. The Rajesh Ranjan Bihar, PRD Muslim, Ram Bilas Paswan, Bihar, Hannan Mollah from West Bengal took leading part but Government has not taken decision despite the moral pressure due to their past traditional attitude for minorities specially Muslims and Christians.

During 14th Parliament the new UPA Government gone in deep to sought out the major problems issue of Muslim minority of India constituting the high level seven-member committee under Justice Rajendra Sachchar, presidentship to prepare a detailed report on the socio-economical and educational status of Muslim community of India, considering the fact a lack of authentic information about the socio economic and education status which comes in the way of planning formulating and implementing specific interventions, polices and programmes to the Government and their benefit to socio-economic backwards of the community on 9th March 2005 and suggestion were offered by OSD Dr. Zafar Mohmood on 7-point ToR for the major backward linkages of the Muslim of India. SEVAK the NGO already working on issues since 2000 with few social notable activists and organization like AIMBMM Bihar Dr. M Ejaz Ali, Mr HR Siddiqui, IRS Udit Raj.

SEVAK sent a detailed report on minority issues problems including five year long case study work on Muslims, Dalits and OBCs in May 2005 to Justice Sachcher. 200 pages report was appreciated by PMHLC and call for state level Muslim Minority issues discussion on 25 July 2005 and sit together with UP state 20-25 government-non government representative on arrival of Sachchar committee on 5th to 7th August, 2005, at Yojana Bhawan Lucknow. SEVAK mainly emphasises mainly that socio-economic and education status of declared OBC people is below the Scheduled Caste (Dalit Hindus), no systematic efforts has been made by Government since independence sense of equality, constitutional rights are overruled in Schedule Caste Presidential order 1950 in article 341, Muslim are more backward than other backward due to lack of development agenda in community and government both, after division of country, Indian Muslims suffered a vacuum in intellectual and middle class and before division education and socio-economic proper agenda was not followed by Muslim rulers and British agency, communal agenda during division, insecure sense in Muslim minority non-implementation of recommendation of several commission reports. Due to law of development agenda and education Muslim women 7 crore mostly population is with in boundaries of home, health facility is profile is very adverse comparatively otherce clean drinking water, sanitation, education standard is also very remarkable dropout problem is highly observed population stabilization counselling efforts are not effectively.

SEVAK is interested for the separate packages of Drop out educations, health, self employment, packages in Muslim headed districts innovative programme and other national issue social justice right of equality should be implemented by the Central Government as amendment in Presidential Order 1950 to include rest minorities like Sikhs and Buddhists and State Government where Muslims are more than 15 per cent and OBC headed separate reservation for Muslim OBC as per their population share should be given within the criteria adopted by the Government. NCEUS (National Commission for Enterprises in Unorganized Sector) reports say in Oct 07 that unorganized Hindu Schedule Caste and Muslim OBC are same in poverty and they are 40 per cent in total population Muslim OBC poverty status 39.7 in comparison Hindu OBC 27.5 recorded, it is also found in study that 77 per cent poor families are above BPL line earning 12 rupees per day and they are mostly Schedule Caste, Tribe and OBC Muslim category imposed by Government of India in Article-342 of the Constitution. The Commission Chairman Dr. Arjun Sen Gupta says about the working population 86 per cent people work in unorganized sector among them 80 per cent earns only Rs 20/-per day without any service guarantee like pension and funds, chairman says these are the downtrodden poor of Indian society.

In fact 17 Nov 2006 the Justice Sachchar handover the report to Prime minister of India presenting the socio-economic educational mirror of Muslim Minority in secular, democratic India's journey of 60 year. First time a detailed report of database situation tells all about itself.

Although committee has not recommended the reservation inside story of the reports says that if social justice starts from reservation of socio-economic educational backward Muslim caste as other Hindus. So many present backward linkages automatically change into forward linkages a environmental already created for the development social activists of Muslim class in comparison the hardcores, mainly responsible not to highlighted the development agenda due to their monarchy trends like since Mughal Muslim rulers.

SEVAK emphasize after reports that immediate action plan should be started by GOI and state government a resolution has also passed in national workshop of Indian Muslim NGO's on December 22 to 24th, 2006 at Delhi by MOEMIN to introduce priority work for Muslim socio-economic educational upliftment, state wise priority were decided in between national veteran Muslim social workers intellectuals, working NGO's and government diplomats. Again meet was made on 4th-6th Jan 2008 at Jamia Millia Islamia to start the development agenda for Muslim as reported condition of Muslim in Indian states.

SEVAK feels that Muslim structural work based active grassroot working NGO can do a lot to uplift Muslim backward needy class of BPL family at present in absence of reservation decision of the Government. We should start the innovative projects in Muslim forum districts for the BPL OBC families in dropout education sector opening residential non-residential bridge courses, Kasturba Gandhi Awasiya School for Muslim girls in education sector to uplift the basic education for next generation and public health sector efforts to start mobile clinic with special concentration in Muslim head districts town and village for the RCH-2, narrative and curative health also.

It is observed that Muslim needs modern education but due to poverty they prefer madarsa package (with food and shelter) and primary schools, for drop outs, CBSE, ISC, based central school for Minority with 100% subsidy GOI aid started with collaboration of experienced NGO's in specifies district for needy minority family.

SEVAK is running with their own resources educational basic such as schools in pedagogy system and drop out programme are managed as non-residential residential bridge course and making efforts to uplift the poor backward Muslim education status by giving the quality education in cluster also in UP state where 3 crore 18.2% and 62% Muslim mostly Dalit OBC Muslim living together highest in India comparatively other states by selecting the Muslim headed population district Barabanki, Lakhimpur, Sitapur, Rai Barelly district in Lucknow division, Bareilly Pilibhit, Badaun, Shahjahapur, in Bareilly division, Rampur, Moradabad, in Moradabad division and Meerut including Uttarakhand district Deharadun, Haridwar, and US Nagar to make some model work in Muslim minority sector by involving as 20 year work experience in the field of social work to count down the adverse development, social, health and education profile as Sachchar committee indicate to govt. that Muslim would require additional funds to be earmarked from the ongoing programme such as Sarwa Shikasha Abhiyan SSA, Public Health, Jawaher Lal Nehru Urban Renewal Mission etc. and increased allocation to institution, quality development programme as per every development sector govt. and factual better possible reports collected and analysis made by committee.

NGO also thinks that due to lack of priority agenda of Muslim socio-economic educational development programme foreign grant and govt. aid remain unutilized and some time it is consumed in place of utilization only compliant case study worked grass root voluntary organization having required qualification and experience can do better in field of operation.

NGO has a complete innovate action plan to implement the GOI and state govt. minority related development programmes in minority headed district as indicated in Sachchar committee reports high lights of socio-economic education status of Muslims down trodden society and innovative efforts for socio-economic health and drop out and academic education works as per recommendations in National Muslim NGO's workshop organized by national reputed organizations MOEMIN on 24th Dec-2006 at India Islamic Cultural Centre New Delhi and resolution passed again as IInd meet of 4-6 Jan-2008 at Jamia Millia Islamia central university Delhi by MOEMIN in collaboration and support of South ASIAN council for minorities, Indian Muslim relief and charities USA, shackle Hind educational and charitable trust Delhi, God Grace Foundation Delhi.

CASTE SYSTEM AMONG SOUTH ASIAN MUSLIMS

Caste system among South Asian Muslims refers to units of social stratification that have developed among Muslims in South Asia.

Origins

Sources indicate that the castes among Muslims developed as the result of close contact with Hindu culture and Hindu converts to Islam. Religious scholar Yoginder Sikand elaborates that the caste system among Muslims was not due to the "influence of Hinduism among a previously 'pure', 'uncontaminated' Muslim community," but rather to "the continued impact of Hindu beliefs and customs on the converts who still remained within a largely Hindu cultural universe and retained many of its associated beliefs and practices".

Stratification

In some parts of South Asia, the Muslims are divided as Ashrafs and Ajlafs. Ashrafs claim a superior status derived from their foreign ancestry. The non-Ashrafs are assumed to be converts from Hinduism, and are therefore drawn from the indigenous population. They, in turn, are divided into a number of occupational castes. Sections of the ulema (scholars of Islamic jurisprudence) provide religious legitimacy to caste with the help of the concept of kafa'a. A classical example of scholarly declaration of the Muslim caste system is the *Fatawa-i Jahandari*, written by the fourteenth century Turkish scholar, Ziauddin Barani, a member of the court of Muhammad bin Tughlaq, of the Tughlaq dynasty of the Delhi Sultanate. Barani was known for his intensely casteist views, and regarded the Ashraf Muslims as racially superior to the Ajlaf Muslims.

He divided the Muslims into grades and sub-grades. In his scheme, all high positions and privileges were to be a monopoly of the high born Turks, not the Indian Muslims. Even in his interpretation of the Koranic verse "Indeed, the pious amongst you are most honored by Allah", he considered piety to be associated with noble birth.

Barrani was specific in his recommendation that the "sons of Mohamed" [i.e. Ashrafs] "be given a higher social status than the low-born [i.e. Ajlaf]. His most significant contribution in the fatwa was his analysis of the castes with respect to Islam. His assertion was that castes would be mandated through state laws or "Zawabi" and would carry precedence over Sharia law whenever they were in conflict. In the Fatwa-i-Jahandari (advice XXI), he wrote about the "qualities of the high-born" as being "virtuous" and the "low-born" being the "custodian of vices". Every act which is "contaminated with meanness and based on ignominity, comes elegantly [from the Ajlaf]". Barani had a clear disdain for the Ajlaf and strongly recommended that they be denied education, lest they usurp the Ashraf masters. He sought appropriate religious sanction to that effect. Barrani also developed an elaborate system of promotion and demotion of Imperial officers ("Wazirs") that was primarily on the basis of their caste.

In addition to the Ashraf/Ajlaf divide, there is also the *Arzal* caste among Muslims, who were regarded by anti-Caste activists like Babasaheb Ambedkar as the equivalent of untouchables. The term "Arzal" stands for "degraded" and the Arzal castes are further subdivided into Bhanar, Halalkhor, Hijra, Kasbi, Lalbegi, Maugta, Mehtar etc. The Arzal group was recorded in the 1901 census in India and are also called Dalit Muslims "with whom no other Muhammadan would associate, and who are forbidden to enter the mosque or to use the public burial ground". They are relegated to "menial" professions such as scavenging and carrying night soil.

Some South Asian Muslims have been known to stratify their society according to *Quoms*. These Muslims practise a ritual-based system of social stratification. The Quoms who deal with human emissions are ranked the lowest. Studies of Bengali Muslims in India indicate that the concepts of purity and impurity exist among them and are applicable in inter-group relationships, as the notions of hygiene and cleanliness in a person are related to the person's social position and not to his/her economic status. Muslim Rajput is another caste distinction among Indian Muslims.

Some of the backward or lower-caste Muslim communities include Ansari, Kunjra, Churihara, Dhobi and Halalkhor. The upper caste Muslim communities include Syed, Sheikh, Pathan, Mirza, and Mallik. Genetic data has also supported this stratification.

The Sachar Committee's report commissioned by the government of India and released in 2006, documents the continued stratification in Muslim society.

Interaction and Mobility

Interactions between the *oonchi zat* (upper caste) and *neechi zat* (lower caste) are regulated by established patron-client relationships of the jajmani system, the upper castes being referred to as the 'Jajmans', and the lower caste as 'Kamin'. Upon contact with a low-caste Muslim, a Muslim of a higher *zat* can "purify" by taking a short bath, since there are no elaborate rituals for purification. In Bihar state of India, cases have been reported in which the higher caste Muslims have opposed the burials of lower caste Muslims in the same graveyard.

Some data indicates that the castes among Muslims have never been as rigid as that among Hindus. The rate of endogamous marriage, for example, is less than two thirds. An old saying also goes "Last year I was a Julaha (weaver); this year a Shaikh; and next year if the harvest be good, I shall be a Sayyid." However, other scholars, such as Ambedkar, disagreed with this thesis.

Castes in Pakistan

The social stratification among Muslims in the "Swat" area of North Pakistan has been meaningfully compared to the Caste system in India. The society is rigidly divided into subgroups where each Quom is assigned a profession. Different Quoms are not permitted to intermarry or live in the same community. These Muslims practice a ritual-based system of social stratification. The Quoms who deal with human emissions are ranked the lowest. Lower castes are often persecuted by the upper castes. A particularly infamous example of such incidents is that of Mukhtaran Mai in Pakistan, a low caste woman who was gang raped by upper caste men.

Stephen M. Lyon of University of Kent has written about what he calls "Gujarism", the act of Gujjars in Pakistan seeking out other Gujjars to form associations, and consolidate ties with them, based strictly on caste affiliation.

Criticism

Some Muslim scholars have termed the caste-like features in Indian Muslim society as a "flagrant violation of the Qur'anic worldview." Other scholars tried to reconcile and resolve the "disjunction between Qur'anic egalitarianism and Indian Muslim social practice" through theorizing it in different ways and interpreting the Qur'an and Sharia to justify casteism.

While some scholars theorize that the Muslim Castes are not as acute in their discrimination as that among Hindus, Dr. B.R.Ambedkar argued otherwise, writing that the social evils in Muslim society were "worse than those seen in Hindu society".

Babasaheb Ambedkar was an illustrious figure in Indian politics and the chief architect of the Indian Constitution. He was extremely critical of the Muslim Caste System and their practices, quoting that "Within these groups there are castes with social precedence of exactly the same nature as one finds among the Hindus but worse in numerous ways". He was critical of how the Ashrafs regarded the Ajlaf and Arzal as "worthless" and the fact that Muslims tried to sugarcoat the sectarian divisions by using euphemisms like "brotherhood" to describe them. He was also critical of the precept of literalism of scripture among Indian Muslims that led them to keep the Muslim Caste system rigid and discriminatory. He decried against the approval of Shariah to Muslim casteism. It was based on superiority of foreign elements in society which would ultimately lead to downfall of local Dalits. This tragedy would be much more harsher than Hindus who are ethnically related to and supportive of Dalits. This Arabian supremacy in Indian Muslims accounted for its equal disapproval by high and low caste Hindus during 1300 years of Islamic presence in India. He condemned the Indian Muslim Community of being unable to reform like Muslims in other countries like Turkey did during the early decades of the twentieth century.

Pakistani-American sociologist Ayesha Jalal writes, in her book, "Democracy and Authoritarianism in South Asia", that "Despite its egalitarian principles, Islam in South Asia historically has been unable to avoid the impact of class and caste inequalities. As for Hinduism, the hierarchical principles of the Brahmanical social order have always been contested from within Hindu society, suggesting that equality has been and continues to be both valued and practiced in Hinduism."

CASTE SYSTEM AMONG INDIAN CHRISTIANS

The Caste system among Indian Christians is attributed to the assimilation of local Hindu practices, which has caused caste distinctions to be retained after conversion. Some Christian groups have adapted the Indian caste system in diverse ways across the subcontinent, often reflecting their own stratification by sect, location, and the castes of their predecessors. Social practices among certain Indian Christians parallel much of the discrimination faced by lower castes in other religious communities, as well as having features unique to this community. The Catholic church in India has encouraged caste system among new converts even since the time of the Portuguese. Roberto de Nobili (1577 – 16 January 1656) was an Italian Jesuit missionary to Southern India. He used a novel method of adaptation (accommodatio) to preach Christianity, adopting many local customs of India which were, in his view, not contrary to Christianity. Roberto de Nobili was an Italian missionary who arrived in Goa on May 20, 1605. After a short stay in Cochin, he took residence in Madurai. He soon called himself a "teacher of wisdom" and began to dress like a Sannyasin. He took advantage of his noble parentage to approach high caste people and was willing to dialogue with Hindu scholars on the truths of Christianity. He thus justified the continuation of caste system among new converts to Catholicism.

Caste distinctions among Indian Christians are breaking down at about the same rate as those among Indians belonging to other religions. There exists evidence to show that Christian individuals have mobility within their respective castes. But, in some cases, social inertia cause old traditions and biases against other castes to remain, causing caste segregation to persist among Indian Christians. About 70-80% of Indian Christians are Dalit Christian, members of the Dalit or backward classes.

CHRISTIAN CASTES BY REGION

Kerala

Christians in Kerala are divided into several communities, including Syrian Christians and the "Latin" or "New Rite" Christians. The Roman Catholic Church consists of three rites namely the Syro-Malabar rite, the Syro-Malankara rite and the Latin Rite. The Syro-Malabar and Syro-Malankara rites maintain their traditional Syrian rites and practices.

Syrian Christians, especially Knanaya Christians tend to be endogamous, and tend not to intermarry with other Christian castes. Also, very rarely are there intermarriages between Syrian Christians and Latin Rite Christians (converted in the 16th and 19th centuries) in Kerala; the latter were converted mainly from lower castes where fishing was the traditional occupation. Due to active conversion by Latin Missionaries in the coastal belt of Kerala, the new Latin converts were poor and deprived. So the Government of India gave them the social benefit of OBC status (Other Backward Classes) so that the deprived members of that community can be uplifted. It is a matter of great significance that Missionary activities were done by Western Latin rite missionaries who did not understand the significance of the caste system in India. None of the Syrian

Churches ever indulged in these kinds of activities among the scheduled castes of India because they were aware of the prejudices of the caste system.

Syrian Christians derive status within the caste system from the claim that they are converted Nambudiris, who were evangelized by St. Thomas. There are also significant numbers of converted Christians, Nadar Protestants (SIUC & Pentecostals) forming 5 % of Kerala population and Nadar Catholics (mainly Malankara Church) forming 1% of Kerala population.

Anthropologists have noted that the caste hierarchy among Christians in Kerala is much more polarized than among the Hindus in the surrounding areas, due to a lack of jatis. Also, the caste status is kept even if the sect allegiance is switched (i.e. from Syrian Catholic to Syrian Orthodox).

Goa

In the Indian state of Goa, mass conversions were carried out by Portuguese Latin missionaries from the 16th century onwards. The Hindu converts retained their caste practices. The continued maintenance of the caste system among the Christians in Goa is attributed to the nature of mass conversions of entire villages, as a result of which existing social stratification was not affected. The Portuguese colonists, even during the Goan Inquisition, did not do anything to change the caste system. Thus, the original Hindu Brahmins in Goa now became *Bamonns* and the Kshatriya became Christian noblemen called *Chardos*. The Christian clergy became almost exclusively Bamonn. Vaishyas who converted to Christianity became *Gauddos*, and Shudras became *Sudirs*. Finally, the Dalits or "Untouchables" who converted to Christianity became *Maharas* and *Chamars* (an appellation of the anti-Dalit ethnic slur *Chamaar*). The upper caste Gaonkar Christians have demanded that only their community be given positions on the Pastoral Council of Goa's Catholic Church.

Tamil Nadu

The cohesion of jatis among caste Christians (eg. Paravas) and the strength of caste leadership are noted by scholars to be much stronger than comparable predominantly Hindu castes in Tamil Nadu. However, discrimination still persists. Lourdunathan Yesumariyan, Jesuit activist notes that "over 70% of Catholics are Dalit converts. But only four out of 18 bishops are from the Dalit-Christian community."

Andhra Pradesh

60-70 % Catholics are Kammas and Reddys in Andhra Pradesh; the remaining are from various castes. In India, Christians prefer marrying other Christians of the same caste..

Under the Law

Indian law does not provide benefits for "Dalit Christians", however Christians have been agitating for the same rights given to Hindu, Buddhist, and Sikh Scheduled castes. Despite the activists point of discrimination due to social tag or status, which doesn't go away, Justice K. G. Balakrishnan asked:

"Could the Christians admit that they practise caste system and that Dalits (among them) face social discrimination requiring reservation to uplift their cause? This is not all that easy."

Some Christians also oppose the proposed labelling of "Christian Scheduled castes" because they feel their identity may be assimilated. Pastor Salim Sharif of the Church of North India notes "We are becoming another class and caste."

8

Stratification of Social Class

SOCIAL CLASSES AND STRATA IN CONTEMPORARY CAPITALISM

According to the Marxist tradition social classes are large social groups defined by their insertion in the fundamental relations of production within a particular economic and social system. Two basic classes exist in capitalism: the dominant class, which controls the state and appropriates economic surplus in the form of profits and interests, and the working class. These two classes are defined by the roles they play in production, the direct result of the social division of labour. Aside from the various smaller subdivisions, there is a fundamental division between those who own the means of production, and consequently control them, and those who do not.

It is this basic relation of production that gives a structural definition to social classes. It establishes the essential functions that social agents fulfil in the productive process as well as the corresponding forms of participation in the social product. Supported by the state apparatus, which it controls, the dominant class in each mode of production appropriates surplus for itself. This appropriation takes the form of taxes in the Asiatic economic and social system, slave labour in slavery, the corvée in feudalism, speculative profit or primitive accumulation in mercantile capitalism, and surplus value or profit in capitalism. Until almost the end of the nineteenth century, workers were forced to accept remuneration for their labour, which corresponded to mere subsistence. Surplus was fully appropriated by the dominant class. Classical economists and Marx defined wage labour precisely as the subsistence level. They developed a theory of income distribution in which wages were given as this subsistence level, yet historically determined, while profits appeared as the residuum, as the consequence of the increase (or decrease, in the stagnation theories of Ricardo and Marx) of productivity. The tremendous increase in productivity brought by capitalism and the increasing organizational capacity of workers changed this picture. Wages began to increase above the subsistence level, in proportion to the increase in productivity, while profits remained relatively constant in the long run, only fluctuating cyclically. Thus, today, in technobureaucratic or contemporary capitalism, workers also appropriate economic surplus: they share with capitalists and technobureaucrats the productivity gains.

To define dominant and dominated social classes in terms of appropriation of surplus does not make sense anymore. But to define classes in terms of their position in the relations of production continues to be valid, as long as we do not translate relations of productions into levels of income. Society today is much more complex, and the division of labour is much more advanced than in the past. Dividing society into classes, according to the position of each individual in the relations of production, is not as direct as it was in the past. But this position continues to be essential in defining social classes. Either you directly own means of production, or you control the bureaucratic organization that owns the means of production, or you perform direct labour. This means you will belong either to the capitalist, to the technobureaucratic middle class, or to the working class.

Major Actors in History

The structural definition of the social classes based on relations of production is not meant to be merely descriptive. In terms of the Marxist thought, which underlies the argument, social classes are the privileged players in history, and their action takes the form of class struggle. Social classes define themselves in terms on conflict, in terms of struggle for state power and in terms of the dispute over the appropriation of surplus. In Marx and Engels' words: The separate individuals form a class only insofar as they have to carry on a common battle against another class... (1846: 82)

Yet, aside from class struggle, the conflicts between nations and between fractions within the dominant class must also be considered. Basically, war is a strategy of the dominant classes, a form of appropriating external surplus and also a form of neutralizing internal class conflict. Struggles among fractions of the dominant class take place primarily when the dominant class is so hegemonic that it can afford internal conflicts. Although they are still significant today, these struggles were more important in the past, when the balance of forces between the dominant and dominated classes greatly favoured the former.

According to the Marxist tradition it is impossible to understand society and history if we do not use social classes as basic tools. Yet, conservative sociology always underestimated the role of classes in history. In denying class struggle as a basic motor of history, functionalist sociology must, as a consequence, play down the role of social classes. Marxist and neo-Marxist class theory resisted quite well this type of attack up to the 1970s. Following, however, the general crisis of the left and of Marxism, 'the past decade witnessed, as it were, the erosion of class theory and of other fundamentals of traditional Marxism'. A basic reason for this, besides the conservative wave of the last ten or twenty years, lies in the emergence of the new class: the technobureaucracy. As we shall see in this part of the book, the social structure of modern technobureaucratic capitalism became much more gradual, much less dichotomic, than the existing one in classical capitalism – the capitalism that Marx described. Social classes remain the basic actors in history. Capitalists and workers continue to act according to their own logic: the logic of profit and accumulation for capitalists, the logic of wage demands for workers. Class struggle and class consciousness continue to be essential factors in history, but the existence of a new middle class between capitalists and workers demand a different type of analysis.

A Historical Perspective

We have seen that social classes are agents par excellence of history. Yet we have also observed that they are the products of relations of production changing with history. Consequently, the concept of social class varies through different historical periods and keeping with of different modes of production. Classes exist in all antagonistic modes of production where a minority, initially through force or coercion, appropriates effective control of the means of production.

Relations of production are the determinant factor, so that the economic base is what underlies the essential split between classes. However, it is only in the capitalism that classes take on such a clear and explicit economic character, with political and religious aspects as only secondary concerns. Thus it is correct to say that social classes, in the strict sense of the word, are a phenomenon specific to capitalism.

It is only in a broad and imprecise sense that Marx and Engels may use this term when they assert: 'the history of all hitherto existing society is the history of class struggles' (1848: 2). In many other writings it is clear that they use the concept of class as a theoretical tool which is particularly useful in explaining how capitalism functions. It is only with the rise of capitalism that the dominant class can appropriate surplus through explicitly economic means: the mechanism of surplus value. In this way relations between classes defined as economic groups become much clearer, no longer clouded by tradition or religion.

Capitalism brings with it liberalism, that postulates equal treatment before the law. What this signifies in terms of the capitalist ideology is that class distinctions have no legitimation based in the legal and ideological superstructure of society. Thus the economic basis of class becomes more apparent. Some sell and others buy labour in the market; this is where class differences originate. In pre-capitalist modes of production, it was always necessary for the dominant class to use direct force either alone or joined with tradition and religion, in order to extract surplus. With capitalism the use of force occurs indirectly. To the extent that capitalism is based on the generalization of commodities, the capitalist can appropriate surplus through an essentially economic mechanism, surplus value. While in pre-capitalist modes of production the dominant class's appropriation of surplus had a decisively economic component, it always implied a kind of violence or use of power which is not market power, nor power derived from capital. The taxes imposed by the sovereign in the Asiatic mode of production is clearly a violent means of appropriating surplus. The same can be said for slavery, where the violence is even more apparent. The feudal corvée is still violent, though mitigated by the master's reciprocal obligation of military protection and justified by a strong ideological apparatus.

When surplus is appropriated in these pre-capitalist situations, the economic aspect by which classes are defined tends to be weakened or obscured. The dominant class finds it more important to develop political, legal and religious justifications to legitimate the coercion and violence by which it appropriates surplus. It is also essential to set up institutional mechanisms, which divide and stratify the dominated classes in order to facilitate their domination. The basically economic nature of social class is thus doubly obscured: on one hand by the introduction of ideological elements and on the other by dividing up society into castes or status groups which would replace classes in terms of social structure. As Lukács notes: This is true above all because class interests in pre-capitalist society never achieve full (economic) articulation. Hence the structuring of society into castes and estates means that economic elements are inextricably joined to political and religious factors. In contrast to this, the rule of the bourgeoisie means the abolition of the estates-system and this leads to the organization of society along class lines (1922: 55).

Castes and Status Groups

It is characteristic of pre-capitalist societies to establish castes and status groups or some other kind of social division of labour which are hereditary, rigid and backed up by religious values and the law. We are often led to believe that castes and status groups play the social classes' role in pre-capitalist economic formations. But this is not correct, or it is not the whole truth. India's castes and countless sub-castes and the many types and sizes of status groups or estates in feudal society are not real alternatives to classes, but rather a strategy of the dominant class to hierarchically order and regulate the social system. Basic social classes still exist, based on their participation in production. But they are further divided into smaller and more stable groups for which rights, and more importantly, responsibilities and limitations are defined. It is said that on the eve of the French Revolution society was divided into three estates: the nobility, the clergy and the people. But the people were further divided into smaller sub-status groups. The situation is similar among the castes in India. On the other hand, status groups are also forms of stratifying the dominant class. Accordingly Hans Freyer observes:

> The military, the priesthood, public office and landholding are ordinarily sectors which the dominant status groups reserve for themselves (1931: 169).

Weber was correct in comparing status groups with castes: 'a caste is doubtless a closed status group' (1916: 39). Nevertheless he was one of those responsible for the proposition spread widely today that social classes and status groups are alternative forms of social organization. For example, he states that 'classes are groups of people who, from the standpoint of specific interests, have the same economic position', while status group are a 'quality of social honour or the lack of it' (1916: 39). In the same vein, the First Part of Economy and Society, 'Status and Classes.' Here he defines class in function of market position, that is, based on 'a probability which derives from the relative control over goods and skills and from their income producing uses within a given economic order', whereas 'status (*standische lage*) shall mean an effective claim to social esteem in terms of positive or negative privileges.' (1922: 302-305). The notion of social honour, which forms part of the concept of a status group, in fact refers principally to the higher status groups formed by the dominant class and its associates as the pre-capitalist bureaucracy. For a member of the lower class to belong to a professional status group is also viewed by the dominant class and accepted by the dominated class as an indication of social honour. It is an 'honour' and a 'privilege' to belong to the status group of masons or butchers, especially if we consider that the monopoly over this distinction derives from 'appropriation of political or hierocratic powers.' The strategic importance that this kind of distinction holds for the dominant class is apparent.

By establishing castes and status groups, the dominant class neutralizes class struggle. Thus some authors view as a fundamental difference between the two the presence of conflict in relations between classes versus the absence of conflict between status group. Toennies states that 'estates change over into classes, when they engage in hostile actions or engage one another in war.' (1931: 12). In fact status groups never reach the point of questioning the class structure itself. The farthest they go is to engage in local or private clashes with other status groups in order to win certain rights or limit those of others. What is important to remember is that the status group is a subdivision of a class, not an alternative to it. More precisely, it is a subdivision of classes, an internal ranking of the dominant and dominated class. Social classes here are understood in their broad sense as derived from the insertion of social groups in antagonistic relations of production. The status group would be an alternative to the social class if we limit the latter concept to capitalism. This limited conception of class has a certain historical foundation to the extent inhabitants, the census of 1901 identified nearly nine hundred caste names which were subsumed, however, by classification under two hundred real castes." (1931:15).

that classes only appeared in their purest form with capitalism, but we should not lose sight of the more general nature of class and class struggle throughout history. Nevertheless it is conceivable for a status group to become a class. On one hand there would have to be new relations of production, which place the status group in a strategic position, and on the other, this social group, as a result, would have to gain critical mass, a universal nature and finally, a vocation for both conflict and domination. Marx and Engels are quite clear about the bourgeoisie's transformation from a status group to a class when they state that:

By the mere fact that it is a class and no longer an estate, the bourgeoisie is forced to organize itself no longer locally, but nationally, and to give a general form to its mean average interest (1846: 80). This transformation took place when the relations of production for which the bourgeoisie served as vehicle became dominant in society while this new class was gaining critical mass and consciousness of its own interests. The transformation of the bureaucratic status group into the technobureaucratic class is occurring through a similar process in the second half of the twentieth century.

Thus estates or status groups do not constitute an alternative to the class structure since social classes and status groups are common to all antagonistic modes of production, but on a lower level of abstraction, they can be considered as the feudal alternative to the capitalist class structure. This is why status groups when contrasted with specific classes in capitalism become a useful theoretical tool. This tool helps us to understand the historical differences not only between pre-capitalist and capitalist class structures, but also between the latter and the specific class structure of the technobureaucratic mode of production. While a class structure is common to all antagonistic modes of production, each mode structures classes in its own particular way. Status groups played a fundamental role in feudalism, while with capitalism classes tend to appear in a pure form and in statism we will see that the concept of 'layer' or 'social stratum' is essential to understanding its class system.

CLASS AND CLASS CONSCIOUSNESS

As class theory must be the object of a reappraisal in the context of technobureaucratic capitalism, the role of class consciousness must also be revised. The process of class struggle involves not only concrete measures aimed at organization and control of the state, but also the definition of class interests in ideological terms. Conservative or revolutionary ideologies are politically oriented values and beliefs systems. They are expression of class interests, and their proponents seek to endow them with universal validity. Within this framework, class consciousness is an important, but not necessary, element in the definition of class. All classes possess their respective ideology, but not necessarily class consciousness. The technobureaucratic class is endowed of class consciousness, but this only true as much as it has as project or *raison d'être* to control the large corporations and the state.

Class consciousness would be a necessary element in the definition of class if we were to adopt Lukács' conception, in which class consciousness is not the sum or common denominator of what its members think, but rather an 'objective possibility'. According to Lukács, class consciousness is constituted of... the thoughts and feelings which men would have in a particular situation if they were able to assess both it and the interests arising from it in their impact on immediate action and on the whole structure of society. Therefore class consciousness exists potentially in everyone-given some specific historic conditions this potential consciousness 'could be conscious.' (1922: 51-52 and 59). Although this concept is attractive to the extent that it emphasizes the dialectical relationship between relations of production and class consciousness, I am rather defining social class here as a concrete historical process originating from that dialectical relationship. The dominant class always had class consciousness and exercised its domain not only through control of the means of production and the repressive apparatus, but also through ideological hegemony, while the dominated class is not necessarily endowed with it. In order to maintain its dominant position, the dominant class transmits its ideology to the dominated through the ideological apparatuses existing in society.

In the pre-capitalist period, religion was the main ideological apparatus. In capitalism, educational institutions, political parties, the press, television and radio have performed this function. If the dominant class can achieve full ideological hegemony, it can annul or neutralize the consciousness of the dominated class. For this reason, the attainment of some consciousness by the dominated is a recent historical phenomenon, and yet a partial one. It appears with capitalism, taking shape when workers organized into unions and political parties, and acquiring stability through the spread of socialist and Marxist ideas. Yet, given the success of capitalism in promoting economic development and transferring productivity gains to workers without endangering a satisfactory profit rate, this attainment is partial.

Thus, class consciousness is not an essential element in defining a class if the class to be defined is the working class. Yet it is a real class, it possess its own collective interests and ideology in opposition to the dominant class. But it cannot be considered an effective actor in history. A class only becomes an effective historical force once it attains some degree of class consciousness, organizes itself politically and fights for state power. For Therborn (1980: 60), the acceptance or the resistance to class exploitation is not essential to the definition of the ideology of the dominated classes. A purely dominated class is endowed with an ideology based on the ideas of authority and obedience. Class struggle will take place, but, contrarily to Marx's expectation, it will not tend to be revolutionary. In pre-capitalist societies the dominant class was the only effective historical factor. Fractions of the dominant class disputed state control, but only very rarely did the exploited class take part in these struggles. The latter may have revolted or escaped, or even gained more political space. Dominant class power, however, only suffers a threat with the advent of capitalism and the working class, precisely because the working class is the first dominated class that has ever become organized and developed a consciousness of its own interests. The economic success of capitalism, however, did not permit that this threat did not turn into revolution. On the contrary, revolution turned increasingly into an unrealistic alternative in contemporary capitalism.

THE NEW CLASS AND THE SOCIAL STRATA

The essential condition for the emergence of a new class is the rise of corresponding relations of production. The new class may or may not have class consciousness, but it is essential that it is not confused with social strata. In principle, in pure modes of production, we only have a dominant and a dominated class: the 'middle class' will correspond to the less rich fractions of the dominant class and the richer fractions of the dominated one. Small and medium sized capitalist on one hand, and skilled workers in the other fall in the first category. Alternatively, in a mixed social formation, the middle class will represent the emergence new relations of production and of corresponding social relations. The technobureaucratic middle class that emerges in technobureaucratic capitalism falls in this second category.

This notion of social class has little in common with the functionalist theories of social stratification. Nor is it the same as the Weberian theories of social class that emphasize purchasing power or market position. It also differs significantly from those Weberian theories developed by Dahrendorf (1957) and Lenski (1966), that focus on power rather than on relations of production to delineate social class. While these theories have a certain utility, especially from a functionalist perspective, in terms of a descriptive and static view of society, they obviously do not meet our needs as a theory that helps to explain the historical process of social and political change. Rather we are interested in a theory of social classes providing us with tools for the analysis of contemporary capitalism, where the technobureaucratic middle class plays an increasingly decisive role.

Social classes are social groups that are defined by the roles they play, dominant or dominated, within society's basic relations of production. Through the inherent process of class struggle, they became the prime players of history. On one hand, this can be explained by the development of the productive forces, which establishes new material conditions for the relations of production, and, on the other, as a function of class struggles which originates in each class' insertion in the relations of production and their resulting class consciousness. Therefore, in order to a new class establish itself, it is essential that this class takes part in new emerging relations of production, that these new relations of production should be basic to the definition of a new mode of production, and that, as a result, the new social group should be of sufficient size or critical mass to formulate a historical project designed to eventually make it the new dominant class. The emerging technobureaucratic class, that characterizes technobureaucratic capitalism, fully meets these requirements. In a previous essay (1977) I discussed the concept of class in terms of pure modes of production rather than in terms of concrete social formations. The capitalist mode of production in its purest form (that of England in the nineteenth century) was compared with the technobureaucratic mode of production dominant in the Soviet social formation. Adopting this strategy I was able to define the technobureaucratic relation of production and identify the technobureaucracy as the dominant class in this mode of production.

While in pure capitalism we have two classes, the bourgeoisie and the workers, and a respective relation of production, capital, in the pure statist mode of production, we also have only two classes, the technobureaucracy and the workers, and a respective relation of production, organization. Capital as a relation of production ceases to exist to the extent that private ownership of the means of production disappears. What replaces it is something I have been calling 'organization': the collective ownership of the means of production by the new professional or technobureaucratic class. While technobureaucrats do not hold legal ownership of the means of production as capitalists do, they are similar to the latter in that they hold their effective control.

The most important difference, however, does not concern legal ownership but the fact that capitalism property is private, individual, whereas in the technobureaucratic mode of production property is collective. In the capitalism system, each capitalist either directly owns the means of production, or a proportion of them directly in the form of stocks, or indirectly in the form of credits. In contrast, the technobureaucrats cannot say that they own a business enterprise or even a given part of it. Rather, the technobureaucrats own the bureaucratic organization to the extent that they occupy a position in its organizational hierarchy, and use the organization's resources for their own benefit.

Technobureaucratic capitalism, being a mixed social formation, that remains dominantly capitalist, but shares some statist or technobureaucratic characteristics, is the realm where emerge the new middle class: the technobureaucratic or professional class.

Combining Classes and Strata

A fundamental question in class theory is 'the middle class question', that I will examine ahead. Now it is enough to say that according to Marxist class theory there are no middle classes. Marx and Engels certainly used the expression 'middle class', but this was a way to designate the bourgeoisie, which was in the middle of the social structure, between the working class and the land-owning aristocracy. In this way, Marx and Engels were basically coherent with their own conception of social class, defined by the role large social groups play in the relations of production.

The concepts of social layers or social strata have been utilized as synonyms for class by functionalist sociologists. They consider social class to be a question of social stratification, which, according to Talcott Parsons, is a hierarchical ranking of the individuals of a particular social system. It is the way that individuals occupy positions in the social structure in terms of status. In Parsons words:

> Social stratification is regarded here as the differential ranking of the human individuals who compose a given social system their treatment as superior and inferior relative to one another in certain socially important respects (1940: 841).

If we understand social classes as part of a system of stratification, the concept of class is no longer derived from relations of production. Instead, it becomes a mere expedient for the hierarchical division of society into strata in order to better describe it. It is also possible, more or less arbitrarily, to increase the number of strata, as Lloyd Warner did, so that we have an upper-upper class, a lower upper class, an upper middle class, a lower middle class, an upper lower class and lower-lower class (1941).7 Nonetheless it is important to point out that the concept of middle class is not merely a functionalist notion. Social scientists from various theoretical perspectives, including Marxists, have utilized it. It prevails because it forms part of our everyday language, and because it is frequently used to describe reasonably well-defined sectors of society.

Strictly speaking, it is more correct to speak of upper, lower and middle strata, rather than upper, lower and middle classes.

The former constitutes a criterion for social classification which is distinct from that of class, and are valid and useful as a tool for sociological analysis. We could define a stratum as a portion of society sectioned off horizontally in accordance with a series of criteria which allow us to establish a hierarchical order. These more or less arbitrary criteria refer to individuals' economic power and social prestige. The functionalist sociologists examined in depth the correlations which are present and those lacking between social prestige and wealth, occupation, education, race and religion middle class" as synonymous with technobureaucracy. What makes no sense is to speak simply of the middle class, since then we confuse social classes with social strata.

MARX'S THEORY OF SOCIAL CLASS AND CLASS STRUCTURE

For Marx, the analysis of social class, class structures and changes in those structures are key to understanding capitalism and other social systems or modes of production. In the *Communist Manifesto* Marx and Engels comment that the history of all hitherto existing society is the history of class struggles. (Bottomore, p. 75).

Analysis of class divisions and struggles is especially important in developing an understanding of the nature of capitalism. For Marx, classes are defined and structured by the relations concerning (i) work and labour and (ii) ownership or possession of property and the means of production. These economic factors more fully govern social relationships in capitalism than they did in earlier societies. While earlier societies contained various strata or groupings which might be considered classes, these may have been strata or elites that were not based solely on economic factors – e.g. priesthood, knights, or military elite.

Marx did not complete the manuscript that would have presented his overall view of social class. Many of his writings concern the class structures of capitalism, the relationship among classes the dynamics of class struggle, political power and classes, and the development of a classless society, and from these a Marxian approach to class can be developed. Note that Hadden does not discuss class in any detail, although the class structure of capitalism is implicit in the labour theory of value and can be derived from this theory.

Classes in Capitalism

The main classes in capitalism are the bourgeoisie and the proletariat. However, other classes such as landlords, petty bourgeoisie, peasants, and lumpenproletariat also exist, but are not primary in terms of the dynamics of capitalism.

Bourgeoisie. The bourgeoisie or capitalists are the owners of capital, purchasing and exploiting labour power, using the surplus value from employment of this labour power to accumulate or expand their capital. It is the ownership of capital and its use to exploit labour and expand capital are key here. Being wealthy is, in itself, not sufficient to make one a capitalist (e.g. managers in the state sector or landlords). What is necessary is the active role of using this wealth to make it self-expansive through employment and exploitation of labour.

Historically, the bourgeoisie began cities of medieval Europe, with the development of traders, merchants, craftspersons, industrialists, manufacturers and others whose economic survival and ability to increase wealth came from trade, commerce, or industry. In order for each of these to expand their operations, they needed greater freedom to market products and expand economic activities. In the struggle against the feudal authorities (church and secular political authorities) this class formed and took on a progressive role. That is, they helped undermine the old hierarchical and feudal order and create historical progress. For a segment of this class, wealth came by employing labour (industrial capital), for others it came through trade (merchant capital), banking and finance (finance capital), or using land in a capitalist manner (landed capital). It was the industrial capitalists who employed labour to create capital that became the leading sector of the bourgeoisie, whose economic activities ultimately changed society. In Britain, this class became dominant politically and ideologically by the mid-nineteenth century. By employing workers, industrial capital created the surplus value that could take on the various forms such as profit, interest and rent.

Proletariat. The proletariat are owners of labour power (the ability to work), and mere owners of labour power, with no other resources than the ability to work with their hands, bodies, and minds. Since these workers have no property, in order to survive and obtain an income for themselves and their families, they must find employment work for an employer. This means working for a capitalist-employer in an exploitative social relationship.

This exploitative work relationship recreates or reproduces itself continually. If the capitalist-employer is to make profits and accumulate capital, wages must be kept low. This means that the proletariat is exploited, with the surplus time (above that required for creating subsistence) worked by the worker creating surplus products. While the worker produces, the products created by this labour are taken by the capitalist and sold – thus producing surplus value or profit for the capitalist but poverty for workers. This occurs each day of labour process, preventing workers from gaining ownership of property and recreating the conditions for further exploitation.

The antagonistic and contradictory nature of this system is evident as capitalists attempting to reduce wages and make workers work more intensively, while workers have exactly the opposite set of interests. Work and the labour process in the capitalist mode of production are organized so that workers remain propertyless members of the proletariat. The surplus products and value created by workers turns into capital, which is accumulated.

Historically, the proletariat emerged as the aristocracy began to suffer financial difficulties in the later middle ages. Many of those who were supported by working for the aristocracy lost their livelihood – the "disbanding of the feudal retainers and the dissolution of the monasteries." Using enclosures, changing the conditions of production in agriculture, and denying peasants access to common lands and resources, landowners transformed land into pasture land for raising sheep, or sold land to farmers who began to develop grain and livestock production. People who had subsisted on the land were denied the possibility of making a living on the land, and they become propertyless. Population growth was also considerable, and in some areas forced labour (slavery, indentured servants, poor, prison) was used. While some people subsisted in rural industry and craft production, factory production began to undermine these as well in the eighteenth and nineteenth centuries. Together these changes created a large class of landless and propertyless people who had no choice but to become members of the proletariat – many working in factories. These people became free wage labourers, free from feudal ties and free from a source of livelihood. Today we still talk of free labour markets and the dual meaning is much the same.

While the relationship between workers and capitalists, or between labour and capital may appear to be no more than an economic relationship of equals meeting equals in the labour market, Marx shows how it is an exploitative social relationship. Not only is it exploitative, it is contradictory, with the interests of the two partners in the relationship being directly opposed to each other. Although at the same time, the two opposed interests are also partners in the sense that both capital and labour are required in production and an exploitative relationship means an exploiter and someone being exploited.

This relationship is further contradictory in that it is not just two sets of interests, but there is no resolution of the capital-labour contradiction within the organization of capitalism as a system. The contradictory relationship has class conflict built into it, and leads to periodic bursts of strikes, crises, political struggles, and ultimately to the overthrow of bourgeois rule by the proletariat. Class conflict of this sort results in historical change and is the motive force in the history of capitalism.

Landlords. In addition to the bourgeoisie and the proletariat, Marx discussed a number of other classes. First, Marx mentions landowners or landlords as a class in Britain. While these were historically important, and many still retain their wealth even today (e.g. the Royal Family), they were considered by Marx to be a marginal class, once powerful and dominant but having lost their central role in production and the organization of society. In order to retain their wealth, some of these landowners were able to transform their wealth in land into landed capital. While this constituted a somewhat different form than industrial capital, this meant that the land was also used as capital, to accumulate. Labour may not be directly employed by landowners, but the land is used as a means by which capital can be expanded.

Petty Bourgeoisie and Middle Class. The lower middle class or the petty (petite) bourgeoisie (the bourgeoisie was sometimes called the middle class in this era), constitutes "the small manufacturer, the shopkeeper, the artisan, the peasant". The characteristic of this class is that it does own some property, but not sufficient to have all work done by employees or workers. Members of this class must also work in order to survive, so they have a dual existence – as (small scale) property owners and as workers. Because of this dual role, members of this class have divided interests, usually wishing to preserve private property and property rights, but with interests often opposed to those of the capitalist class. This class is split internally as well, being geographically, industrially, and politically dispersed, so that it is difficult for it to act as a class. Marx expected that this class would disappear as capitalism developed, with members moving into the bourgeoisie or into the working class, depending on whether or not they were successful. Many in this class have done this, but at the same time, this class seems to keep recreating itself in different forms.

Marx considers the petite bourgeoisie to be politically conservative or reactionary, preferring to return to an older order. This class has been considered by some Marxists to have been the base of fascism in the 1920s and 1930s. At other times, when it is acting in opposition to the interests of large capital, it may have a more radical or reformist bent to it (anti-monopoly).

Note on the Middle Class. The issue of the middle class or classes appears to be a major issue within Marxian theory, one often addressed by later Marxists. Many Marxists attempt to show that the middle class is declining, and polarization of society into two classes is a strong tendency within capitalism. Marx's view was that the successful members of the middle class would become members of the bourgeoisie, while the unsuccessful would be forced into the proletariat. In the last few years, many have argued that in North America, and perhaps on a world scale, there is an increasing gap between rich and poor and there is a declining middle.

While there have been tendencies in this direction, especially among the farmers and peasantry, there has been no clear long run trend toward decline of the middle class. At the same time as there has been polarization of classes, there have been new middle groupings created. Some of these are small business people, shopkeepers, and small producers while others are professional and managerial personnel, and some intellectual personnel. Well paid working class members and independent trades people might consider themselves to be members of the middle class. Some segments of this grouping have expanded in number in recent years. While it is not clear that these groups hold together and constitute a class in any Marxian sense of being combined in opposition to other classes, they do form a middle grouping. Since Marx's prediction has not come true, sociologists and other writers have devoted much attention to explaining this middle grouping – what is its basis, what are the causes of its stability or growth, how it fits into the class structure, and what are the effects of its existence on proletariat and bourgeoisie.

Lumpenproletariat. Marx also mentions the "dangerous class" or the social scum. Among the members of this group are "ruined and adventurous offshoots of the bourgeoisie, vagabonds, discharged soldiers, discharged jailbirds.. pickpockets, brothel keepers, rag-pickers, beggars" etc. (Bottomore, p. 292). This is the lumpenproletariat. He does not consider this group to be of any importance in terms of potential for creating socialism, if anything they may be considered to have a conservative influence. Other writers and analysts have considered them to have some revolutionary potential. One of the main reasons for mentioning them is to emphasize how capitalism uses, misuses and discards people, not treating them as humans. Today's representative of this class of lumpenproletariat are the homeless and the underclass.

Peasantry and Farmers. Marx considered the peasantry to be disorganized, dispersed, and incapable of carrying out change. Marx also expected that this class would tend to disappear, with most becoming displaced from the land and joining the proletariat. The more successful might become landowners or capitalist farmers. With respect to family farmers as a group, much the same could be said. However, Marx was not really very familiar with these as a group, and had little to say about these. The various analyses of the role of farmers in the Prairies constitute a more adequate view of what may be expected from this group. They could be considered to form a class when they act together as a group. In the early days of Prairie settlement, farms were of similar size, farmers had generally similar interests, and the farm population acted together to create the cooperative movement and the Wheat Board. More recently, Prairie farmers are often considered to be split into different groups or strata, dependent on type of farming, size of farm, and whether or not they employ labour. Farmers have not been able to act together as a class in political and economic actions in recent years. Lobbying by some farm groups have been successful, but these do not usually represent farmers as a whole.

Features of Marx's Analysis

Group Basis. For Marx, classes cannot be defined by beginning observation and analysis from individuals, and building a definition of a social class as an aggregate of individuals with particular characteristics. For example, to say that the upper class is all families with incomes of $500,000 or more is not an adequate manner of understanding social class. The latter is a stratification approach that begins by examining the characteristics of individuals, and from this amassing a view of social class structure as a whole. This stratification approach often combines income, education, and social prestige or status into an index of socioeconomic status, creating a gradation from upper class to lower class. The stratification approach is essentially a classification, and for Marx classes have meaning only as they are real groups in the social structure. Groups mean interaction among members, common consciousness, and similar types of behaviour that are connected in some way with group behaviour. Categories such as upper class, middle class and lower class, where those in each category may be similar only in the view of the researcher are not fully Marxian in nature.

Classes are groups, and Marx discusses the bourgeoisie and the proletariat, not individual capitalists and individual workers. As individuals, these people may be considered members of a class, but class only acquires real meaning when it the class as a whole and the social relationships defining them that are considered. For example, "The bourgeoisie... has put an end to all feudal, patriarchal, idyllic relations.... " (Giddens and Held, p. 21). Here the bourgeoisie is historically created and is an actor in politics, economics and history.

In terms of individuals as members of classes, they are members of a class as they act as members of that class. For example, Marx notes that burghers or members of the bourgeoisie in early capitalist Europe: the class in its turn achieves an independent existence over against the individuals, so that the latter find their conditions of existence predestined, and hence have their position in life and their personal development assigned to them by their class, become subsumed under it. (Giddens and Held, 20).

To the extent that individuals are considered in the social system, they are defined by their class. For Marxists, class structures exist as objective facts, and a researcher could examine class and membership of a class, but would have to understand the nature of the whole social and economic structure in order to do so. To the extent that these members act in society, they act as representatives of their class, although Marx would leave some room for individual freedom of action.

Property and Class. Classes are formed by the forces that define the mode of production, and classes are an aspect of the relations of production. That is, classes do not result from distribution of products (income differences, lender and borrower), social evaluation (status honour), or political or military power, but emerge right from relationship to the process of production. Classes are an essential aspect of production, the division of labour and the labour process. Giddens notes:

Classes are constituted by the relationship of groupings of individuals to the ownership of private property in the means of production. This yields a model of class relations which is basically dichotomous [since some own and others do not, some work and others live off the fruits of those who labour]: all class societies are built around a primary line of division between two antagonistic classes, one dominant and the other subordinate. (Giddens, p. 37).

In describing various societies, Marx lists a number of classes and (antagonistic) social relationship such as "freeman and slave,... lord and serf,... oppressor and oppressed" that characterize different historical stages or modes of production. While Marx also mentions various ranks and orders of society, such as vassals and knights, the forms of struggle between classes are primarily viewed as occurring around control and use of property, the means of production, and production as a whole, and the manner in which these are used. The basic struggle concerns who performs the labour, and who obtains the benefits from this labour.

An elite is not necessarily a class for Marx. Examples of elites are military elites, priests or religious leaders, and political elites – these may may very powerful and oppressive, and may exercise formal rule at a certain time or place. An elite could form a class, but a political or military elite is not necessarily a class – an elite may be based on recruitment (rather than ownership) and may not have much ultimate say in determining the direction of society. Or the elite may be based on religious, military, political or other structures. This would especially be the case in pre-capitalist or non-capitalist societies. For Marx, and especially in capitalism, domination came from control of the economy or material factors, although it was not confined to this. Thus, the dominant class was the class which was able to own, or at least control, the means of production or property which formed the basis for wealth. This class also had the capability of appropriating much of the social surplus created by workers or producers. An elite may have such power, but might only be able to administer or manage, with real control of the means of production in the hands of owners.

Class as Social Relationship – Conflict and Struggle. At several points, Marx notes how the class defines itself, or is a class only as it acts in opposition to other classes. Referring to the emergence of the burghers or bourgeoisie as a class in early capitalist Europe, Marx notes how

> The separate individuals form a class only insofar as they have to carry on a common battle against another class; otherwise they are on hostile terms with each other as competitors. (Giddens and Held, p. 20).

Both competition and unity can thus characterize a class; there can be very cut-throat competition among capitalists, but when the property relations and existence of the bourgeois class is threatened, the bourgeoisie acts together to protect itself. This becomes apparent when rights of private property or the ability of capital to operate freely comes under attack. The reaction of the bourgeoisie may involve common political action and ideological unity, and it is when these come together that the bourgeoisie as a class exists in its fullest form. In commenting on France, Marx notes that the French peasantry may be dispersed and lacking in unity, but

> In so far as millions of families live under economic conditions of existence that separate their mode of life, their interests and their culture from those of the other classes, and put them in hostile opposition to the latter, they form a class. (Giddens, p. 37)

It is when the peasantry as a group is in opposition to other classes that the peasantry form a class. These quotes do not provide an example of the same with respect to the proletariat, but in his other writings Marx noted that the proletariat is a true class when organized in opposition to the bourgeoisie, and creating a new society.

Class, for Marx, is defined as a (social) relationship rather than a position or rank in society. In Marx's analysis, the capitalist class could not exist without the proletariat, or vice-versa. The relationship between classes is a contradictory or antagonistic relationship, one that has struggle, conflict, and contradictory interests associated with it. The structure and basis of a social class may be defined in objective terms, as groups with a common position with respect to property or the means of production. However, Marx may not be primarily interested in this definition of class. Rather, these classes have meaning in society and are historical actors only to the extent that they do act in their own interests, and in opposition to other classes. Unlike much other sociology, Marx's classes are defined by class conflict.

SOCIAL MOBILITY AFFECT ANTAGONISTIC ATTITUDES

Empirical research has shown convincingly that educational achievement and social class are among the most important predictors of antagonistic attitudes toward ethnic out-groups, such as prejudices, ethnocentrism and opposition to ethnic intermarriage. The sociological literature consistently finds that less educated persons hold less favourable attitudes toward ethnic out-groups than more educated persons and that manual workers and the self-employed hold less favourable attitudes toward ethnic out-groups than other social classes.

Besides one's current social position, one's social origin – parental educational attainment and social class of the father during the formative years – also explains attitudes toward ethnic out-groups, although it seems to a lesser extent than current social position (Tolsma, Lubbers, and Coenders 2008). If social mobility has an impact on antagonistic attitudes, newcomers into a specific social position may differ in their level of antagonistic attitudes from members who hold the same social position but who have not experienced social mobility. The relative impact of social origin and destination positions on antagonistic attitudes remains unclear as the impact of social mobility may have been underestimated in previous studies because standard approaches are inadequate for modelling mobility effects.

Many theories in the Durkheimian tradition hypothesize that social mobility leads to instability, identity conflict, and subjective feelings of deprivation (Durkheim 1987[1897]). Social mobility – both upward and downward – is expected to cause alienation and abnormal strain. Without social and personal control, this may be manifested in dissatisfaction with life, antagonistic attitudes toward ethnic out-groups, and, in extreme cases, in suicide (Durkheim 1987[1897]). Despite these longstanding theoretical predictions, we know of no empirical research that has shown that experiences of social mobility affect prejudice through anomie or any other mechanism (Marshall and Firth 1999).

Conceptually, we view individuals' attitudes toward out-groups as affected both by the social position of their parents and by their own social position in adulthood. In addition, the experience of social mobility itself may affect attitudes independent of the social origin and destination (Marshall and Firth 1999).We stress that the two views are not in contrast with one another but rather complementary. Diagonal mobility models, which we apply in the present contribution, offer a parsimonious and elegant representation of origin, destination, and mobility effects and are well suited to model these potential mechanisms simultaneously.

In addition to the theoretical literature on causes of prejudice, our research contributes to the theoretical literature on the consequences of social mobility. Several scholars have applied diagonal mobility models to assess the relationship between mobility on the one hand and, on the other, voting behaviour, culture and material consumption behaviour, fertility, and lifestyles. These studies showed that the level of acculturation depends on the specific origin and destination positions. Until now, consequences of intergenerational mobility on antagonistic attitudes toward ethnic out-groups have been neglected in the body of research on social mobility.

Both educational achievement and social class are important determinants of antagonistic attitudes. We, therefore, examine the effects of mobility in terms of both educational achievement and social class on attitudes toward out-groups. We employ three distinct measures of antagonistic attitudes toward out-groups: ethnic stereotypes, ethnic threat, and opposition to ethnic intermarriage. We use two data sets from The Netherlands that are distinctive in their inclusion of measures of antagonistic attitudes, education, and class: SOCON and NKPS.

EXPECTATIONS: CLASS ORIGIN AND DESTINATION STATUS

Class of origin and class of destination are distinguished for individuals in that they occur at different points in the life course. Individuals experience their class of origin – their parent's class – most strongly during childhood and adolescence when they reside with their parents. They experience their destination class as adults after the completion of formal schooling. Persons who climb or fall from the social ladder thus experience two different class positions. We expect that both origin and destination class status may have an impact on attitudes, but their relative importance depends to a large extent on the relative importance of early socialization into the attitudes typical of the origin class by parents and other members of the origin class versus later circumstances on the formation of attitudes toward ethnic out-groups in adulthood.

Since socialization takes place primarily early in life (Alwin and Krosnick 1991) and many attitudes tend to be rather stable during the life course (Glenn 1980), a 'socialization' perspective would expect a larger role for origin position than destination position. As antagonistic attitudes are in part transmitted during childhood (Dalhouse and Frideres 1996), 'Once prejudices appropriate to one's class position are accepted, they may become traditions which are passed by childhood socialization from one generation to the next.'. Re-socialization may also occur later in life, but most theory and research suggests that socialization is a process that operates most strongly in childhood and adolescence, and thus class-based socialization influences should largely reflect origin class position. Under the view that socialization experiences are of primary importance in the formation of negative attitudes toward ethnic out-groups, we expect the *'Class Origin Hypothesis'* to hold: *The impact of the destination class on antagonistic attitudes is weaker than* the impact of the origin class on antagonistic attitudes.

Another approach suggests that attitudes toward out-groups are more closely related to individuals' perceptions of their material self-interest and related collective identities, especially their current class position. In line with this view, ethnic competition theories state that members of ethnic groups compete with each other for scarce resources such as jobs, housing, and income. Especially in conditions in which new competitors come from ethnically distinct groups, many individuals perceive this competition as reflecting collective competition between ethnic groups. Since workers and the self-employed can rely on fewer resources and are more directly in competition with ethnic out-groups than other social categories, these categories perceive competition most strongly. Perceived ethnic threat evoked by perceptions of ethnic competition enhances in turn negative sentiments against ethnic out-groups. According to ethnic threat theories, members of a social class thus share similar attitudes toward ethnic out-groups because of their shared competitive economic environment and because of their perceived mutual interest to protect their social class from ethnic outgroups. These theories suggest the *'Class Destination Hypothesis': The impact* of the destination class on antagonistic attitudes is stronger than the impact of the origin class on antagonistic attitudes.

Educational Origin and Destination Status

Past research has consistently found that level of education is one of the strongest correlates of prejudice and attitudes toward out-groups, with higher education associated with lower prejudice. Many have theorized that this holds in part because schools are socializing agents and transmit the prevailing norms of society, which in most Western societies favour tolerance. Moreover, education develops cognitive competence, increases open mindedness, and reduces authoritarian attitudes, all of which tend to foster a more tolerant stance toward ethnic out-groups. Studies have generally not examined the relative impact of parental level of education versus own educational achievement on attitudes toward ethnic out-groups. Applying the distinction we made earlier between socialization and instrumental theories of class position, socialization theory predicts that more educated parents are likely to transmit their tolerant attitudes to the child during both school and pre-school years. This suggests the *'Educational* Origin Hypothesis': The impact of one's own educational achievement on antagonistic attitudes is weaker than the impact of father's educational achievement on antagonistic attitudes.

While parental education is also likely to have an impact on attitudes, we expect a stronger impact of respondent's own education, consistent with past research. There are two reasons for this. First, education itself has a socializing influence that increases acceptance of norms of tolerance, at least in societies in which tolerance is the dominant value orientation. Second, education is important because it has a strong impact on job and class position, and thus affects perceptions of ethnic competition experiences. In fact, Hello, Scheepers, and Sleegers (2006) find education affects social distance attitudes toward ethnic out-groups largely because of its effect on perceived ethnic competition, suggesting this second mechanism is predominant. Because of the combined effect of these mechanisms, we suggest that the more likely hypothesis with regard to education is the '*Educational Destination Hypothesis*': *The impact of* one's own educational achievement on antagonistic attitudes is stronger than the *impact of father's educational achievement on antagonistic attitudes.*

Tolerance and the National Culture

Individuals are influenced by 'the social pressure resulting from the shared values of the other members of the group' (Blau 1960: 191). We assume that this social pressure will not only originate from one's 'educational group' or one's 'social class' but also from the group formed by the people of a nation. The stronger the value climate of tolerance is in a country, the more individuals are thus stimulated to subscribe to these values. The Netherlands, like many other societies, officially condemn intolerance and discrimination. Although support for discrimination has been more widespread in times of high levels of immigration and during times of increasing unemployment, the Dutch majority did not support ethnic discrimination in the period from 1979 to 2002 (Coenders et al. 2008). Even after experiencing an ideological shift from multiculturalism toward assimilation (2001 to 2004), tolerance is the dominant attitude among older and younger generations in The Netherlands. The majority of the Dutch people do not agree that ethnic minorities form a threat, do not hold ethnic stereotypical attitudes, and do not oppose ethnic intermarriage.

Intolerant attitudes are therefore difficult to express without facing social criticism; pressures of social conformity favour more tolerant attitudes. We expect that general social pressures make it less difficult for individuals to adopt attitudes that are in congruence with the dominant norms of society. In the case of prejudice toward ethnic out-groups, these happen to be more tolerant. In summary, we expect the *'Tolerance Dominance Hypothesis'* to hold: *Someone who moves to a social destination of which the immobile* members are in general more tolerant than the immobile members of the social origin will be more likely to adopt the attitudes of the destination than someone who is mobile into a social position of which the immobile members express less tolerant attitudes than the social origin.

Losers of Modernization

The importance of social mobility for attitudes toward ethnic out-groups is also found in the 'losers of modernization' thesis (Scheuch and Klingemann 1967). Downward mobility may determine that people lose connections with society and that problems accumulate among those who experience downward mobility (Bernhardt 2001; Durkheim 1987[1897]). Downward mobility is likely to fuel feelings of subjective deprivation and economic competition. Since intergenerational progress is an important expectation in society, lack of mobility may lead to frustration. Feelings of subjective deprivation, perceptions of competition, and frustration may find a release in antagonistic attitudes toward ethnic out-groups whom become scapegoats (Bettelheim and Janowitz 1964). Consequently, the downward mobile may be especially likely to develop antipathy toward ethnic out-groups. These theories suggest the *'Frustration Hypothesis': Intergenerational downward* mobility induces antagonistic attitudes toward ethnic out-groups above and beyond social origin and destination effects on attitudes.

We test our hypotheses on two different datasets, for two types of mobility (educational and class) and on three different attitudes. We assume that the same mechanisms apply and our results should therefore be consistent.

Data and Methods

The Netherlands *Kinship and Panel Study* (NKPS) wave 2002.2 Within the SOCON a random stratified sampling method is followed: 81 municipalities were randomly selected according to their level of urbanization, followed by a random selection of residents aged 18–70. The response rate of these surveys is approximately 50 per cent. The cooperation rates are: SOCON 1995 51.5 per cent; SOCON 2000 43.7 per cent; SOCON 2005 66.2 per cent. The NKPS is a random sample of individuals within private households in The Netherlands, with a minimum age of 18 and a maximum age of 79. To collect data from the main respondents, Computer Aided Personal Interviewing (CAPI), supplemented with self-completion questionnaires, was used. The overall response rate was 44.7 per cent. Response rates tend to be rather low in The Netherlands, and the response rates of the SOCON and the NKPS are not exceptionally low. The samples of the SOCON are to a large extent representative for the Dutch population. The distribution by sex, urbanization, and matrimonial status in the NKPS sample significantly differs from that in the comparison population. Results based on a weighted sample do not lead to different conclusions as those presented below (results available on request). For further information with regard to the sampling procedure, response rates and the construction of the weight variable we refer to the respective codebooks.

With regard to the educational mobility analyses, we only included respondents older than 25 at which age most people finished their educational career. For the class mobility analyses we excluded all students. The sample sizes used in this contribution depend on the type of intergenerational mobility (educational or class) and the dependent variable in question. Based on the SOCON data sets, we constructed an *ethnic stereotype* scale and an *ethnic threat scale* as dependent variables. The ethnic stereotype scale score was based on the mean score of the following items: 'With Moroccans you never know for certain whether they are going to be aggressive or not', 'Most people from Surinam work quite slowly', 'Gypsies are never to be trusted', 'Turks have so many children because they do not know better yet', and 'When you do business with Jews, you have to be extra careful' With answer categories: (4) agree entirely, (3) agree, (2) don't agree/don't disagree, (1) disagree, and (0) disagree entirely. The Cronbach's alpha of the ethnic stereotype scale is 0.79. For the 1995, 2000, and 2005 waves this is 0.78, 0.83, and 0.76, respectively. If a respondent had one or two missing values on these ethnic stereotype items, we substituted these with the mean values based on the other stereotype items. Missing values were distributed more or less equally across these items (approximately 4 per cent). Results based on a sub-sample of respondents who had valid scores on all five items do not lead to substantially different results (available on request). The ethnic threat scale was a mean score of the items 'The day will come that Dutch people will be fired to give jobs to ethnic minorities' and 'The coming of ethnic minorities to The Netherlands is a threat to our own culture', both with answer categories: (4) agree entirely, (3) agree, (2) don't agree/don't disagree, (1) don't agree, and (0) don't agree at all. The inter-item Pearson correlation coefficient is 0.52. For the 1995, 2000, and 2005 waves this is 0.51, 0.62, and 0.48 respectively. Confirmatory factor analysis showed that the stereotype and ethnic threat dimension are empirically distinguishable (results available on request).

Based on the NKPS data we constructed an *opposition to ethnic intermarriage* scale by adding the scores on three items on views related to ethnic intermarriage with specific ethnic groups. The question is: 'Would it bother you if one of your children decided to marry someone of [Turkish/Moroccan/Surinamese] descent?', with answer categories (4) 'bother me a lot', (3) 'bother me a little', (2) 'neutral', (1) 'not bother me', (0) 'not bother me at all'. Opposition to mixed marriages is an indicator of ethnic exclusionism and is highly related to prejudice and other antagonistic attitudes toward ethnic out-groups. The Cronbach's alpha of the opposition to ethnic intermarriage scale is 0.95.

Social destination is measured either as respondent's current social class or as respondent's highest achieved educational degree. Social origin is either father's social class when the respondent was 15 or father's highest achieved educational degree. The *social class* of respondent's current class position and *father's social class* when the respondent was 15 were measured using a condensed version of the original eleven-category EGP classification scheme created by Erikson, Goldthorpe, and Portocarero (Goldthorpe 2000). In The Netherlands, the majority of the employed male population works in the service class, i.e. as high-and low-grade professionals and managers (classes I and II of the EGP class scheme). Güveli, Need and De Graaf (2007a) argue that in post-industrial societies, within this service class two sub-classes may be distinguished: the socio-cultural specialists (e.g. social workers, teachers, lawyers) and the technocrats (e.g. engineers, accountants, and office managers).

These subclasses are defined according to two criteria: controllability of the work performance and the socio-cultural character of the work tasks. It is relatively harder for employers to monitor sociocultural specialists than technocrats in their work tasks. Furthermore, sociocultural specialists have specific skills and knowledge involving social services and social-cultural issues. Extensive validation tests strongly supports this class distinction for The Netherlands. The final class background categories we used were: (1) technocrats, (2) socio-cultural specialists, (3) routine nonmanual occupations; (4) small employers, (5) manual supervisors and skilled manual occupations, and (6) semi-unskilled manual occupations and farm labourers.

We measured the *education* of the respondent and *father's education* in six categories: (1) university (WO), (2) college (HBO), (3) O and A levels (HAVO/VWO), (4) secondary vocational (MBO), (5) lower secondary education (MAVO) and (6) elementary school and lower vocational school (LBO).

Although the impact of class and educational intergenerational social mobility on antagonistic attitudes is the main focus of this contribution, we also take into account other relevant variables which are likely to affect antagonistic attitudes and which possibly intervene with the impact of social origin and destination positions on these attitudes. *Sex* was coded as (0) male and (1) female. *Church attendance* was used as an indicator for religiosity and was measured in times per year. With regard to the class mobility analyses we controlled for respondent's educational attainment since both father's class position and respondent's educational attainment are causally prior to respondent's class destination. To take into account over time changes in antagonistic attitudes we included the variable *birth cohort.* Birth cohort was coded as survey year minus age at time of survey. Taking into account social position specific birth cohort trends in antagonistic attitudes did not alter our findings (results on request).

We are aware of other alternative explanations for negative attitudes, such as, for example, contact with ethnic minorities and neighbourhood contexts. However, only omitted variables that are related to both the specific negative attitude *and* social mobility possibly bias our estimation of mobility effects. We expect to find mobility effects due to socialization mechanisms or due to a change of competition environment following mobility. Testing whether mobility effects could be explained by for example more or less contact with ethnic minorities or due to a change in residential environment following mobility, although interesting, is beyond the scope of this paper.

MARX AND CLASS CONFLICT

It is important to recognize that Marx viewed the structure of society in relation to its major classes, and the struggle between them as the engine of change in this structure. His was no equilibrium or consensus theory. Conflict was not deviational within society's structure, nor were classes functional elements maintaining the system. The structure itself was a derivative of and ingredient in the struggle of classes. His was a conflict view of modem (nineteenth century) society.

The key to understanding Marx is his class definition. A class is defined by the ownership of property. Such ownership vests a person with the power to exclude others from the property and to use it for personal purposes. In relation to property there are three great classes of society: the bourgeoisie (who own the means of production such as machinery and factory buildings, and whose source of income is profit), landowners (whose income is rent), and the proletariat (who own their labour and sell it for a wage).

Class thus is determined by property, not by income or status. These are determined by distribution and consumption, which itself ultimately reflects the production and power relations of classes. The social conditions of bourgeoisie production are defined by bourgeois property. Class is therefore a theoretical and formal relationship among individuals. The force transforming latent class membership into a struggle of classes is *class interest*. Out of similar *class situations*, individuals come to act similarly. They develop a mutual dependence, a community, a shared interest interrelated with a common income of profit or of wages. From this common interest classes are formed, and for Marx, individuals form classes to the extent that their interests engage them in a struggle with the opposite class.

At first, the interests associated with land ownership and rent are different from those of the bourgeoisie. But as society matures, capital (i.e., the property of production) and land ownership merge, as do the interests of landowners and bourgeoisie. Finally the relation of production, the natural opposition between proletariat and bourgeoisie, determines all other activities. As Marx saw the development of class conflict, the struggle between classes was initially confined to individual factories. Eventually, given the maturing of capitalism, the growing disparity between life conditions of bourgeoisie and proletariat, and the increasing homogenization within each class, individual struggles become generalized to coalitions across factories. Increasingly class conflict is manifested at the societal level. Class consciousness is increased, common interests and policies are organized, and the use of and struggle for political power occurs. Classes become political forces.

The distribution of political power is determined by power over production (i.e., capital). Capital confers political power, which the bourgeois class uses to legitimatize and protect their property and consequent social relations. Class relations are political, and in the mature capitalist society, the state's business is that of the bourgeoisie. Moreover, the intellectual basis of state rule, the ideas justifying the use of state power and its distribution, are those of the ruling class. The intellectual-social culture is merely a superstructure resting on the relation of production, on ownership of the means of production.

Finally, the division between classes will widen and the condition of the exploited worker will deteriorate so badly that social structure collapses: the class struggle is transformed into a proletarian revolution. The workers' triumph will eliminate the basis of class division in property through public ownership of the means of production. With the basis of classes thus wiped away, a classless society will ensue (by definition), and since political power to protect the bourgeoisie against the workers is unnecessary, political authority and the state will wither away.

Overall, there are six elements in Marx's view of class conflict.

- Classes are authority relationships based on property ownership.
- A class defines groupings of individuals with shared life situations, thus interests.
- Classes are naturally antagonistic by virtue of their interests.
- Imminent within modern society is the growth of two antagonistic classes and their struggle, which eventually absorbs all social relations.
- Political organization and Power is an instrumentality of class struggle, and reigning ideas are its reflection.
- Structural change is a consequence of the class struggle.

Marx's emphasis on class conflict as constituting the dynamics of social change, his awareness that change was not random but the outcome of a conflict of interests, and his view of social relations as based on power were contributions of the first magnitude. However, time and history have invalidated many of his assumptions and predictions. Capitalist ownership and control of production have been separated. Joint stock companies forming most of the industrial sector are now almost wholly operated by non-capital-owning managers.

Workers have not grown homogeneous but are divided and subdivided into different skill groups. Class stability has been undercut by the development of a large middle class and considerable social mobility. Rather than increasing extremes of wealth and poverty, there has been a social levelling and an increasing emphasis on social justice. And finally, bourgeois political power has progressively weakened with growth in worker oriented legislation and of labour-oriented parties, and with a narrowing of the rights and privileges of capital ownership. Most important, the severest manifestation of conflict between workers and capitalist—the strike—has been institutionalized through collective bargaining legislation and the legalization of strikes.

These historical events and trends notwithstanding, the sociological outlines of Marx's approach have much value. His emphasis on conflict, on classes, on their relations to the state, and on social change was a powerful perspective that should not be discarded. The spirit, if not the substance, of his theory is worth developing.

9

Concept of Patriarchy

The concept of patriarchy has evolved from the struggles of women all over the world. It encompasses the totality of structures of Domination and Exploitation that affect women's position in society.

The term patriarchy essentially means the rule of the father or the patriarch (a male member of the household or society). In feminist theory and practice, patriarchy has been looked at differently from the liberal to socialist feminism. Defined simply however, it implies a system in which the father or a male member who is considered as the head of the family, controls all economic and property resources, makes all the major decisions of the family and thereby maintains ongoing control over all members of the family and those related to it. Very clearly, this system establishes male dominance and control over women in society, in general, and particularly so within the family. The "unequal power relationship" between men and women, accrues power to men in an important institution of society. Thus, it is important to see patriarchy as both an ideology of women's subordination and control, and, a concept of struggle against the same.

The origins of patriarchy can be traced through different stages of civilisation and, several views have been expressed regarding the origins of patriarchy and its universality. Its roots have been traced in history, religion and in nature. For some, patriarchy as a system has a beginning in history, is man made and thus can be ended by historical processes in the future. For others, patriarchy is a natural phenomenon, i.e., it is based on biological differentiation of human beings into male and female categories. It is understood that, patriarchy is universal, God given, natural and cannot be questioned. Therefore to change patriarchy would amount to changing nature. Still others, have not accepted the above explanations and have talked about the existence of a stage in society prior to patriarchy – that of a matriarchal or matrilineal society, where have had a dominant status. Evidence for such a society is quoted till today, through religious myths and symbols over different periods in history, citing examples of matrilineal heritage in some parts of India, especially Kerala.

While we can endlessly debate on the differing perceptions about the origins of patriarchy, it is more significant to understand the modes of patriarchal control and its institutional manifestations as it has impacted upon processes of women's subordination in society.

In this context, one would also like to analyse the often asked question "Do women have no power at all?" It has been seen that women are not totally powerless or totally deprived of rights, influence and resources, but that they are subservient to male control. Men have laid down the acceptable social norms for women – the role models for women in society. Women are thus made unwitting partners in the perpetuation of the patriarchal system, in different ways: "Gender indoctrination (i.e., role stereotyping of men and women), denial of education and knowledge of their own history, dividing women from one another, by defining norms of behaviour i.e., respectability and deviance according to their sexual activities, by discriminating women in access, and/or control over economic resources and political power, etc."

Since patriarchy is perpetuated through a process of institutionalisation of the social, cultural and religious practices in society, as well as legitimised through the political, legal and economic systems of society, it leads women to internalise, as well as further perpetuate patriarchal ways of thinking, both in values and behaviour. Therefore, women are not part of this system or out of it by choice alone. The system is so complex with interplaying factors such as sex, gender, class, caste, ethnicity, and race that it encircles women within its control of exploitation, discrimination and oppression. It is this cycle that needs to be understood by women themselves and by those who are working to support women's struggles in society.

WOMEN'S EQUALITY

The rising demand for women's equality began to take shape in the middle of the nineteenth century and continues as a transformative force today (Brown 1993). Early on, American feminists mobilized to abolish discrimination that legally subordinated women to men and basically made a mockery of the nation's claim to be a community of equals (Brown 1993). Success came when the Nineteenth Amendment to the Constitution was ratified in 1920, and over time the right to vote became a reality for all women, as poll taxes and other racial restrictions were eliminated, thus today women exercise the franchise on an equal footing with men (Brown 1993). In 1923, the Supreme Court struck down a Washington, D.C. minimum wage law that applied only to women (Brown 1993).

Although in the beginning, women came in small numbers, today their numbers equal or surpass their male classmates in graduation rates (Meirowitz 2005). Over the past 150 years, the long-term shift toward gender equality: activities and power shifted out of the household into modern economic, political, and educational institutions whose logic and structure gave men less interest in womens subordination (England 1999). The Nineteenth Amendment brought women into political citizenship after centuries of exclusion by men (Brown 1993). By 1990, approximately 70 percent of wives between ages 20 and 54 were in the labour force, compared to less than 20 percent in 1940, and only 5 percent in 1900 (Oppenheimer 1994). Although married womens employment increased gradually throughout the first 40 years of the twentieth century, the major transformation in economic behaviour came after 1940 (Oppenheimer 1994). Between 1940 and 1960, wives labour force participation either doubled or tripled, depending on the age group; and between 1960 and 1980 there was another leap in work rates, especially for younger wives, and these rates continued to increase during the 1980 (Oppenheimer 1994).

Since the founding of American universities in the seventeenth century, educators and students have been divided concerning the roles of women in institutions of higher learning (Meirowitz 2005). This decision marked a sharp reversal in the Courts approach to female-specific labour laws, and the court justified its move by endorsing an equality for women, thus women had stepped forward from an oppressive past to claim the vote and with it, a full measure of equality (Brown 1993). While many American universities have been coeducational since their inception, the majority of colleges and universities only provided single-sex education until the middle of the twentieth century (Meirowitz 2005). After the civil rights and feminists movements in the 1960, many single-sex colleges and universities began admitting both men and women, diversifying by gender as well by race, religion, and class (Meirowitz 2005). pital is known as one of the Courts liberty of contract decisions, which nullified various labour laws as infringements of the constitutional rights of employers and workers to negotiate the terms of employment freely (Brown 1993). Although some women were attending coeducational and womens colleges in the nineteenth and early twentieth centuries, it was really not until the civil rights and feminist movements of the 1960 and 1970 that most mens colleges began to admit women (Meirowitz 2005).

THEORIES OF PATRIARCHY

Assess the claim that gender inequalities in the domestic and occupational divisions of labour are best understood with reference to the concept of patriarchy. You should illustrate your answer with reference to a range of feminist perspectives. Western female thought through the centuries has identified the relationship between patriarchy and gender as crucial to the women's subordinate position. For two hundred years, patriarchy precluded women from having a legal or political identity and the legislation and attitudes supporting this provided the model for slavery. In the late 19th and early 20th centuries suffrage campaigners succeeded in securing some legal and political rights for women in the UK. By the middle of the 20th century, the emphasis had shifted from suffrage to social and economic equality in the public and private sphere and the women's movement that sprung up during the 1960s began to argue that women were oppressed by patriarchal structures. Equal status for women of all races, classes, sexualities and abilities-in the 21st century these feminist claims for equality are generally accepted as reasonable principles in western society.

The feminist engagement with theories of patriarchy criticised pre-existing theoretical positions and their ideological use, tracing theoretical progenitors of popular views about gender, gender roles etc (Cooper, 1995; Raymond, 1980). Coole et al (1990) point out that the functional needs served by the nuclear element of the nuclear family are neither exclusive nor universal which indicates that differentiation it is not essential to the performance of the vital functions of the family. The differential relationships that identify the roles of wife and mother are part of the nuclear family model promoted by patriarchal ideologies for more than one hundred and fifty years. The male patriarch in the household is both the oppressor and recipient of womens subordination. For example, Irigaray (1985) proposed that this be done through the promotion of entre-femmes, a kind of social form specific to women. These activities are imposed and remunerated in a specific and unequal manner. It was not until feminists in the 1960s began to explore the features and institutions of patriarchy, that the power of the concept to explain womens subordinate position in society was proven (Seidman, 1994).

GENDER AND POWER IN THE WORKPLACE

This paper is an analysis of contemporary issues associated with gender and power in the workplace; which will specifically include a discussion of gender relations, stereotyping, women's identity, the structuring of formal and informal power, sources of inequality, and sexual harassment. The concept of gender in relation to the division of labour in the workplace, and in relation to issues of power and control is an unfortunate, groundless stereotype. Suzanne Tallichet notes that the gendered division of workplace labour is rooted in erroneous ideology of innate sex differences in traits and abilities, and operates through various control mechanisms. (Tallichet 1995: 698) These control mechanisms are primarily exercised by men over women and serve to exaggerate differences between the sexes, especially surrounding women's presumed incapability for doing male identified work. Tallichet notes that most forms of workplace control take the form of harassment, sexual bribery, and gender based jokes and comments, and profanity, which passively but succinctly make gender differences a salient aspect of work relations.

Monica Boyd (1997: 64) proposes that power inequality in the workplace between genders has been maintained through occupational segregation, because it is the occupations themselves which differ in the capacity that incumbents have to impose their will upon others. Boyd is able to back her claims by noting that Canadian women are employed in positions with fewer decision making powers; women are more likely to supervise other women only; and although women have increased their presence in the workforce, this presence is mostly in the service industry only, and that this increase in presence has not converted into a presence of power. The organizational model suggests that the structural aspects of organizations promote power inequalities between individuals and set the stage for sexual harassment; while sociocultural models reflect a feminist perspective, conceptualizing sexual harassment as an outcome of patriarchal systems that enable men to exercise sexual power to assert and maintain male dominance. " Australian New Zealand Journal of Sociology. "Gendered Relations in the Mines and the Division of Labour Underground. Perhaps a strategy then for the exploited female subordinate class could be to develop an autonomous informal power structure to balance against the patriarchal dominance of their supervisors. Perhaps the most common and widely accepted form of inequality in the workplace is the hiring and treatment of part-time workers. " American Journal of Sociology. These traditional roles and consequently womens identities have been formed and maintained by the workplace, therefore understanding any gendered differences in labour requires an examination in this light.

UNDERSTANDING PATRIARCHY

Subordination of women to men is prevalent in large parts

of the world. We come across experiences where women are not only treated as subordinate to men but are also subject to discriminations, humiliations, exploitations, oppressions, control and violence. Women experience discrimination and unequal treatment in terms of basic right to food, health care, education, employment, control over productive resources, decision-making and livelihood not because of their biological differences or sex, which is natural but because of their gender differences which is a social construct. "Sex is considered a fact-one is born with either male or female genitalia. Gender is considered a social construction-it grants meaning to the fact of sex. Conversely, it could be said that only after specific meanings came to be attached to the sexes, did sex differences become pertinent" (Geetha, 2002: 10). Gender based discriminations and exploitations are widespread and the socio-culturally defined characteristics, aptitudes, abilities, desires, personality traits, roles, responsibilities and behavioural patterns of men and women contribute to the inequalities and hierarchies in society. Gender differences are man made and they get legitimised in a patriarchal society. This paper attempts to link the theoretical dimensions of patriarchy with its empirical experiences to engage in the ongoing debates and discussion on "patriarchy" which manifests itself in various forms of discriminations, inequalities, hierarchies, inferior status and position of women in society. Thus it is important to understand patriarchy in terms of its multiplicity, complexities and dynamics.

What is Patriarchy?

Patriarchy literally means rule of the father in a male-dominated family. It is a social and ideological construct which considers men (who are the patriarchs) as superior to women. Sylvia Walby in *"Theorising Patriarchy"* calls it "a system of social structures and practices in which men dominate, oppress and exploit women" (Walby, 1990). Patriarchy is based on a system of power relations which are hierarchical and unequal where men control women's production, reproduction and sexuality. It imposes masculinity and femininity character stereotypes in society which strengthen the iniquitous power relations between men and women. Patriarchy is not a constant and gender relations which are dynamic and complex have changed over the periods of history. The nature of control and subjugation of women varies from one society to the other as it differs due to the differences in class, caste, religion, region, ethnicity and the socio-cultural practices. Thus in the context of India, brahminical patriarchy, tribal patriarchy and dalit patriarchy are different from each other. Patriarchy within a particular caste or class also differs in terms of their religious and regional variations. Similarly subordination of women in developed countries is different from what it is in developing countries.

While subordination of women may differ in terms of its nature, certain characteristics such as control over women's sexuality and her reproductive power cuts across class, caste, ethnicity, religions and regions and is common to all patriarchies. This control has developed historically and is institutionalized and legitimized by several ideologies, social practices and institutions such as family, religion, caste, education, media, law, state and society, which are discussed in the later sections. Patriarchal societies propagate the ideology of motherhood which restrict women's mobility and burdens them with the responsibilities to nurture and rear children. The biological factor to bear children is linked to the social position of women's responsibilities of motherhood: nurturing, educating and raising children by devoting themselves to family.

"Patriarchal ideas blur the distinction between *sex and gender* and assume that all socio-economic and political distinctions between men and women are rooted in biology or anatomy" (Heywood, 2003: 248). Gender like social class, caste, race or religion is a significant social cleavage and it is important to analyse it to understand social inequalities, oppressions and unequal relationship between men and women. It has been explained by feminist scholars/thinkers/writers who believe that the theory of 'sexual politics' and 'sexism' are conscious parallels with theory of 'class politics' and 'racism' to understand oppression of women. The traditionalist view accepts patriarchy as biologically determined and as the biological functions of men and women are different, the social roles and tasks assigned for women are also different. Sigmund Freud stated that for women 'anatomy is destiny' and it is women's biology which primarily determine their psychology and hence their abilities and roles. Similarly the traditional notion of 'public-private divide' which located politics in the public sphere and family and personal relationships in private sphere as non-political, believed that sexual inequality is natural and not political. While the political sphere was preserved for men the private sphere was reserved for women as housewives and mothers who were excluded from politics. These theories of male supremacy have been challenged and opposed by feminists as they lack historical or scientific evidence. Feminists argue that the biological difference might lead to some difference in their roles, but the former should not become the basis of a sexual hierarchy in which men are dominant. The dismantling of these theories enables us to acknowledge that patriarchy is man-made and has developed historically by the socio-economic and political processes in society.

Gerda Lerner in *"The Creation of Patriarchy"* (1986) has argued against single cause theories and against looking for one historical moment when patriarchy was established. Patriarchy has been conceptualized and analyzed by several feminist scholars in different ways. Feminists have challenged patriarchal knowledge, ideology, values and its practice. Despite a range of common themes within feminism, disagreements exist amongst the feminists in understanding patriarchy. All feminists do not like the term "patriarchy" for various reasons and prefer the term "gender" and "gender oppression". Patriarchy has remained a relatively undefined concept and some feminist scholars are at unease with the use of the concept of 'patriarchy' when it involves the notion of a general system of inequality. Michele Barrett argues that the use of the term patriarchy assumes that the relation between men and women is unchanging and universalistic. She suggests that it can only be appropriate if it is defined very narrowly and refers to specific aspects of ideological relations such as those of father-daughter relationship described in Virginia Woolf's Three Guineas (Barrett, 1980: 15). The use of the term often involves confusion between 'patriarchy' as rule of the father and 'patriarchy' as men's domination of women (ibid, 16). However, Sylvia Walby critiques Barrett as the problem is not with the concept itself but with the way it is used in specific texts as it involves problems of reductionism, biologism, universalism, and therefore the inconsistent definition of patriarchy needs be overcome in an adequate analysis of gender inequality (Walby, 1986: 28). Sheila Rowbotham also argues that 'the term patriarchy necessarily implies a conception of women's oppression that is universalistic, ahistoric and essentially biologistic and that it incorrectly leads to a search for a single cause of women's oppression either in a base super-structure model or as quest for ultimate origins from capitalist relations'.

Suma Chitnis (2004) argues that because of the inadequate note of historical circumstances and values that render women's issues different in India, a large section of the population recoils from the feminist rhetoric. Similarly the unease with the term patriarchy is because of the role that men have played in the emergence and growth of women's question in India. In a hierarchical society often gender oppression is linked with oppressions based on caste, class, community, tribe and religion, and in such multiple patriarchies "men as the principal oppressors" is not easily accepted. However, Mary E. John argues that multiple patriarchies which are byproducts of discrimination along class, caste and communal lines, are diverse in nature and it is because of the unequal patriarchies that "there is a need to conceptualize the complex articulation of different patriarchies, along with the distinct and equally challenging question of how subaltern genders are relating to questions of power in the current conjuncture" (John, 2004: 66).

The assertion of autonomous dalit women's organizations have thrown up several crucial theoretical and political challenges besides underlying the brahmanism of feminist movements and patriarchal practices of dalit politics. Within the framework of 'difference' the issues of caste is primarily responsible for oppression of dalit women (Rege, 2004: 211). Sharmila Rege argues that the category of 'difference' has been brought to the centre of feminist analysis by the black and third world feminists who question the sex/class debate of the 1970s and argue that the complex interplay between sex, class, race need to be underlined. Vaid and Sangari make a distinction between "the modernizing of patriarchal modes of regulating women" and the "democratizing of gender relations" both at home and work place and underline both the revolutionary potential and inherent contradictions that the democratizing movements constituted for peasants and working class women. Thus feminist historiography made radical breakthroughs in redefining gender and patriarchies in the context of hierarchies of caste, class, community and ethnicity. Therefore it is pertinent to underline several perspectives of feminism for a comprehensive understanding of patriarchy in terms of its origin, characteristics, nature, structures and persistence.

Feminism

"Feminism is an awareness of patriarchal control, exploitation and oppression at the material and ideological levels of women's labour, fertility and sexuality, in the family, at the place of work and in society in general, and conscious action by women and men to transform the present situation" (Bhasin and Khan, 1999: 3). It is a struggle to achieve equality, dignity, rights, freedom for women to control their lives and bodies both within home and outside. As a cross cutting ideology feminists have different political positions and therefore address a range of issues such as female suffrage, equal legal rights, right to education, access to productive resources, right to participate in decision-making, legalization of abortion, recognition of property rights and abolition of domestic violence. Thus feminism passed through several paradigms which are referred to as first wave and second wave of feminism. Since the origin of patriarchy and establishment of male supremacy can be traced to different factors and forces feminists differ in their approach to understand patriarchy and adopt different strategies to abolish it. One way to understand the various dimensions of feminist theories and their theoretical approaches to understand patriarchy is to locate them within the broader philosophical and political perspectives that have been broadly classified as Liberal, Marxist, Socialist and Radical. However, despite the ideological differences between the feminist groups, they are united in their struggle against unequal and hierarchical relationships between men and women, which is no longer accepted as biological destiny.

Feminist theorists generally share four concerns (i) They seek to understand the gendered nature of all social and institutional relations, which determines who does what for whom, what we are and what we might become. (ii) Gender relations are considered as problematic and as related to other inequalities and contradictions in social life. "Family, education and welfare, worlds of work and politics, culture and leisure are socially structured through relations of gender, power, class, race and sexuality". (iii) Gender relations are not viewed as either natural or immutable but as historical and socio-cultural productions, subject to reconstitution. In particular feminist analysis deconstructs errors and myths about women's empirical realities, and constructs theories by and about women. (iv) Feminist theorists tend to be explicitly political about their advocacy about social change. They challenge the traditional race-class-sexuality-power arrangements which favour men over women, white over non-whites, adults over children and their struggle to embrace inclusivity continues.

Since feminism is not ahistoric, understanding several perspectives of it engages us in understanding the history of feminism. An uneasy relationship with western 'feminism' and the claim for an "indigenous feminism" led to the search for the indigenous roots of feminism, which is often linked to our colonial past. Kumari Jayawardena defines feminism as "embracing movements for equality within the current system and significant struggles that have attempted to change the system". She asserts that these movements arose in the context of i) the formulation and consolidation of national identities which modernized antiimperialist movements during the independence struggle and ii) the remaking of pre-capitalist religion and feudal structures in attempt to modernize third world societies. Indian feminists like Veena Mazumdar link the antiimperialist struggle of the national movement with awareness of women's issues as "the independence of the country and of women has become so intertwined as to be identical".

Whether women's movements from the Seventies onwards can only be termed as feminist is an equally important question of concern to some feminist scholars. With the women's movement gaining momentum sharp critiques of mainstream conceptualization of work, development, legal process and the state emerged, which led to several theoretical and praxiological reformulations. It led to the debates of class v/s patriarchy, caste v/s patriarchy and women's movements have addressed issues concerning women of working class, dalit, tribal and minorities. Gopal Guru located the need for dalit women to talk differently in a discourse of descent against the middle class women's movement by dalit men and the moral economy of peasant movement. He argues that social location determines the perception of reality and therefore representation of dalit women by non-dalit women was less valid and less authentic. A dalit feminist standpoint is seen as emancipatory as it places emphasis on individual experiences within socially constructed groups and focuses on the hierarchical, multiple, changing structural power relations of caste, class, ethnic, which construct such a group (Rege, 2004: 222). Since dalit women is not a homogeneous group, the dalit feminist standpoint is open to interrogations and revisions and the subject of dalit women's standpoint is multiple, heterogeneous and contradictory (ibid).

Since in the Indian context questions of cultural identity, difference, plurality and diversity have been important, some Indian feminists in their effort to counter attacks of being western have turned out to "Hindu iconography and Sanskrit idioms denoting women's power, thus inadvertently strengthening communal identity that Indian, Hindu and Sanskrit are synonymous". Flavia Agnes critiques such feminist groups. Maitrayee Chaudhuri also argues that in India the battle for recognition of 'difference' had to be worked out independently without the accepted terminology of today's western feminism or multiculturalism Chaudhuri, 2004: xxii). "Within the Indian sub-continent there have been infinite variations on the status of women diverging according to cultural milieu, family structure, class, caste, property rights and morals" (Thapar, 1975: 6). Therefore despite several debates and discussion on Indian women's movement there have been no clear ideological lines drawn and no major trends have emerged. In fact, the women's issues taken up in the women's movement since 1975 have arisen out of the movement itself and have been taken up by women's groups representing all ideologies and tendencies (Omvedt, 2004: 180). The effort to characterize the specificity of women's oppression and to analyse the links with other forms of social oppression is more an ongoing theoretical research rather than an ideological dividing line (ibid, 181). In India almost all feminists agree that women's movement has to be linked to broader movements against all kinds of social oppression (ibid, 183). While in the West there have been a wide variety of feminist positions, from those stressing male power and sexual dominance to "Marxist – Feminist" positions stressing social production, in India it has been mainly the Marxist who have dealt with the issue of women's oppression and subjugation though there have been varying approaches.

Approaches to Understand Patriarchy

Liberal Feminism: Liberal feminists have championed equal legal and political rights for women to enable them to compete with men in the public realm on equal terms. The philosophical basis of liberal feminism lies in the principle of individualism and they campaigned for all individuals to participate in public and political life. Several women's movement demanded female suffrage during the 1840s and 1850s in United States and United Kingdom. The famous Seneca Falls Convention in 1848 marked the birth of women's rights movement which among other things called for female suffrage. Women were granted the right to vote in the US Constitution in 1920. In UK though franchise was extended to women in 1918 for a decade they did not exercise equal voting rights with men. Mary Wollstonecraft's *"Vindication of the Rights of Women"* (1972) was the first text of modern feminism which campaigned for women's right to vote/female suffrage. Wollstonecraft claimed that if women gained access to education as rational creatures in their own right the distinction of sex would become unimportant in political and social life. John Stuart Mill in collaboration with Harriet Taylor in *"The Subjection of Women"* (1970) proposed that women should be entitled to the citizenship and political rights and liberties enjoyed by men. It indicts traditional arrangements of work and family as tyrannizing women and denying them freedom of choice. Thus, liberal feminists believed that female suffrage would do away with all forms of sexual discrimination and prejudice. Walby contends that "first wave feminism was a large, multifaceted, long-lived and highly effective political phenomenon" (Walby, 1997:149).

Betty Friedan's *"The Feminine Mystique"* marked the resurgence of liberal feminist thought in the 1960s and is often credited as stimulating the emergence of 'second wave' feminism. She referred to the cultural myth that women seek security and fulfilment in domestic life and that their feminine behaviour serves to discourage women from entering employment, politics and public life in general. In *"The Second Stage"* (1983) Friedan "discussed the problem of reconciling the achievement of personhood by making it possible to open up broader opportunities for women in work and public life while continuing to give central importance to family in women's life which has been criticized by radical feminists as contributing to 'mystique of motherhood"(Heywood, 2003: 254).

Therefore, liberal feminism is essentially reformist and does not challenge the patriarchal structure of society itself. Critics suggest that the liberal reforms to increase opportunities for women, prohibit discriminations and to increase public consciousness of women's rights have not been shared equally by all women because these changes have not addressed issues of socially structured inequalities (Mandell, 1995: 8). Thus, while the first wave feminism ended with winning suffrage rights the emergence of second wave feminism in 1960s acknowledged that political and legal rights were insufficient to change women's subordination. Feminist ideas and arguments became radical and revolutionary thereafter.

Marxist Feminism: Marxist feminist believed that both subordination of women and division of classes developed historically with the development of private property. Frederick Engels in *"The Origin of Family, Private Property and the State"* (1884) stated that with the emergence of private property, women's housework sank into insignificance in comparison to man's productive labour. 'The world historical defeat of the female sex with the establishment of capitalism based on private property ownership by men did away with inheritance of property and social position through female line'. Thus maternal authority gave place to paternal authority and property was to be inherited from father to son and not from woman to her clan. The bourgeois families which owned private property emerged as patriarchal families where women were subjugated. Such patriarchal families became oppressive as men ensured that their property passed on only to their sons. Therefore bourgeois family and private property as a byproduct of capitalism subordinated and oppressed women. Marxist feminists unlike the radical feminists argue that class exploitation is deeper than sexual oppression and women's emancipation essentially requires social revolution which will overthrow capitalism and establish socialism. Engels believed that "in a socialist society marriage will be dissolvable and that once private property is abolished its patriarchal features and perhaps also monogamy will disappear". Therefore Marxist feminists like many socialist feminists connect structural changes in kinship relations and changes in the division of labour to understand women's position in society. They argue that it is not women's biology alone but, private property and monogamous marriage, economic and political dominance by men and their control over female sexuality which led to patriarchy. However, the Marxist feminists have been criticized for differentiating working class women and bourgeois women and also for the focus on economic factors to explain subordination of women. Recent socialist feminists critique traditional Marxist feminists as the later emphasize only on economic origins of gender inequality and state that female subordination occurs also in pre-capitalist and socialist systems (Mandell, 1995: 10). In fact socialist feminists accuse Marxists feminists of being 'sex blind' and only adding women to their existing critique of capitalism (Hartmann, 1979).

Socialist Feminism: Unlike the liberal feminists, socialist feminist argue that women do not simply face political and legal disadvantages which can be solved by equal legal rights and opportunities but the relationship between sexes is rooted in the social and economic structure itself. Therefore women can only be emancipated after social revolution brings about structural change. Socialist feminists deny the necessary and logical link between sex and gender differences. They argue that the link between child bearing and child rearing is cultural rather than biological and have challenged that biology is destiny by drawing a sharp distinction between 'sex and gender'. Therefore, while liberal feminist takes women's equality with men as their major political goal, socialist feminism aim at transforming basic structural arrangements of society so that categories of class, gender, sexuality and race no longer act as barriers to share equal resources (Mandell, 1995: 9). Gerda Lerner's (1986) explains how control over female sexuality is central to women's subordination. She argues that it is important to understand how production as well as reproduction was organized. The appropriation and commodification of women's sexual and reproductive capacity by men lies at the foundation of private property, institutionalization of slavery, women's sexual subordination and economic dependency on male.

Most socialist feminists agree that the confinement of women to the domestic sphere of housework and motherhood serves the economic interests of capitalism. Women relieve men of the burden of housework and child rearing, and allow them to concentrate on productive employment. Thus unpaid domestic labour contributes to the health and efficiency of capitalist economy and also accounts for the low social status and economic dependence of women on men. But, unlike the Marxist feminists, socialist feminists look at both relations of production as well as relations of reproduction to understand patriarchy. Unlike orthodox Marxists who have prioritized class politics over sexual politics, modern socialist feminists give importance to the later. They believe that socialism in itself will not end patriarchy as it has cultural and ideological roots.

In *'Women's Estate'* (1971) Juliet Mitchell believes that gender relations are a part of the super structure and patriarchy is located in the ideological level while capitalism in the economical level (Mitchell, 1975: 412). Like traditional Marxist analysis she fails to consider the significance of sexual division of labour as an economical phenomenon (Walby, 1986: 34). She argues that patriarchal law is that of the rule of the father, which operates through the kinship system rather than domination of men. Mitchell stated that women fulfil four social functions (i) They are members of workforce and are active in production, (ii) they bear children and thus reproduce human species (iii) they are responsible for socializing children and (iv) they are sex objects. Therefore "women can achieve emancipation only when they liberate from each of these areas and not only when socialism replaces capitalism". Walby critiques Mitchell as she fails to consider the material benefits that men derive from women's unpaid domestic labour and the significance of men's organized attempts to limit women's access to paid work. On the other hand, Delphy argues that the basis of gender relations is the domestic mode of production in which the husband expropriates the wife's labour (Delphy, 1977: 37). Women share a common class position and are exploited by men as a class. Thus it is not women's position within the domestic mode of production which is the basis of their class oppression alone but it is their main form of subordination. The forms of oppression outside the family therefore derive from oppressions within the family (Walby, 1986: 38). She further argues that women's relation to production is not determined by content of the task but by the nature of the social relations under which they labour. Therefore it is the relations of production which explain why their work is excluded from the realm of value (ibid, 4). Delphy has been critiqued by Molyneux for placing all women in one class without making a distinction between the bourgeoisie and proletariat (Molyneux. 1979: 14).

Similarly Zillah Eisenstein in *"Capitalist Patriarchy and the Case for Socialist Feminism"* (1979) argues that 'male supremacy and capitalism are the core relations which determine oppression of women' She defines patriarchy as a "sexual system of power in which the male possesses superior power and economic privilege' (Eisenstein 1979:17). Patriarchy is not the direct result of biological differentiation but ideological and political interpretations of these differentiations. "On the one hand the capitalist live a process in which exploitation occurs and on the other the patriarchal sexual hierarchy in which the women is mother, domestic labourer and consumer and in which the oppression of women occurs". Social relations of reproduction are therefore important and they are not the result of capitalist relations but cultural relations. Thus, while in her early work in 1979 there was greater stress on the synthesis between capitalism and patriarchy, in her later work in 1984, there is more recognition of conflict and tensions between the two (Walby, 1986: 31). Heidi Hartmann (1979) argues that both patriarchy and capitalism are independent yet are interacting social structures. She believes that "We can usefully define patriarchy as a set of social relations between men who have a material base who through hierarchical, establish/create interdependence and solidarity among men and enable them to dominate women (Hartmann, 1979: 11). She argues that historically both had important effects on each other as the material base upon which patriarchy rests lies most fundamentally in men's control over women's labour power. "In capitalist societies a healthy and strong partnership exists between patriarchy and capitalism" (ibid, 13). She has been critiqued for paying insufficient attention to tension and conflict between capitalism and patriarchy (Walby, 1986: 44).

Maria Mies, in her paper *"The Social Origins of the Sexual Division of Labour"* refers to women's labour as 'shadow work'. She suggests that we should no longer look at the sexual division of labour as a problem related to the family, but rather as a structural problem of a whole society. The hierarchical division of labour between men and women and its dynamics form an integral part of dominant production relations i.e. class relations of a particular epoch and society and of the broader national and international divisions of labour. She argues that the asymmetric division of labour by sex, once established by means of viclence was upheld by such institutions as the family and the state and also by the powerful ideological systems. The patriarchal religions have defined women as part of nature which has to be controlled and dominated by man (ibid, 33).

Thus, socialist feminists have advanced theoretical boundaries by analysing the ways class and gender relations intersect. Economic class relations are important in determining women's status but gender relations are equally significant and therefore eradicating social class inequality alone will not necessarily eliminate sexism. Patriarchy existed before capitalism and continued to exist in both capitalism and other political-economic systems (Mandell, 1995: 11). However, patriarchy and capitalism are concretely intertwined and mutually supportive system of oppressions. Women's subordination within capitalism results from their economic exploitation as wage labourers and their patriarchal oppression as mothers, consumers and domestic labourers (ibid, 13).

Sylvia Walby in *'Patriarchy at Work'* (1986) attempts to conceptualise patriarchy not only in terms of the complexity of relationships of gender but also subtleties of interconnections of patriarchy with capitalism, which is a relationship of tension and conflict and not of harmony and mutual accommodation. Domestic labour is a distinct form of labour and core to patriarchal mode of production which is essential to exploitation of women by men and is independent of exploitation of proletariats by the capitalists (Walby, 1986: 52). Within the household women provide all kinds of services to their children, husband and other members of the family, in other words in the patriarchal mode of production, women's labour is expropriated by their husbands and others who live there. The control over and exploitation of women's labour benefit men materially and economically. "Patriarchy is a system of interrelated social structures through which men exploit" (ibid, 51). She states that gender relations need to be explained at the level of social relations and not as individuals. Within the patriarchal mode of production, the producing class comprises of women and domestic labourer and husbands are the non-producing and exploiting class. And domestic labourer works to replenish/produce his/their labour power, she is separated from the product of her labour and has no control over it, while the husband always has control over the labour power which the wife has produced. She is separated from if at every level, physically, in the ability to use it, legally, ideologically etc. (ibid, 53). Thus the domestic labourer is exploited as the husband has the control over the wage he receives from the capitalist in exchange of his labour. The relations of production in such a mode of production are personalized relations between individuals (ibid, 54). When the patriarchal mode of production articulates with the capitalist mode, women are prevented from entering paid work as freely as men and are reinforced by patriarchal state policies.

The state is a site of patriarchal relations which is necessary to patriarchy as a whole as it upholds the oppression of women by supporting a form of household in which women provide unpaid domestic services to male (ibid). Thus capitalism benefits from a particular form of family which ensures cheap reproduction of labour power and the availability of women as a reserve army. Patriarchy is also located in the social relations of reproduction and masculinity and femininity are not biological givens but products of long historical process. Thus, socialist feminists combine both marxist and radical approach and neither is sufficient by itself. Patriarchy is connected to both relations of production and relations of reproduction. Therefore reactionary feminism differed from conventional feminism challenging the traditional public/private divide and the influence of patriarchy not only in politics, public life and economy but also in all aspects of social, personal, psychological and sexual existence. This was evident in the pioneering work of radical feminists. Kate Millet's *"Sexual Politics"* (1970)) and Germaine Greer's *"The Female Eunuch"* (1970), Simon de Beauvoir's *"The Second Sex"* (1970), Eva Figes's *"Patriarchal Attitudes"* (1970) drew attention to the personal, psychological and sexual aspects of female oppression. It is the because of the 'patriarchal values and beliefs which pervade the culture, philosophy, morality and religion of society that women are conditioned to a passive sexual role, which has repressed their true sexuality as well as more active and adventurous side of their personalities' (Greer in Heywood, 2003: 258). Therefore the emphasis shifted from political emancipation to women's liberation and the second wave feminists campaigned for the legislation of abortions, equal pay legislation, anti-discrimination laws and wider access to education and political and professional life. Women's Liberation Movement during the 1960s and 70s called for radical social changes rather than legal and political reforms and criticized the repressive nature of the conventional society.

Radical Feminism: Unlike the liberal and socialist traditions, radical feminists developed a systematic theory of sexual oppression as the root of patriarchy which preceded private property. They challenge the very notion of femininity and masculinity as mutually exclusive and biologically determined categories. The ideology of motherhood subjugates women and perpetuates patriarchy, which not only forces women to be mothers but also determines the conditions of their motherhood (Bhasin, 199: 8). It creates feminine and masculine characteristics, strengthens the divide between public and private, restricts women's mobility and reinforces male dominance. "While sex differences are linked to biological differences between male and female, gender differences are imposed socially or even politically by constructed contrasting stereotypes of masculinity and femininity" (de Beauvoir, 1970: 258). Simone de Beauvoir in *"The Second Sex"* (1970) pointed out that women are made and not born. She believed that greater availability of abortion rights, effective birth control and end of monogamy would increase the control over their bodies. Judith Butler turned the sex-gender distinction on its head: by making sex the effect of gender, a legitimization subsequently imposed in order to fix the socially contingent through recourse to an unquestioned biology, "the distinction between sex and gender turns out to be no distinction at all".

Kate Millet in *"Sexual Politics"* (1970) defined politics as power structured relationships, which is not only confined to government and its citizens but also to family between children and parents and husband and wife. Through family, church and academy men secure consent of the very women they oppress and each institution justifies and reinforces women's subordination to men with the result that women internalize a sense of inferiority to men (Mandell, 1995: 16). Men use coercion to achieve what conditioning fails to achieve (Millet 1970:8). She proposed that patriarchy must be challenged through a process of conscious-raising and women's liberation required a revolutionary change. The psychological and sexual oppression of women have to be overthrown. Shulamith Firestone in *"The Dialectic of Sex"* (1972) believes that the basis of women's oppression lies in her reproductive capacity in so far as this has been controlled by men. She stated that patriarchy is not natural or inevitable but its roots are located in biology which has led to a natural division of labour within the biological family and liberation of women required that gender difference between men and women be abolished. Firestone's attempt to build a theory of patriarchy in which different sets of patriarchal relations have their place and specify their articulation with class and race relations is one of the most sophisticated and highly developed radical feminist theories (Walby, 1986: 25). However, her analysis of relations of patriarchy with class and ethnicity are rather reductionist as she ignores various structures and institutions which have shaped these relationships through out history (ibid, 26). Walby critiques her for her insufficient analysis of capitalist relations and their interrelationships with patriarchal relations, which Walby sees as a serious omission (ibid). Her believe that the connection between childbirth and child care is a biological rather than a social fact has also been critiqued.

Mackinnon argues that sexuality is the basis of differentiation of sexes and oppression of women and this she considers as parallel to the centrality of work for Marxist analysis of capitalism. "Sexuality is to Feminism what work is to Marxism: that which is most one's own, yet most taken away" (Mackinnon, 1982: 1). She considers that sexuality constructs gender and these are social processes and not biological givens. Walby critiques her for not assessing the relative importance of class/labour for gender equality as compared to sexuality (Walby, 1986: 27). For radical feminists sexual relations are political acts, emblematic of male/female power relationships. The traditional political theory which divide personal and political spheres and believe that family is nonpolitical and personal has been questioned by radical feminists who argue that family is that space where maximum exploitation of women takes place. It is this 'public-private divide' which legitimizes exploitation of women. In fact, it is essential that the private sphere must be mapped in terms of the same values of justice, equality and freedom which are necessary in the public sphere.

Radical feminists aim at the need to redefine individual identity, free language and culture from the clutches of masculinity, re-establish political power, re-evaluate human nature/behaviour and challenge the traditional values. Thus along with legal reforms and the right to franchise the protest against capitalist society is important to transform the traditional sexual identity through sexual revolution. Radical feminists therefore believe that unless sexuality is reconceived and reconstructed in the image and likeness of women, the later will remain subordinate to men (Mandell, 1995: 16).

While radical feminists claim that 'personal is political' liberal feminist warn against the dangers of politicizing the private sphere, which is the realm of public choice and individual freedom. On the other hand the limitation of individualism as the basis of gender politics has been raised by radical feminists as an individualist perspective draws attention away from the structural character of patriarchy. Women are subordinated not as systematic individuals who happen to be denied rights or opportunities but as a sex that is subject to pervasive oppression (Heywood, 2003: 254). They critique individualism which makes it difficult for women to think and act collectively on the basis of their common gender identity. Liberal individualism depoliticizes sexual relations and equal treatment might mean treating women like men. Finally the demand for equal rights only equips women to take advantage of the opportunities and may therefore reflect the interest of white, middle class women in developed countries and fail to address problems of women of colour, working class women and women in developing countries (ibid). Thus while 'egalitarian feminists' link gender difference to patriarchy as a manifestation of oppression and subordination and want to liberate women from gender difference, 'difference feminists' regard the very notion of equality as either misguided or simply undesirable. Alison Jaggar in *"Feminist Politics and Human Nature"* (1971) critiques the radicals for ignoring the causes that led to the origin of patriarchy and its structures which requires theorizing human behaviour and human society. She states that it is not that gender differences determine some forms of social organizations but the later which give rise to gender difference. Therefore instead of controlling their bodies women should be able to control their lives. Marxist feminists critique radical feminists for ignoring the historical, economic and materialist basis of patriarchy and therefore the later are trapped in ahistorical biological deterministic theory.

The new feminist traditions such as psychoanalytical feminism, ecofeminism, postmodern feminism, black feminism, lesbian feminism have emerged since the 1980s. Psychoanalytical feminists analyse the psychological process through which men and women are engendered. They do not hold biological factors as responsible for the construction of sexual difference. Psychoanalytical feminist explore the hidden dynamics at work in personal, interpersonal and social relations and the unconscious dynamics that shape the way we think, feel and act in the world. Freudian psychoanalysis describes women oppression in patriarchy as a process, which need to be altered. After Juliet Mitchell's book *"Psychoanalysis and Feminism"* (1974) the psychological process which determine patriarchy has expanded. Similarly *"Feminism and Psychoanalysis"* (1992) edited by Elizabeth Wright demonstrates the continued interest in this field. Psychoanalysis feminists may share the politics of radical, marxist or socialist feminists but the kind of questions and concerns raised by them are not acknowledged by the later. They analyse gender difference beyond conscious levels of experience and focus on the unconscious levels where gender-specific desires and meanings are constituted and formed. Dorothy Dinnerstein and Nancy Chodorow draw on a school for psychoanalysis called 'objectrelation theory'. Exclusive female mothering is seen to be the cause of gender inequality (Mandell, 1995: 20).

Eco-feminists accept women's attitudes and values as different from men. They believe that in certain respects women are superior to men and possess the qualities of creativity, sensitivity and caring which men can never develop. Vandana Shiva in her conception of ecofeminism critiques development and establishes the connection between ecological destruction and capitalist growth as a patriarchal project.

Postmodern feminists claim that there is no fixed female identity. The socially constructed identities can be reconstructed or deconstructed. Thus the distinctions between sex and gender are criticized from two perspectives: (i) 'difference feminists' who believe that "there are essential difference between men and women and the social and cultural characteristics are seen to refer the biological differences" and (ii) 'postmodern feminists' who "questioned whether sex is a clear-cut biological distinction as is usually assumed". In other words the features of biological motherhood do not apply to women who cannot bear children. Thus "there is a biology-culture continuum rather than a fixed biological/cultural divide and the categories male and female become more or less arbitrary and the concepts of sex and gender become hopelessly entangled".

Linda Nicholson in *"Feminism/Postmodernism"* (1990) claims that there are many points of overlap between a postmodern stance and position long held by feminists. According to Nancy Fraser and Nicholson if feminism pursues a trend towards a more historical non-universalizing, non-essentialist theory that addresses difference amongst women (lesbians, disabled, working class women, black women) then feminism will become more consistent with postmodernism (Nicholson, 1990: 34) This trend means giving up universal claims of gender and patriarchy. However, feminists hostile to postmodernism theory claim that no feminist politics is possible once one has called into question the nature of gender identity and subjectivity (Mandell, 1995: 26). Black feminists have prioritized differences based on race and challenge the tendency within feminism to ignore it. They portray sexism and racism as interlinked systems of oppression and highlight the particular range of gender, racial and economic disadvantages that confront "women of colour". Black feminists argue that women are not subject to common forms of oppression due to their sex but 'women of colour 'in particular are more vulnerable to oppression and subjugation. They criticize the liberal, Marxist, socialist and radical feminists for ignoring race as a category of oppression and analysis. By assuming that gender is primary form of subordination, oppression of class, sexuality and race become extensions of patriarchal domination. Radical feminists' insistence that the elimination of sexism is key to the elimination racism is inadequate to "women of colour" as they experience racism from white women as well as from men. Thus an analysis of the intersection of class, caste, race, sexuality and gender is important.

Similarly lesbian feminists primarily struggle against homophobia which is as important as the struggle against patriarchy. Lesbian feminism and cultural feminism are two types of feminist separations advocating the creation of women identified world through the attachments women have to each other. They believe that since patriarchy is organized through men's relations with other men, unity among women is the only effective means for liberating women. They position lesbianism as more than a personal decision and an outward sign of an internal rejection of patriarchal sexuality (Rich in Mandell, 1995: 14). Lesbianism becomes a paradigm for female-controlled female sexuality which meets women's needs and desires. 'Another popular strategy for resisting patriarchy has been to redefine social relations by creating women-centered cultures that emphasise positive capacities of women by focusing on creative dimensions of their experiences' (ibid).

Therefore while earlier feminists struggled for a legally equal position for women and demanded democratic rights, which included right to education and employment, right to own property, right to vote, right to birth control, right to divorce, today feminists have gone beyond demanding mere legal reforms to end discrimination between men and women. They have raised issues of violence against women, rape, unequal wages, discriminatory personal laws, the sexual division of labour, distribution of power within the family, use of religion to oppress women and negative portrayal of women in media. Emancipation of women necessarily calls for challenging patriarchy as a system which perpetuates women's subordination. Several structures of society such as kinship and family, class, caste, religion, ethnicity, educational institutions and state reinforce patriarchy. Some of the experiences of multiple patriarchies can be illustrated by analysing the dynamics and interface of social forces which institutionalize and legitimize patriarchy in society.

Structures of Patriarchy

The first lessons of patriarchy are learnt in the family where the head of the family is a man/father. Man is considered the head of the family and controls women's sexuality, labour or production, reproduction and mobility. In a patriarchal family the birth of male child is preferred to that of a female. The former is considered as the inheritor of the family while the later is considered as *paraya dhan.* The Indian joint family is the "patriarchal family" and it was constituted by a group of persons related in the male line and subject to absolute power of the senior most male member. In the South Asian context kinship systems are largely based on patrilineal descent which is the foundation of a pervasive patriarchal ideology that rationalizes the differential access of men and women to the material and symbolic resources of society.

According to Gerda Lerner, family plays an important role in creating a hierarchical system as it not only mirrors the order in the state and educates its children but also creates and constantly reinforces that order. Family is therefore important for socializing the next generation in patriarchal values. The boys learn to be dominating and aggressive and girls learn to be caring, loving and submissive. These stereotypes of masculinity and femininity are not only social constructs but also have been internalized by both men and women. While the pressure to earn and look after the family is more on the man, the women are supposed to do the menial jobs and take care of their children and even other members of the family. It is because of these gender stereotypes that women are at a disadvantage and are vulnerable to violence and other kinds of discriminations and injustices. Systemic deprivation and violence against women: rape, sexual harassment, sexual abuse, female foeticide, infanticide, witchkilling, sati, dowry deaths, wife-beating, high level of female illiteracy, malnutrition, undernourishment and continued sense of insecurity keeps women bound to home, economically exploited, socially suppressed and politically passive.

Patriarchal constructions of knowledge perpetuate patriarchal ideology and this is reflected in educational institutions, knowledge system and media which reinforce male dominance. More subtle expressions of patriarchy was through symbolism giving messages of inferiority of women through legends highlighting the self-sacrificing, self-effacing pure image of women and through ritual practice which emphasized the dominant role of women as a faithful wife and devout mother. Laws of Manu insist that since women by their very nature are disloyal they should be made dependent on men. The husband should be constantly worshiped as a god, which symbolized that man is a lord, master, owner, or provider and the shudras and women were the subordinates. It legitimized that a woman should never be made independent, as a daughter she should be under the surveillance of her father, as a wife of her husband and as a widow of her son. While in ancient India (Vedic and Epic periods), women were by and large treated as equal to men, the restrictions on women and patriarchal values regulating women's sexuality and mobility got strengthened in the post-vedic periods (Brahmanical and Medieval periods) with the rise of private property and establishment of class society.

Patriarchal constructions of social practices are legitimized by religion and religious institution as most religious practices regard male authority as superior and the laws and norms regarding family, marriage, divorce and inheritance are linked to patriarchal control over property biased against women. A person's legal identity with regard to marriage, divorce and inheritance are determined by his or her religion, which laid down duties for men and women and their relationship. Most religions endorse patriarchal values and all major religions have been interpreted and controlled by men of upper caste and class. The imposition of parda, restrictions on leaving the domestic space, separation between public and private are all gender specific and men are not subject to similar constraints. Thus the mobility of women is controlled. They have no right to decide whether they want to be mothers, when they want to be, the number of children they want to have, whether they can use contraception or terminate a pregnancy and so on and so forth. Male dominated institutions like church and state also lay down rules regarding women's reproductive capacity.

Similarly caste and gender are closely related and the sexuality of women is directly linked to the question of purity of race. The caste system and caste endogamy retained control over the labour and sexuality of women. Anuloma and pratiloma marriage by definition denigrate women. Caste not only determines social division of labour but also sexual division of labour. Ideologically concepts of caste purity of women to maintain patrilineal succession justified subordination of women. The prohibition of sacred thread ceremony for both women and sudhra, similar punishment for killing a women and sudhra, denial of religious privileges are illustrations which indicate how caste and gender get entrenched. Feminist writings as *'Gendering Caste Through a Feminist Lens'* (2006) illustrates how caste system upholds the patriarchal values and ideology which is used to justify the dominant, hegemonic, hierarchical and unequal patriarchal structures. Therefore it is important to emphasize the substantive question of sub-ordination of certain sections of society and the structures that make their sub-ordination. For feminist scholars the issue is no longer whether the status of women was low or high but the specific nature and basis of their subordination in society. Hence the historical developments of patriarchy/ies and how they have come to stay is important.

Uma Chakravarti argues that the establishment of private property and the need to have caste purity required subordination of women and strict control over their mobility and sexuality. Female sexuality was channelled into legitimate motherhood within a controlled structure of reproduction to ensure patrilineal succession. According to her the mechanism of control operated through three different levels. The first device was when patriarchy was established as an ideology and women had internalized through *stridharma* or *pativartadharma* to live up to the ideal notion of womanhood constructed by the ideologues of the society. The second device was laws, customs and rituals prescribed by the brahmanical social code which reinforced the ideological control over women through the idealization of chastity and wife fidelity as highest duty of women. Like Gerda Lerner she believes that patriarchy has been a system of benevolent paternalism in which obedient women were accorded certain rights and privileges and security and this paternalism made the insubordination invisible and led to their complicity in it. The relationship between women purity and caste purity was important and central to brahmanical patriarchy and women were carefully guarded and lower caste men were prevented from having sexual access to women of higher caste. The third was the state itself which supported the patriarchal control over women and thus patriarchy could be established firmly not as an ideology but as an actuality. Therefore gender relations are organized within the structural frame work of family, religion, class, caste, community, tribe and state.

Thus feminist theories provide explanation for a wide range of particular issues and have been enriched by different approaches and perspectives. The feminist movements need to draw on the strength of all feminist theories as each one on its own is incomplete. In fact, feminism will survive as long as patriarchy persists and 'the challenge is to establish a viable and coherent third wave feminism', which will explain the changing nature of gender relations and explore the 'myth of post-feminism' that society is no longer patriarchal as the most obvious forms of sexist oppression have been overcome.

THE STRANGLEHOLD OF STATE PATRIARCHY

Entrenched patriarchal and class interests continue to be maintained by the denial of basic economic rights to women. And personal laws form the basis of exploitation of women in our society, in the name of religion and family. This continuation of personal laws over years, with changes being resisted by religious leadership, the State and patriarchal interests, is directly linked to women's unequal inheritance rights and lack of control over common property resources. No legislative initiative is ever taken to accord women's right to matrimonial home or property, or even a substantial maintenance. While the State brings no change in the status quo to benefit women, at various times it has instead, made interventions to counter positive measures that were to come about by collective or individual struggle by women. Such situations more often than not have had to do with the question of women gaining more economic rights. This reveals the anti-woman character of the State. It also shows how change in personal law will be resisted by all those who stand to lose if women were to gain more rights.

Though Hindu personal laws have been extensively reformed to give women less of a raw deal, inequalities persist in certain key areas. Property continues to go down the male lineage. Women have no coparcenary rights in ancestral property but are otherwise Class 1 heirs of their father's property.

However, women are deprived of their share even in that. A coparcener has a right to convert self-acquired property to coparcenary property. It is done sometimes to reduce payment of income tax but in this way, the share of the female heirs gets reduced. Secondly, a coparcener has the right to renounce his coparcenary rights and thus deprive the daughter of the property she would have inherited upon the father's death.

Daughters do not have the right to partition but only the right of residence in the ancestral home. Even the right to residence is accorded, if she is unmarried, deserted or widowed without a house. Daughters who are otherwise Class 1 heirs in the father's property are deprived of their rightful share in case dwelling house is the only property.

In March '85, Lata Mittal had filed a writ petition in the Supreme Court challenging the constitutional validity of the Hindu Succession Act, 1956 (HSA), as it violates the right to equality on basis of gender. This Act only allows a male to become the 'karta' or head of a Hindu Undivided Family.

The amendment of the Special Marriage Act (SMA) by the State is yet another instance that highlights how it benefited Hindu men over men of other communities, and how it deprived Hindu women marrying under this Act. The SMA, 1954 made it mandatory for those marrying under this Act to be governed by the Indian Succession Act, 1925. Hindu males marrying under the SMA are deprived of any share in joint family property. The amendment of the SMA in 1976 made it possible for two Hindus marrying under this Act to be continued to be governed by the Hindu Succession Act, 1956. While Hindu male privilege continued as before in property rights, Hindu women marrying under the SMA were deprived of the relative benefit the ISA held for them.

Dispossessed Daughters of the Soil

Women's access to agricultural property and land rights is severely limited. In subsistence economies, women labour hard within the house and also take part in agricultural activities but they have no rights in the land resources. This is the reality of a large majority of women in this country for whom land would be the only asset. Agricultural land does not come under the purview of personal laws. If at all women have very limited rights in other forms of property, these rights become totally inapplicable in case of land rights, as such matters come under state level tenurial legislation or the relevant customary law. This is well illustrated by the Delhi Land Reforms Act 1954, which prohibits married daughters from inheriting land, and gives unmarried daughters very limited right of maintenance from the land. The Act even prohibits a father from willing away his share of agricultural land in a joint family property. Women disadvantaged by these provisions are challenging the Act in a spate of criminal and civil litigations.

The HSA, 1956 granted exemption in favour of special rules providing for devolution of tenures due to which nothing in the Act would affect provisions in matters of tenancy rights in agricultural holdings. In this way, multiple tenancy laws continued. Some states opted for the HSA, some promulgated their own laws, while others continued with existing laws. This ambiguity resulted in customary or personal laws getting de facto recognition in several places, to the disadvantage of women. Furthermore, all tenancy and land reform legislations are under the IX Schedule of the Constitution and therefore cannot be challenged on constitutional grounds, as violations of Fundamental Rights. Although this was done to prevent litigation from slowing down the process of land reform, the fall-out has been that women cannot challenge the gender unequal aspects of these Acts.

Bibliography

Atal, Yogesh: *The Changing Frontiers of Caste*, Delhi, National Publishing House, 1968.

Baldwin, Peter: *The Politics of Social Solidarity: Class Bases of the European Welfare State, 1875–1975,* Cambridge, Cambridge University Press, 1990.

Barnes, Bob.: *Social Survey Division in the 1990s*, Population Trends, 1991.

Benjamin, Joseph: *Scheduled Castes in Indian Politics and Society*, New Delhi, Ess Ess Publications, 1989.

Beteille, Andre.: *The Backward Classes and the New Social Order*, Oxford University Press, Delhi, 1981.

Bhai, P. N.: *Harijan Women in Independent India,* B. R. Publishing, New Delhi, 1986.

Bhattacharya, Sanjay : *Social Work : An Integrated Approach*, Deep and Deep, Delhi, 2003.

Dietrich, Gabriele: *Dalit Movements and Women's Movement*, Horizons India Books, New Delhi, 1992.

Dumont, Louis: *The Caste System and Its Implications*, London, Granada Pub. Ltd., 1970.

Frederic G. Reamer : *Social Work Values and Ethics,* Rawat, Delhi, 2005.

Ghurye, G. S. : *Caste and Class in India*, Bombay, Popular Books, 1950.

Glass, Joseph W.: *The Pennsylvania Culture Region: A View From the Barn*, Ann Arbor, UMI Research Press, 1986.

Gulalia, Akash : *Social Work Practice : With Mobile Population Vulnerable to HIV/AIDS,* Mohit, Delhi 2008.

Gurukal, Rajan: *The Formation of Caste Society in Kerala*, Rawat Publications, New Delhi, 1994.

Heinsath, Charles : *Indian Nationalism and Hindu Social Reform*, Princeton, Princeton University Press, 1964.

Jogdand, P. G.: *Dalit Women in India: Issues and Perspectives*, New Delhi, Gyan Publishing House, 1995.

Mallik, Suneila: *Social Integration of the Scheduled Castes*, New Delhi, Abhinav, 1979.

Mathur, Raj Bala : *Modernisation of Social Work, Planning and Administration*, Book Enclave, Delhi, 2007.

Moddie, A.D.: *The Brahmanical Culture and Modernity*, London, Asia, 1968.

Prakash M Katare : *Social Work and Folk Culture*, Arise Pub, Delhi, 2006.

Ramachandran, S.P. : *Social Work for Minorities*, Sumit Enterprises, Delhi, 2008.

Romanofsky, Peter: *Community Organizing for Urban Social Change, A Historical Perspective,* Greenwood Press, Delhi, 1981.

Sherry Joseph : *Social Work Practice and Men Who Have Sex With Men*, Sage, Delhi, 2005

Silverberg, James: *Social Mobility in the Caste System in India*, Mouton Publishers, The Hague, 1968.

Sinha, Debotosh : *Aspects of Industry and Occupational Social Work*, Abhijeet Pub, Delhi, 2007.

Siva Raju: *Gerontological Social Work in India : Some Issues and Perspectives*, B.R., Delhi, 2000.

Solanki, Jagdish : *Social Work Perspective on Depressed Class Population*, Anmol, Delhi, 2006.

Tripathy, R. B.: *Dalits: A Sub-Human Society*, New Delhi, Ashish Publishing House, 1994.

VanderVennen, R. : *Social Science in Christian Perspective*, Lanham, MD: University Press of America, 1988.

Vijendra Kumar : *Problems and Perspectives on Social Work and Social Welfare,* ABD Pub, Delhi, 2002.

Yolton, J. W.: *John Locke: Problems and Perspectives*, Cambridge Uni. Press, 1969.

Index

S

T

U

❑❑❑